Cultural Journeys

Multicultural Literature for Elementary and Middle School Students

Pamela S. Gates
and
Dianne L. Hall Mark

D1417860

ROWMAN & LITTLEFIELD PUBLISHERS, INC.
Lanham • Boulder • New York • Toronto • Plymouth, UK

Published by Rowman & Littlefield Publishers, Inc.
A wholly owned subsidary of The Rowman & Littlefield Publishing Group, Inc.
4501 Forbes Boulevard, Suite 200, Lanham, Maryland 20706
www.rowmanlittlefield.com

Estover Road, Plymouth PL6 7PY, United Kingdom

British Library Cataloguing in Publication Information Available

Library of Congress Cataloging-in-Publication Data

The hardback edition of this book was previously catalogued by the Library of Congress
as follows:

Gates, Pamela S.
  Cultural journeys : multicultural literature for children and young adults / Pamela S.
Gates, Dianne L. Hall Mark
    p. cm.
  Includes bibliographical references and index.
    1. Children's literature—History and criticism.   2. Young adult literature—History
and criticism.   3. Multiculturalism in literature.   I. Mark, Dianne L. Hall.   II. Title.
PN1009.5.M84G38   2006
809'.89282—dc22   2005037276

  ISBN: 978-0-8108-5079-8 (cloth : alk. paper)
  ISBN: 978-1-4422-0687-8 (pbk. : alk. paper)
  ISBN: 978-1-4422-0688-5 (electronic)

∞ ™ The paper used in this publication meets the minimum requirements of American
National Standard for Information Sciences—Permanence of Paper for Printed Library
Materials, ANSI/NISO Z39.48-1992.

Printed in the United States of America

Contents

Preface

Defining Our Work:
What, Why, and How Do We Begin?

In thinking about the impetus for writing this book, we began to mull over the varied experiences we have encountered in our personal and professional lives. One of our discussions centered on our fascination with the metaphor of the *journey* and its implications. Through this metaphor, we are able to explore the following:

- the *journey* of teaching and learning;
- the *journey* of discovering our place in this world in relation to those around us;
- the *journey* of growth we all need to experience if we are to be lifelong learners; and
- the potential *journey* we can each take as we enter the lives of others through the magic of story.

The metaphor also epitomizes the way we have come to create this text—traveling from different paths and stumbling over different roadblocks to converge finally at this crossing.

A key factor in the creation of this book relates to our job as teachers. We believe that it is our responsibility to find ways to help our students become critical readers, writers, viewers, and thinkers as they acquire habits of lifelong learning. We also believe that one way to do that is through the travels of the literature experience—particularly the multicultural literature experience. No matter what our ethnic or cultural backgrounds are, we are each limited by the experience of our own culture. As teachers, it is essential that we grow beyond our own cultural background and learn about the social, political, and human experiences of others. To do that, we can either travel extensively or open our minds through the experiences of reading literature that authentically relates the experiences of others. It is the latter that we propose in this book.

Though the importance of teaching and learning about multicultural literature is imperative, there is often a sentiment, or a sense, of apology from some who teach multicultural literature and are from the "dominant culture." How could someone from the dominant culture know or express an adequate understanding about the experiences from other cultures? In an article published in the *ALAN Review* in the fall of 1996, Marc Talbert speaks about his own writing. He discusses the significance of his reflections as an author of multicultural novels for young people and making sense of looking at oneself in the mirror versus looking at oneself within the societies in which we live. He suggests that both approaches are multidimensional and that we see ourselves as pieces or portions of a whole—never knowing which image will be strongest on any given day. It is in this same way that we think about the preparation of our teacher-education students for the diverse student body they will teach. Although there is some ethnic diversity within the population of college students we teach, the majority of those students preparing to become teachers are European American, with a very limited exposure to students of other cultures.

A study conducted by Terrill and Mark (2000) finds that the demographics of students enrolled in a particular teacher-education department mirrored the demographic profile of teachers nationwide. These preservice teachers are primarily European American, middle class, and female. They are from rural and suburban communities that are usually within a hundred-mile radius of the higher-education institution they attend.

Many of them believe that they have attended high schools that are ethnically diverse and profess to be aware of the tensions for minority students, yet few have experienced the tensions themselves. In addition, we have found that although they are willing and often eager to learn about other cultures, they have had little to no grounding in the historical struggles of the minority groups of their country. According to Terrill and Mark's research, "the majority of the respondents . . . did not identify high levels of comfort and safety for the schools and communities with children of color" (2000, 152). It would appear that these preservice teachers, as well as others with the same attitudes, would have a difficult time communicating with the families and communities of students of color. One of the primary reasons is because they have not been exposed to other cultures.

It is within these teaching and learning experiences that we have struggled to develop ways of engaging, informing, and initiating our preservice students to social, political, and human experiences that are culturally diverse. As we prepare these students to teach, it is our personal goal that they understand, respect, and invite diversity. On the basis of attitudes, perceptions, misconceptions, and backgrounds of students going into the field of teaching, this challenge goes beyond the occasional snippets of culturally relevant curricula. Most teachers include a multicultural book, some poetry by African American authors, and possibly an invited guest from a nearby Native American reservation into their classes at "appropriate" times throughout the school year, but the journey needs to go beyond those traditional gestures.

Teaching multiculturally allows and even expects teachers to be sensitive to the needs of *all* children. Their teaching styles will adapt to the personality of each classroom, each student, and the many diverse cultures brought to the classroom environment. As teachers incorporate multicultural literature in their classes, they will bring their students closer to understanding the realities, not only in the United States, but globally. We propose, therefore, that multicultural literature is one of the most important avenues for beginning this journey of discovery and understanding.

WORKS CITED

Talbert, Marc. "What Is a Mirror to Do?" *ALAN Review* 24, no. 1 (1996): 2–6.
Terrill, Margueritte, and Dianne L. H. Mark. "Preservice Teachers' Expectations for Schools with Children of Color and Second-Language Learners." *Journal of Teacher Education* 51, no. 2 (2000): 149–55.

Acknowledgments

Writing a book is more than just the research and creative efforts of the authors. In our case, this endeavor has spanned several years and has grown up along with our children.

In an effort to recognize those who have helped and walked with us on this journey, we want to offer a special thank-you to all of our educators who graciously contributed their time, their units, and their special insights into the activities and classroom strategies that extend the information we have gathered about multicultural literature. Their work and the work of all those who use multicultural literature to expand the minds of young people have provided us with a touchstone to what happens daily in classrooms and in school districts. We would also like to thank Cynthia Whitaker for her continued efforts to provide quality literature for our teacher-education students and for her help in finding books for our review. A special thanks goes out to Susan Steffel and Francis Molson, who were my coauthors on an earlier work with Scarecrow Press, *Fantasy Literature for Children and Young Adults*—a work from which we drew heavily for our chapter on folktales and fairy tales. We thank as well our editor, Kim Tabor, and our production editor, Kellie Hagan, for their guidance and support in seeing this project through to completion.

Finally, we are grateful and appreciative to our husbands and families for their love and support over the past few years as we took this wonderful journey to create a book that is an expression of our commitment as educators to this all-important genre of literature. While the written journey for now is complete, the quest for new knowledge, new titles, and new cultural expressions beckon us back to continue the search for quality literature selections.

Chapter One

Why Do We Study Multicultural Literature?

Well over a decade ago, Bernice Cullinan wrote about the metaphors of a mirror and a window for helping us to think about the purposes of children's literature. At that time she said that

> Literature mirrors our perception of life; we see in stories reflections of our own values, disappointments, and dreams. We view both our inner and outer worlds (394). . . . An author invites us to look through a window, and we respond, to see the world through another's eyes. . . . Literature's windows on the world look upon the full range of human experience, including our joys and sorrows, our virtues and vices. (424)

MULTICULTURAL LITERATURE AS A MIRROR

Many have argued the need for multicultural literature on the basis of Cullinan's mirror metaphor. Rudine Sims Bishop states, "[I]f literature is a mirror that reflects human life, then all children who read or are read to need to see themselves as part of humanity" (1993, 43). This is essential; all children need to see themselves and their culture depicted realistically and authentically in picture books and novels. The shortage of quality multicultural literature has plagued educators, and only within the last decade have publishing companies made significant efforts to alleviate the shortage. The mirror metaphor is an apt and appropriate one for all children, especially for children of color.

For too long, these students have not seen positive representations of themselves and their cultures in the books they have read. Also, European American students have missed out on the realities of life that people of color have experienced and, thereby, have not been provided with the opportunity to see the cultural reflections. The mirror metaphor, however, is not a sufficient lens for developing cross-cultural understandings.

MULTICULTURAL LITERATURE AS A WINDOW

It is essential to value the window metaphor as well; for without it, we ignore significant numbers of children who, too, have an opportunity to change the social problems of racism and prejudice. It is essential that all children have the opportunity to read and discuss multicultural literature. We can view the world through our own cultural lenses, which for most of us is limited to a single lens, a single culture. Through the window of literature, however, we are allowed to enter worlds not physically open to us—to view, to empathize, and to participate emotionally in ways that may ultimately change the way we see ourselves and the society in which we live. Only through repeated immersion into those other cultural experiences will we as a society begin to appreciate the struggles, the pain, and the horror that our sisters and brothers of other backgrounds have suffered. Only then will we begin truly to develop the respect needed to appreciate and honor our unique diversity as a country.

DEFINING MULTICULTURAL LITERATURE

Developing a single definition that values all aspects of diversity yet is attentive to cultural specificity is no easy task. Various scholars have created individual definitions that fit the nuances of their specific research interests, but a common thread seems to relate to the inclusiveness of diverse cultural experiences. Many scholars refer to the works of James Banks and Carl Grant, twentieth-century pioneers in multicultural education, focusing on the political nature of the oppression many groups have endured throughout our country's history. Banks identifies a goal of multicultural education that "is to educate citizens who can participate in the workforce and take action in the civic community to help the nation actualize its democratic ideals" (1999, 54). Grant and Gomez discuss the importance of teachers who work in multicultural environments to rethink their own curricular experiences because multiculturalism will challenge some of their stereotypes and misconceptions of the way they think things are or should be. They continue by stating that the rethinking process "enhances the task of taking hard looks at the principles that should guide the presentation of American and more general history selections and interpretations of literature" (2001, 31).

Other scholars cite the works of Violet Harris, Rudine Sims Bishop, and

Sonia Nieto, women who are activists in the promoting of quality and authenticity in literature for children of color. More recently, scholars such as Mingshui Cai have urged us to think about types of definitions—specifically, literary versus pedagogical definitions—as they relate to "its intrinsic literary nature or the pedagogical purposes it is supposed to serve in education" (2002, 3). Still others seem to skirt the issue of defining that which they argue is undefinable, satisfied to move into a discussion about the literature, assuming their readers will fill in the needed gaps.

For the purposes of this text, it seems imperative to develop a definition that honors and represents all the work compiled thus far in the field of multicultural education and literature, embracing the cultural diversity that in itself defines our country. While we may address the pedagogical relationships from time to time, for our literary purposes, we will define and address *multicultural literature* as *a body of literature that spans all literary genres but generally focuses on primary characters who are members of underrepresented groups whose racial, ethnic, religious, sexual orientation, or culture historically has been marginalized or misrepresented by the dominant culture.* Bishop articulates it in this way, "multicultural literature should be defined in a comprehensive and inclusive manner; that is, it should include books that reflect the racial, ethnic, and social diversity that is characteristic of our pluralistic society" (1993, 3). Many scholars choose to specify other groups as well who have felt the sting of discrimination because of age, gender, poverty, and physical or mental disability under the comprehensive heading of multicultural literature. The evaluative criteria used in this text indeed may be broad enough to address all of those groups; however, the discussions will relate primarily to literature written for, about, or by

- African Americans;
- Asian Americans (Chinese, Japanese, Korean, Cambodian, and Vietnamese);
- Latino Americans (Puerto Rican, Mexican, Cuban, Central, and South American); and
- Native Americans.

VALUES: THE SOCIAL, PSYCHOLOGICAL, AND POLITICAL IMPLICATIONS OF USING MULTICULTURAL LITERATURE IN THE CLASSROOM

Although many scholars have provided insight into the relationship of multicultural education and the study of literature for children, Sonia Nieto provides the clearest framework for us to understand the social, psychological, and political implications of the study of multicultural literature. Within her book, *Affirming Diversity: The Sociopolitical Context of Multicultural Education*, Nieto identifies and defines multicultural education by developing a framework to address issues of cultures (both at home and school), language, and discrimination and their impact on learning. She also addresses the expectations and implications for teaching and school reform. By describing seven basic characteristics of multicultural education, Nieto details the components she feels necessary for multicultural educational reform to take place. Her characteristics parallel those needed in a commitment to the use of multicultural literature. Nieto's Components for Multicultural Educational Reform (208) are as follows:

1. Multicultural education is *antiracist education.*
2. Multicultural education is *basic education.*
3. Multicultural education is *important for all learners.*
4. Multicultural education is *pervasive.*
5. Multicultural education is *education for social justice.*
6. Multicultural education is *a process.*
7. Multicultural education is *critical pedagogy.*

Throughout her discussion of characteristics for successful, authentic multicultural education, Nieto insists that we must make our students aware of social and political contexts. For instance, although an antiracist and antidiscriminatory characteristic would seem to be a given, Nieto fears that many schools simply do a superficial response to this issue. Nieto points out that monthly celebrations of ethnic festivals, food, and language sometimes minimize and stereotype cultural perspectives. Key examples such as the celebrations of Hispanic month in November, African American month in February, and Native American month in March imply that those histories need not be addressed during other times of the school year. Instead, she suggests that to be antiracist would be for teachers and students "to take a long hard look at everything as it was and is, which also means considering the effects and interconnections among events, people, and things" (209). It is important to note that Nieto cautions, however, that teachers of the dominant culture not let themselves (or their students) become immobilized by guilt by recognizing that "although everybody is not 'guilty' of racism and discrimination, we are all responsible for it" (211). Finally, Nieto insists that multicultural education must be integrated into all aspects of the teaching and learning spectrum, not simply added on. She states

A true multicultural approach is pervasive. It permeates the physical environment in the classroom, the curriculum, and the relationships among teachers and students and community. It can be seen in every lesson, curriculum guide, unit, bulletin board, and letter sent home . . . [it is] a philosophy, a way of looking at the world, not simply a program or a class or a teacher. (215)

In other words, multicultural education is a style of teaching—a type of attitude on the part of the teacher. In light of Nieto's work, we suggest that with some slight modifications, we could and should substitute the phrase *multicultural literature* for her use of the phrase *multicultural education*. By doing so, we can easily see the importance of multicultural literature in relation to incorporating more fully Hawisher and Soter's (1990) ethical tradition for the purposes of teaching literature:

1. Multicultural literature supports *antiracist education.*
2. Multicultural literature is a part of *basic education.*
3. Multicultural literature is *important for all learners.*
4. Multicultural literature must be *pervasive.*
5. Multicultural literature promotes *education for social justice.*
6. Multicultural literature is a teaching and learning *process.*
7. Multicultural literature is *critical pedagogy.*

Nieto states that since "knowledge is neither neutral or apolitical, neither can be the act of teaching be neutral or apolitical" (219). We would further suggest that a commitment to the teaching of multicultural literature is a social, psychological, and political act—one that insists on viewing the integration of multicultural literature as a dynamic process—which is not meant merely to change the curriculum content, but rather to change the philosophy underlying the curriculum and the classroom teaching and learning of literature. Finally, since this is a philosophy of expanding the canon to include literature of all cultures, it will challenge the status quo of the more traditional canon, and thus further challenge the social structures embedded within schooling and creating a potential model for social justice.

HISTORICAL OVERVIEW AND REVIEW
OF THE LITERATURE

The history of multicultural literature is short but powerful. Many scholars credit the awakening of multicultural literature to two significant publications. Ezra Jack Keats's book *Snowy Day* and Nancy Larrick's article "The All-White World of Children's Books," published in *Saturday Review,* appeared during the politically charged time of the civil rights movement. Up to that point, seemingly fewer than a dozen quality books featuring children of color had been published. Years of negative stereotyping and ridicule were embedded within the stories containing characters of color, and there were few authors of color publishing literature for children. Easily lost in the plethora of books harboring negative stereotypes were the few quality publications prior to 1960. Books such as *Waterless Mountain* (Laura Armer, 1932 Newbery Award), *Moved Outsiders* (Forence Crannell Means, 1946 Newbery Honor), *Pedro, the Angel of Olvera Street* (Leo Politi, 1946 Caldecott Honor), *Story of a Negro* (Arne Bontemps, 1949 Newbery Honor Award), *Song of the Swallows* (Leo Politi, 1950 Caldecott Award), *And Now Miguel* (Joseph Krumgold, 1953 Newbery Award), and *Umbrella* (Taro Yashima, 1959 Caldecott Honor). Some texts often referred to as particularly problematic for negative stereotypes are Mark Twain's *Adventures of Huckleberry Finn* (1885); Joel Chandler Harris's *Uncle Remus and His Friends* (1892); Helen Bannerman's *The Story of Little Black Sambo* (1899); Claire Bishop's *Five Chinese Brothers* (1938); James Daughtery's *Daniel Boone* (1940 Newbery Award); Walter D. Edmonds's *The Matchlock Gun* (1942 Newbery Award); and Elizabeth Yates's *Amos Fortune, Free Man* (1950 Newbery Award). Two of the last three Newbery Award books as well as some of the Laura Ingalls Wilder series have been charged with promoting negative stereotypes of Native Americans as savages while advocating the right of manifest destiny.

The late 1960s and 1970s brought to the focus a significant awareness of discrimination and a demand for change. Discrimination because of race, age, and gender was in the news, and publishers and critics began to respond with a newfound sense of commitment to multicultural literature in the broadest sense. Authors such as Virginia Hamilton, Mildred Taylor, Byrd Baylor, Eloise Greenfield, John Steptoe, Sharon Bell Mathis, Yoshiko Uchida, Murial and Tom Feelings, and Julius Lester made significant contributions to the field of multicultural literature and were recognized with numerous awards. For instance, of the thirty-six Newbery Honor and Awards given for the ten-year period from 1969 to 1978, fourteen books were multicultural in theme with at least eight of those books written by authors of the culture.

A similar review of the Caldecott awards during that same time period revealed that of the thirty-nine awards given, fifteen books were multicultural in nature with at least eight of them written and/or illustrated by people of the culture. Given the significant increase in recognition during that decade, the sudden drop in awards for multicultural literature the following ten years during a somewhat conservative political climate can be seen as shocking. Of the thirty-five Newbery honors and awards given between 1979 and 1988, only three books could be considered multicultural in nature with only one written by someone of color. Many still question the reasons for this sudden drop in recognition. Conversely, we might wonder what caused the sudden increase in multicultural literature during the 1990s. More than likely, the increase in multicultural literature was a result of teachers, librarians, and curriculum administrators insisting on quality literature that reflected the diversity of all of their students. Publishers now have responded by establishing divisions that offer publishing opportunities to new authors of all ethnic groups. As you might expect, with an increased focus, quality pieces of multicultural literature are again receiving award recognition. Of the honor and award books for the Newbery and Caldecott awards during the 1990s, more than one-third could be considered multicultural with one-quarter or more written and/or illustrated by people of the cultures depicted. With the popularity of literature-based reading programs, it is essential that all students are given the opportunity to see themselves and their cultural values represented in the literature they read.

WHAT ARE THE GOALS OF USING MULTICULTURAL LITERATURE IN THE CLASSROOM?

Many articles have been written that speak to the need for teachers to address issues of cultural diversity through children's literature and through the development of study units for reading and writing. Most often, however, the focus has been one of attempting to inform students about cultural diversity by providing authentic reading, writing, and discussion experiences around quality literature selections. Although this is certainly a valuable endeavor, it can skirt the sensitive and hard issues related to the historical and global implications related to racism and prejudice. Two studies that did attempt to address those relationships are found in *Facing History in South Boston High School* (Klein 1993) and *Through Whose Eyes* (Naidoo 1992). *Facing History* is the story of one teacher's attempt to "move students gradually from literary and historical examples of genocide back to present-day experiences of intolerance and racism" (16). Klein tells us about a teacher of sophomore English who attempts to help her students understand issues of racism through an examination of literature about the Holocaust. It becomes clear throughout the article that, although the teacher genuinely tries to provide opportunities for her students to think about racism and prejudice both historically and in their daily lives, she struggles with students' apathetic attitudes about learning that undermines her efforts to raise their social consciousness. Despite this fact, Klein felt that the unit offered multiple chances for students to begin making connections between historical and global actions and their own experiences of racism and prejudice.

Although this study is an important comment on the possibilities and use of history and historical fiction, in particular the Holocaust, as a means to raise the social consciousness of the relationship between the past and present understandings of racism and prejudice for high school students, the very fact that it happens late in a student's learning career poses questions about its effectiveness. Some of the students of the South Boston High School study may have exhibited a deeper understanding or may have made connections between history and personal experiences. However, the obstacles encountered by the teacher indicates that many students were too entrenched in their own "anxiety, shame, and low self-worth related to themselves as learners" (Klein 1993, 19), to address the sociopolitical aspects of cultural diversity in ways that many teachers using multicultural literature with younger children might not have to encounter.

A second study that ultimately influenced my own research (Gates-Duffield 1993) and thinking about multicultural literature was Naidoo's book *Through Whose Eyes* (1992). Within this study, Naidoo designed a yearlong course in which middle school students in a white, working-class Christian school in England read and responded to several texts that contained strong indictments of racism. Her intent was to "extend white students' empathies; to challenge ethnocentric and racist assumptions and concepts; and to develop critical thinking about the nature of our society" (21). Although she encountered difficulties with teacher support and inconsistent level of student commitment, her finding raised several questions that had a direct impact on my own research and ultimately the framework of this text. The following quotation highlights some important implications for the study of multicultural literature:

> The major question remains of how to create a supportive framework for challenging racism and the racist society to which the young people belong in ways that enable them to question, and indeed change, aspects of their own identity. The problem is that while racism is seen as something "out there," it can perhaps be faced and decried. But it is another matter when it is identified as something functioning "in here" i.e. in one's own school or worse still in one's own head. (141)

This implication has a direct relationship on what teachers' goals and objectives are, for developing a literature-based multicultural curriculum. A general intent to help students make connections between historical and global aspects of racism and prejudice and what is "out there" and "in here" is noble, but not always sufficient to redesign a literature curriculum. Naidoo identified the following *needs* as important features to a successful restructuring:

- A culturally diverse curriculum
- A combined focus on language and literature
- An ability for students to deconstruct their own "knowledge"
- The integration of cognitive and affective learning
- The creation of space for girls' voices
- The development of a pedagogy that encourages self-esteem, open-mindedness, and collaboration
- The ability for teachers to be both supportive and challenging
- The ability for teachers to develop their own awareness of racism
- The ability for the wider school context to reflect the collaborative, supportive but challenging context of the classroom (141, 142)

As the list indicates, many factors are necessary to create change, not the least of which is the willingness of teachers and administrators to take risks to address issues that continue to inhibit our growth as a nation.

WHY IS THE STUDY OF MULTICULTURAL LITERATURE IMPORTANT?

There are many obvious reasons that we, as teachers, as prospective teachers, and as students should undertake the study of multicultural literature. For one thing, as mentioned earlier in this chapter, it offers a mirror through which children can see representations of themselves, and it provides a window by which children not of the represented culture can see into worlds and experiences not personally accessible to them. We believe, however, that in order to answer the question of why we should study multicultural literature, we should review the benefits of studying any literature for children and young adults.

In 1990, I had the privilege to begin working with two outstanding sixth-grade teachers. During the early spring and fall of 1992, we worked together to design a full-year curricular unit using multicultural literature to teach about issues of racism and prejudice. Once the design was completed, I was given the charge of observing the implementation and evaluating the unit's strengths and weaknesses. Our work together over the years offered many opportunities to frame the process of exploring the history and current issues of racism and prejudice through the study of multicultural literature. The initial book choices were made on particular teaching and learning beliefs related to quality literature and with a certain willingness to take a risk to enable their students an opportunity to understand themselves and their place in society.

Regarding beliefs on the traditions of why and how literature is taught seems to influence teachers' decisions about what to read and how to make sense of those readings. For instance, Hawisher's essay "Content Knowledge versus Process Knowledge: A False Dichotomy" examines the traditions and methods of teaching literature. She states

> that at least three traditions have informed our decision for teaching literature: (1) the ethical tradition in which students through literature should learn those values prized by our society; (2) the classical tradition in which students should develop disciplined minds through close analysis of language in text; and (3) the nonacademic tradition in which students through reading should come to appreciate the joys of good literature. (Hawisher and Soter 1990, 4)

Although the classical tradition and the nonacademic tradition generally are used by teachers, the use of the ethical tradition is necessary for multicultural literature. For example, although most teachers want their students to have an enjoyable (aesthetically pleasing) experience reading novels and picture books—and often allow class time for reading—teachers also develop lessons to examine the literary elements of story, including stereotyped imagery. By using the ethical tradition, teachers can provide a vehicle for developing awareness and understanding of cultural diversity and the issues of racism and prejudice.

MAKING DECISIONS ABOUT WHAT TO STRESS

Many of the teachers with whom I have worked revealed that they became somewhat frustrated when they tried to deal with the distinctly different values for literature. For example, we can help our students learn to use literature as a source for gathering information. For another example, we can help our students understand that literature is a thing in itself, and as such it has characteristics or features that can be appreciated apart from the information that is conveyed. What these teachers saw as problematic, at least initially, not only was how to teach their students such different values of literature, "efferent" and "aesthetic," (Rosenblatt 1978) without compromising any of them but also how to do this without compromising their students' enthusiasm for literature. Although she is a strong advocate for aesthetic appreciation, one educator warns us against stifling our students' naive, uninstructed response to literature:

Some direct instruction about the structure or elements of story, [for example] . . . has a place in teaching . . . literature in elementary grades. But, none of this should precede or restrict the reading of a selection for the kind of literary experience or response each child is capable of and inclined to make on his/her own. (Cianciolo and VanCamp 1991)

The teachers with whom I work are very aware of the desirability for their students to respond critically and aesthetically to literature. However, they hope that their students' exposure to a variety of multicultural texts also will help to inform them about issues of cultural diversity and to encourage them to continue the literary experience in their own particular ways.

In addition to making decisions about what to stress, we, as teachers, must also make decisions on how students are to make sense of those readings. Without realizing it, many teachers employ Robert Probst's (1988) *Five Kinds of Knowing* into their thinking and decision making for book choices (105–8):

Knowledge of self. Personal significance of literary experience
Knowledge of others. Literacy serves also to create society
Knowledge of texts. Learning how texts suggest values and beliefs
Knowledge of contexts. The circumstances in which a text is read helps to shape meaning
Knowledge of processes. Expressive and inferential

By thinking about and integrating Probst's roster into their decision making about multicultural book choices, teachers are cognitive about those choices and the potential impact on their classroom discussions. If the curricular expectation is to immerse students into a particular period or culture, for example, then we must choose books that will best serve that expectation. Thus, what becomes immediately obvious is that in order to make cognitive choices about classroom texts, we must know fully how to evaluate those texts with a full range of criteria. The development of these criteria and their application to a variety of genres are the purposes of this text.

BUILDING A MULTICULTURAL LITERATURE-BASED CURRICULUM

As the studies and discussions indicate, there are teachers who are attempting to study and document the impact of the use of multicultural literature with children and young adults. There are many resources available to help teachers create a literature-based program that infuses multicultural literature into curriculum. Many resources are available on the Internet, although we must caution novice teachers and preservice teachers about pulling whole units that are developed by someone else. As teachers, it is very important for us to remember that we know the expectations and limits of our students, district, and community best. The units you will find on the Internet and the strategies that we offer are intended only as general suggestions—ideas that have worked for some teachers. You should not unilaterally copy and use these resources randomly. Let us reiterate this statement. The resources you may find on the Internet or in this text are intended as strategies to use after a thorough and thoughtful process of creating an adaptation that is appropriate to your own classroom of students on the basis of curricular and community mandates and expectations. You are the professionals in the field and your decisions have a major impact on the teaching and learning that happens in your classrooms. Please remember that any of us can face the challenges related in the studies done by Klein and Naidoo; it is important to create literature units that both infuse multicultural literature into our programs and remain flexible and current.

CONCLUSIONS

The study of multicultural literature is an important undertaking for teachers and students at all levels. If we are to grow as a nation, we must ensure that respect for our diverse racial, ethnic, and cultural heritage is embedded into our educational process. Multicultural literature is an important avenue for change. Through literature, we can come to a greater understanding of the historical foundations of racism and prejudice that have continued to undermine our society. Bishop (1993) argues eloquently for this as well; she states

> Multicultural literature is one of the most powerful components of a multicultural education curriculum, the underlying purpose of which is to help to make the society a more equitable one. (Bishop, 40)

Through this book, it is our intent that you have a better understanding of, application, and appreciation for using multicultural literature. If we use the mirror metaphor in looking at multicultural literature, we hope that our students will be able to view both their inner and outer world. This view will make students more aware and enable them to ask questions; questions that we will answer or that they will explore on their own. In any event, they will become better prepared to take on their role as productive citizens in our global world.

WORKS CITED

Banks, James A. "Multicultural Citizenship Education." *Teaching and Learning in the New Millennium*, 54–61. Ed. Barbara Day. Indianapolis, Ind.: Kappa Delta Pi, 1999.

Bishop, Rudine S. "Multicultural Literature for Children: Making Informed Choices." In *Teaching Multicultural Literature in Grades K–8*, 37–54. Ed. Violet J. Harris. Norwood, Mass.: Christopher-Gordon, 1993.

Cai, Mingshui. *Multicultural Literature for Children and Young Adults*. London: Greenwood Press, 2002.

Cianciolo, Patricia J., and Mary Ellen VanCamp. *The Analysis of Commonly Used Curriculum Materials*. East Lansing: Michigan State University Center for Learning and Teaching Elementary Subjects, 1991.

Cullinan, Bernice. *Literature and the Child*. New York: Harcourt Brace Jovanovich, 1989.

Gates-Duffield, Pamela. *A Qualitative Analysis of the Use of Language Arts Instruction in Two Sixth-Grade Classrooms to Develop Awareness and Understanding of Cultural Diversity*. PhD diss., East Lansing: Michigan State University, 1993.

Grant, Carl A., and Mary Louise Gomez, eds. *Campus and Classroom: Making Schooling Multicultural*. 2nd ed. Upper Saddle River, N.J.: Merrill-Prentice, 2001.

Harris, Violet J., ed. *Using Multiethnic Literature in the K–8 Classroom*. Norwood, Mass.: Christopher-Gordon, 1997.

Hawisher, Gail, and Anna O. Soter, eds. *On Literacy and Its Teaching: Issues in English Education*. Albany: State University of New York Press, 1990.

Keats, Ezra Jack. *Snowy Day*. New York: Viking, 1962.

Klein, Thomas. "Facing History at South Boston High School." *English Journal* 82, no. 2 (1993).

Larrick, Nancy. "The All-White World of Children's Books." *Saturday Review* 11 (September 1965).

Naidoo, Beverley. *Through Whose Eyes? Exploring Racism: Reader, Text, and Context*. Staffordshire, England: Trentham Books, 1992.

Nieto, Sonia. *Affirming Diversity: The Sociopolitical Context of Multicultural Education*. New York: Longman, 1992.

Probst, Robert. *Response and Analysis: Teaching Literature in Junior and Senior High School*. Portsmouth, N.H.: Heinemann, 1988.

Rosenblatt, Louise M. *The Reader, the Text, the Poem: The Transactional Theory of the Literary Work*. Carbondale: Southern Illinois University Press, 1978.

Chapter Two

Defining Literary Standards

How do we evaluate and select multicultural literature for children and young adults? With thousands of new books for children and young adults being published each year, it is essential that we as teachers, librarians, and parents be able to select the very best for our children. Literary critics and associations produce lists of recommended titles, while well-respected committees honor the very best each year with awards such as the Newbery, Caldecott, Boston Globe, Coretta Scott King, National Book, and many others internationally. With these high recommendations, it seems as though most of us need to look at the lists only and decide which books to add to our collection. To be sure, their recommendations should enter into our selection process, but to be lulled into a false sense of security would be a dangerous step indeed. Critics, associations, and committees are fine support systems to our own decisions, but it is essential that we evaluate and reevaluate the appropriateness of book selections for the children with whom we work. Many of us can tell stories of lessons gone bad—topics or books that were wild successes with one class only to fall flat with another. Only you know the children and young adults who sit in your classrooms day after day. Only you know what issues are acceptable discussion points for your particular community or grade level. Only you can make the final decisions of what books would be appropriate whole-class reads while other choices are best left for individual readings. We cannot depend on outsiders to make our decisions; that is why we must have clear criteria by which to evaluate every book that is on our shelf.

This text is designed to help you become comfortable and confident in choosing appropriate selections of multicultural texts to use with your students. Within this chapter, we will review the literary elements used to foster understanding about literature in general—plot, setting, characterization, theme, style, mood, tone, and point of view. In addition, we will establish some basic criteria used to evaluate multicultural literature specifically. Finally, we will discuss the tensions surrounding the ongoing debate of credibility and roles of authors of the culture versus authors who are outside the culture about which they write. The discussion of specific genres, and appropriate criteria to evaluate texts within those genres, is left to individual chapters.

LITERARY STANDARDS OF EVALUATION

Literary analysis is the process by which scholars evaluate and critique works of literature. Although the phrase may seem intimidating, the process itself should not be if we share a common vocabulary of terms and concepts. For those of us who are readers, mostly we are very aware of what we like or dislike in a book. We can tell a friend with a few words whether a particular book is worth her time. Our literary tastes may vary, but all the elements are found to some degree in all books—plot, setting, characterization, theme, style, mood, tone, and point of view. As adults, we may expect these elements to exist in our own complex literature, but what of literature for children? Should we expect the same levels of complexity and expertise to exist in the literature we give to children? Yes, absolutely. To expect any less is to sell our children short. Every social issue or problem expressed in literature for adults eventually finds its way into literature for children and young adults. Authors and illustrators of books for children and young adults are charged with creating believable yet sensitive stories that articulate the joys and sorrows of life. They often provide messages of hope yet must not be didactic or simplistic nor distort the realities of life. The challenge of writing well for children and young adults may be one of the most important things authors can do for society, since through stories, children are able to see themselves and others reflected in ways that can help to prepare them for the formidable task of growing into adulthood.

PLOT

When a student asks, "What's the story about?" he is asking about the plot of the story. The order of events, the action, and the pattern by which the story unfolds are all part of the plot. When an author writes a story, she must make decisions about how to tell the story so that it retains the reader's interest. The author needs to consider how the characters and conflict will be introduced, how the suspense will be sustained, how the climax will be reached, and finally how the resolution will be achieved. There are basic structures or story forms that an author may choose to order the events of the story. A *chronological* or *linear* plot is one in which the beginning, middle, and end of the story follow a direct route with the problem or conflict introduced early. This is followed by a sense of rising action and suspense to the moment of climax when a major event occurs to lead the story into a fairly swift resolution. An example of this type of structure can be found in *Mississippi Bridge* by Mildred Taylor. Within this story, the Logan children and other African Americans are denied seats on the bus that is leaving their town. In the midst of a rainstorm, they watch the full bus careen off the bridge and plunge into the raging river. Despite the rudeness and hostility displayed to them moments earlier, the black children risk their lives in attempts to save the white passengers who had taken their seats. The plot is linear with the pace of the action set as fast as the swift waters that threaten to take all of their lives.

A second type of structure is a *cumulative* plot in which an event is added on top of a previous one to create a more complete story. An excellent example of this structure is found in Francisco Jimenez's novel *The Circuit*. A collection of independent stories about a migrant family moving from one labor camp to another over several seasons and over the years; the complete collection reveals the life structure of one family with all its joys and heartaches.

Episodic plot structure is a popular form in early chapter books for young people. Within each chapter, the author introduces a situation or problem that is followed by action and is ultimately resolved in some form by the end of the chapter. One book that uses this form with great effectiveness is *Black Hands, White Sails: The Story of African American Whalers*, written by Patricia and Fredrick McKissack. Each chapter details the dangers and prejudices faced by these men, and by the time the reader has completed the entire text, she has a clearer sense of the whaling profession and the role that African Americans played in its history.

Another type of plot structure usually reserved for more mature readers is the use of *flashback*. When an author uses flashback, the reader often discovers the end of the story first. The author then is able to tell the story of the events that led up to the end result. *Walk Two Moons*, by Sharon Creech, informs the reader early that Sal's mother is dead. Many readers, however, read over that bit of information and travel with Sal and her grandparents to reach her mother by her birthday. The cross-country trip allows us to discover with Sal the meanings of life, death, love, and family. By using the flashback structure, readers can focus on the story of Sal, her grandparents, and Phoebe without wondering about the outcome.

The order of story events does not happen in a vacuum. Within whatever structure is used, it is the conflict—the protagonist's struggle—that is the centerpiece for the action. The kinds of conflict are contained within four common categories: person against self, person against person, person against society, and person against nature. Each type of conflict can be found in a variety of genres but a few examples are listed below.

Person against Self is displayed through the internal conflict of the protagonist: *From the Notebooks of Melanin Sun* by Jacqueline Woodson and *Scorpions* by Walter Dean Myers.

Person against Person is displayed through the protagonist facing her or his foe: *SLAM!* by Walter Dean Myers and *April and the Dragon Lady* by Lensey Namioka.

Person against Society is evidenced through the protagonist's role against society: *The Watsons Go to Birmingham* by Christopher Paul Curtis and *April Raintree* by Bernice Culleton.

Person against Nature is often seen in survival fiction where the protagonist must battle nature itself: *Dragon's Gate* by Laurence Yep and *Julie of the Wolves* by Jean Craighead George.

Although the titles listed above were classified into the four categories, readers will find other types of conflict happening within the stories as well. For instance, many pieces of multicultural literature will have the conflict of person against society coexisting with another type of conflict as in *The Watsons Go to Birmingham*. Kenny must battle with his own sense of guilt from the time he ran away frightened from the bombing and fully aware that his sister may have been inside the church. Further, it is essential that we consider the authenticity of the plot in multicultural literature. If, as critics have suggested, the resolution to problems seems too easy, then the value and credibility of the conflict is minimized. We must question whether the resolution fits the reality of the situation in ways that do not reinforce stereotyped social order. For instance, in his essay "Reading Multiculturally," Daniel D. Hade argues that there is "a stark difference in how race is read by different readers" (1997, 250). Using Ouida Sebestyen's book *Words by Heart* as an example, Hade states that "It is oppressive when someone from a dominant group uses a less powerful as a sign. . . . Real issues of race, class, and gender are ignored when the sign is appropriated for other reasons by dominant groups" (250). According to a formalist reading, for the character of Ben Sills to ask his family to forgive his murderer is consistent and necessary; given Sills's strong religious beliefs, he would be expected to do the Christian act of forgiving one's enemies. However, as Hade explains that while he's "had more than one white colleague defend *Words by Heart* as brilliant and as accurate," he has "yet to have an African American student read the book and find it anything but abhorrent" (250). In order to evaluate the elements of plot and conflict within multicultural texts, we must look beyond their meeting the literary criteria and attempt to read critically, attending to the sociopolitical aspects of racism and discrimination.

SETTING

While the plot and conflict of a story may be the map that guides readers through the sea of darkness, it is also the setting that anchors the story in time and place. Readers can travel to other locations and various periods in history by the stroke of a pen, grounding them for experiences otherwise impossible to be had. Historical fiction and fantasy both act as genres that provide readers with optimum choices for creative and informative experiences in setting. In Jane Yolen's *The Devil's Arithmetic*, readers can experience both genres when they are transported back in time to the Holocaust with a young Jewish girl. This time-warp fantasy allows readers to experience the horrors of one of Hitler's death camps in a historically accurate portrayal. The setting—time and place—is believable through its detailed description of the people and events of the period. My students are stunned by Yolen's portrayal of the life-and-death experiences of the camp and often express that they had forgotten that the story was classified as a time-warp fantasy, experiencing a barrage of emotions at the end of the story. The setting, through Yolen's use of authentic detail, is as powerful as the plot in *Devil's Arithmetic*. Through the clear descriptions of time and place, readers can feel a whole range of emotions from apprehension and fear of the unknown to idyllic levels of comfort. The use of authentic settings in multicultural literature is key if credibility is to be assured.

CHARACTERIZATION

If the elements of plot and setting provide readers with a map and an anchor for the story voyage, the characters are then the traveling companions with whom they make the voyage. Within any story, readers will find primary and secondary characters, antagonists and protagonists, characters who mature and develop and those who do not. The elements of characterization help us to identify people we admire and respect and those who epitomize ignorance or evil. Authors help readers to develop understandings about characters through the use of language, appearance, and actions. Through these devices, a character can become a fully developed and complex or *round* character or he can remain undeveloped and *flat*. It is the use of these devices that provide readers with the opportunity to understand how a character thinks about and reacts to particular events within the story. It is also through these devices that the characters become believable and "real"—an important element in all literature but one that is particularly so in multicultural literature. It behooves authors to know how people of a culture and from a specific period might react to, speak about, and appear in specific situations. It is the nuance of understanding how and why characters behave in certain ways that can create an emotionally engaging character or create instead a character who reinforces stereotypes. Stereotypes in characterization are sometimes used to minimally present a secondary or stock character such as the character of Mr. Zukerman, the farmer who owns Wilber the pig in *Charlotte's Web* (White 1952). Through his actions and language, readers see Zukerman as someone who owns farm animals, has a hired hand who slops the pig, and attends county fairs. We know little of what he thinks outside of his simple nature that can be easily fooled by a spider. The character of Mrs. Zukerman briefly calls attention to the fact that it is the writing spider who is special not the pig, but she is quickly dismissed by her husband—another stereotype. Though these stereotypes may help readers to form a picture of Mr. Zukerman, it is not a very complimentary one. Zukerman, like his hired hand Lurvy, is seen as a simpleton, backward, and easily tricked and as one who dismisses his wife. Though stereotypes have been used often in literature, it is important to be mindful of them since they do a disservice by perpetuating negative images of people and cultures.

Another important element in characterization is the role of growth within a character. Primary or main characters in a story often undergo a change or an awakening that moves them toward maturity or a deeper understanding about the purposes of life. When this happens, a character is considered to be a *dynamic* character. For instance, in Laurence Yep's *Ribbons*, we see a young girl who is angry because she must give up dance lessons to help the family save money to bring her grandmother from China. Throughout the story, she is angry about the sacrifice and is bitter when her grandmother finally does arrive because she must share her room. Not until a major event occurs between them is she ready to move to a level of understanding and respect for her grandmother. At that point, we see an awakening that indicates growth and maturation for the young girl and the reader recognizes that there has been a significant change in the character.

On the opposite end of the spectrum are characters who do not change and who are considered *static*. These characters display character traits—good or bad—that remain virtually unaffected by the events of the story. A common example of a static character is seen in Charlotte of *Charlotte's Web*. In the beginning of the story, we see a spider who is thoughtful and kind to Wilber the pig. She does everything she can to protect him and to save his life. In the end, she dies after doing yet one final good deed. Charlotte is good and loving in the beginning, the middle, and the end of the story; she doesn't grow or change and therefore, is static in nature.

Readers come to know characters through descriptions of their actions, use of language, and their appearance. We respond to the positive and negative traits of certain characters and find ourselves remembering some of them long after we've finished the book. Certain characters are so believable that we grab for sequels so we can experience an adventure with them again. It matters not whether the characters are human like ourselves or fantastic creatures of the author's imagination; if we like the character and what she or he represents, we believe in the character. That is why it is so important to have believable characters in multicultural literature; we need to see ourselves in the reflection of strong characters, characters who stand up to the injustices of the world, thereby modeling for us what is possible in our world.

THEME

Map, anchor, and voyage act well not only as a metaphor for the sea but also as a metaphor for the elements of literature. In keeping with the metaphorical language, one might think of the theme of a story as the ship's cargo. Sometimes the cargo is obvious to all of us by the type of ship—oil tanker, cruise ship, or barge—and at other times, the cargo is hidden and not obvious to casual observers of ships. The theme or main idea of a story is often the same in that sometimes a reader can discover early in the text or just by the cover that a book will be about growing old (*Grandpa's Face*), coming to terms with death (*Everett Anderson's Goodbye*), or being different (*The Skin I'm In*). In those cases, we refer to the theme as being *explicit*; it is obvious. The other type of theme is like the hidden cargo of the ship; we have to get into the cargo and explore its contents. Those themes are *implicit* and are not always easy to spot or articulate. Sometimes, like the cargo of a ship, we may find multiple cargoes or multiple themes. Stories with implicit themes challenge us to sort through ideas settling on those kernels of truth that comment on human nature, society, or the human condition. These themes, universal by nature, are articulated throughout all genres of literature and will be explored in depth in later chapters. Authors of multicultural literature invite us to enter cultures that are not our own to seek the truths that lie within the themes of the stories they tell. Although the universality of human nature, society, and the human condition crosses all cultures, the darkness and pain found in stories such as *Amistad, Dragon's Gate, April Raintree*, and many others underlie themes that address the very foundations of racism and prejudice found in our country.

STYLE, MOOD, AND TONE

The arrangement of words on a page—the way an author uses language to tell a story—relates to the literary element of style. Style is what gives each story a personal voice in much the same way that a mast and sail differentiate a sailing ship from an ore barge. We are drawn into the mystery of a story by its style. It controls how we react and think about particular characters, settings, and events. By arranging a story in diary form, we feel personally connected to the character. By using long, embedded sentences, an author can pull us into a complicated event or character. We are manipulated by the formal or informal tone of the language and by the length of the sentences. Uses of figurative language, irony, humor, personification, alliteration, symbolism, allusion, and even metaphor all capture us as readers and move us through stories. Some of the most interesting indicators of the style of an author happen in the first few pages, acting as a hook to pull readers into story. An author who pulls his readers into a world of terror is Robert Cormier in *We All Fall Down*:

> They entered the house at 9:02 p.m. on the evening of April Fool's Day. In the next forty-nine minutes, they shit on the floors and pissed on the walls and trashed their way through the seven-room Cape Cod cottage. They over-turned furniture, smashed the picture tubes in three television sets, tore two VCRs from their sockets and crashed them to the floor . . .
>
> There were four of them and although their vandalism was scattered and spontaneous, they managed to invade every room in the house damaging everything they touched.
>
> At 9:46 p.m., fourteen-year-old Karen Jerome made the mistake of arriving home early from a friend's house. She was surprised to find the front door ajar and most of the lights on. The sounds of yelling and whooping greeted her as she stepped into the foyer.
>
> One of them, still holding the hammer that had demolished the piano, greeted her.
>
> "Well, hello . . ." he said.
>
> No one had ever looked at her like that before.
>
> At 9:51 p.m., the invaders left the house, abandoning the place as suddenly as they had arrived, slamming the doors, rattling the windows, sending shudders along the walls and ceilings. They left behind twenty-three beer cans, two empty vodka bottles, and damage later estimated at twenty thousand dollars, and worst of all,

Karen Jerome, bruised and broken where she lay sprawled on the cellar floor. (1991,
1–2)

The litany and crudeness of events spilling forth for the first three hundred
words will frighten most readers to the core but capture their attention for the
next 192 pages. What creates this? Style, of course. Cormier captures young
adult readers for years, and his style is what keeps readers coming back.

Another gifted writer who uses her writing style to capture readers is Mildred Taylor. In her book *The Well*, Taylor uses language and dialect consistent
with those in Mississippi during the early 1900s to bring her readers into a
time and place ravaged by racism and prejudice. The power of her style
speaks to us of injustice and hatred.

Charlie Simms was always mean, and that's the truth of it. Thing is we never knew
just how mean he was until that year back when all the wells in our part of Mississippi went dry. All the wells except ours, that is. We was blessed. We had good sweet
water in a well that ran deep. Most folks said our land must've been sitting on an
underground lake, if there is such a thing. Well, I don't know about that. All I know
is that well of ours never went dry. Now some folks wouldn't t've shared their water,
but Mama, and Papa too, weren't those kind of folks. They believed in sharing what
they had, and they tried to teach us boys—my brothers Mitchell and Kevin, Hammer
and me—the same thing; but sometimes it was real hard to do, to share, especially
when some of the folks you had to share with were folks the likes of Charlie Simms
and his family, folks who hated your guts. (1995, 9)

Readers of Taylor's earlier works will recognize David Logan as a young
child and the Logan family's arch enemy, Charlie Simms. Her writing style,
like her earlier works, promises a tale most readers will not soon forget.

Style, then, is the essential component of good storytelling. Authors capti-
vate us with their language and manipulate our emotions by giving the story
a voice.

POINT OF VIEW

To complete the sea metaphor, the point of view could be compared to the
ship's logs kept by the captain, his first mate, and galley cook. Each member
of the crew would have made the same voyage, but the experiences and
details recorded would vary from one to the other on the basis of the individual interpretations. The point of view an author chooses is determined by who
will narrate the story. The options are fairly limited, and the choice of point
of view will control what information is allowed to reach the readers.

First Person Point of View is used when the story is told through the eyes of one character—often the protagonist. In this view, the thoughts, feelings, and actions of the story are interpreted by one character only. (*The Well* by Mildred Taylor is a good example of first person point of view with David Logan telling the story.)

Omniscient Point of View is provided by a third person who is all knowing about every action, thought, and feeling present for all the characters in the story. (Robert Cormier's *We All Fall Down* is told with an omniscient point of view.)

Limited Omniscient Point of View offer the reader the sense of the story being told in the third person with some closer attention paid to a particular character's feelings. (*Grandpa's Face* by Eloise Greenfield employs this point-of-view technique.)

STEREOTYPES

It is important that we evaluate multicultural literature on the basis of literary merit and with an eye for stereotypes that reflect negatively upon the people of a culture. Earlier discussions revealed areas where stereotyping can occur, but the following lists specific questions to address that are consistent with the literary evaluative framework. If, in evaluating a text for children or young adults, you can answer yes to any of the following questions, you have reason for concern and should evaluate its appropriateness for classroom use on the basis of it being a positive example of multicultural literature. The following is a list of stereotypes to avoid in a plot:

- Does the conflict reflect bias?
- Does the resolution fit the reality of the situation or does it perpetuate the stereotyped social order?
- Does the resolution to a conflict happen because someone outside the culture resolved the problem?

Stereotypes to avoid in setting are as follows:

- Are historical events or periods inaccurately portrayed?
- Are cultural settings limited to "long ago and far away"?
- Do illustrations of the period appear generic rather than culturally specific?

The following are stereotypes to avoid in characterization:

- Are characters from diverse cultures depicted as outsiders rather than part of American society?
- Are characters from diverse cultures fraught with problems of poverty, drug abuse, alcohol abuse, or dysfunctional families?
- Are characters from diverse cultures portrayed as part of a group rather than as individuals?
- Are characters from diverse cultures portrayed as less intelligent, less attractive, or less successful?
- Do illustrations portray insulting or dated caricatures?
- Do characters of diverse cultures have "funny" clothing, hair styles, or nicknames?
- Do the illustrations show characters as looking the same?

Stereotypes to avoid in style are as follows:

- Is the text paternalistic in tone?
- Is the language spoken by the characters inappropriate for the period or social background?
- Does the text contain language that is offensive?
- Is the mood and tone of the story hopeless?

Stereotypes to avoid in theme are as follows:

- Are cultural differences viewed as a negative?
- Are universal themes of human nature, society, and the human condition not visible?

And the following is a stereotype to avoid in point of view:

- Is the story told from the point of view of a character from the dominant culture?

AUTHENTICATING DETAILS AND
THE ROLE OF AUTHORS

The debate between scholars about who should write and evaluate multicultural literature is often a hotly contested argument. Issues of cultural authenticity are tied closely to issues of power and oppression. Those cultures that have not been accurately depicted in the literature canon and whose depictions have been misrepresented and misappropriated have good reason to be distrustful of those outside their culture. As educators, we must insist on the very best examples of multicultural literature for our students and that means literature free of stereotyped images and inaccurate cultural information. There is no guarantee that racial, ethnic, or cultural heritage can ensure accuracy of content or literary quality; all authors must be attentive to the details. It does, however, suggest a degree of acculturation not available to those outside a culture.

There is also the question of ownership. In other words, who should tell the story. Folktales and fairy tales have long been part of the public domain as well as an appreciation for the tales that have crossed the cultural boundaries. But even in the folk literature, it is essential that stereotyped images be eliminated. The tale of the *Five Chinese Brothers* has long been criticized for its offensive illustrations, yet it is still on the shelves of bookstores around the country. No one will disagree that authentic and accurate depictions of a culture and its people are essential. What is still under debate, however, is who we should accept as authors of multicultural literature. In her 1997 article for the *New Advocate*, Jane Yolen asks that we not confine writers to the narrow corridors of their own personal experiences. She cites a number of books that she would not have been able to write had she been limited to her own cultural and geographical experiences (Yolen 1997).

The debate is far from over, but with clear criteria for evaluating the literature that we bring into our classrooms, we can provide the best examples to our students. The value of multicultural literature is important to our students and should not be discouraged by the debates. Instead, we need to be aware of the issues and concerns and make informed decisions as best we can about the literature we teach.

WORKS CITED

Bishop, Claire. *The Five Chinese Brothers*. New York: Putnam, 1938.

Clifton, Lucille. *Everett Anderson's Goodbye*. Illustrated by Ann Grifalconi. New York: Holt, Rinehart, and Winston, 1983.

Cormier, Robert. *We All Fall Down*. New York: Delacorte Press, 1991.

Creech, Sharon. *Walk Two Moons*. New York: HarperCollins, 1994.

Culleton, Beatrice. *April Raintree*. Winnipeg: Pemmican, 1984.

Curtis, Christopher Paul. *The Watsons Go to Birmingham—1963*. New York: Delacorte, 1995.

Flake, Sharon G. *The Skin I'm In*. New York: Hyperion, 1998.

George, Jean C. *Julie of the Wolves*. New York: Harper & Row, 1972.

Greenfield, Eloise. *Grandpa's Face*. New York: Philomel Books, 1988.

Hade, Daniel D. "Reading Multiculturally." In *Using Multiethnic Literature in the K–8 Classroom*. Ed. Violet J. Harris. Norwood, Mass.: Christopher-Gordon, 1997.

Jimenez, Francisco. *The Circuit.* New York: Houghton Mifflin, 1997.

McKissack, Patricia, and Fredrick L. McKissack. *Black Hands, White Sails: The Story of African-American Whalers.* New York: Scholastic, 1999.

Myers, Walter Dean. *Scorpions.* New York: Harper & Row, 1988.

———. *SLAM!* New York: Scholastic, 1995.

Namioka, Lensey. *April and the Dragon Lady.* New York: Harcourt Brace, 1994.

Paulsen, Gary. *Harris and Me.* New York: Yearling, 1995.

Sebestyen, Ouida. *Words by Heart.* Boston: Little, Brown, 1979.

Taylor, Mildred. *Mississippi Bridge.* New York: Dial Books, 1990.

———. The Well. New York: Dial Books, 1995.

White, E. B. *Charlotte's Web.* New York: Harper, 1952.

Woodson, Jacqueline. *From the Notebooks of Melanin Sun.* New York: Blue Sky Press, 1995.

Yep, Laurence. *Dragon's Gate.* New York: HarperCollins, 1993.

———. *Ribbons.* New York: Putnam, 1996.

Yolen, Jane. *The Devil's Arithmetic.* New York: Viking Kestrel, 1988.

———. "Taking Time: or How Things Have Changed in the Thirty-Five Years of Children's Publishing." *New Advocate* 10, (Fall 1997): 285–91.

Chapter Three

Picture Books

Some of the earliest memories we have about literature and reading are rooted in our experiences with picture books. As parents, we are encouraged to begin reading to our children almost immediately. One of my fondest early memories of my oldest child is captured in a picture of him lying on his back at about four months of age holding a cloth book up in the air and babbling cooing sounds as if reading. Despite the fact that he is holding the book upside down and unaware of decoding or formal structures of reading, he is in the act of reading—looking at the colorful pictures and reacting in a verbal sense.

The images we set before our children influence their view of the world, and picture books help them make sense of that world through artistic illustrations and photographs. Because of their early role in the lives of children, and because they are usually the first books children see, picture books are an essential component for us in the study of multicultural literature. While picture books in general tell stories, introduce concepts, and provide information, multicultural picture books do it specifically and with special attention to the details of diversity. Captivating illustrations and lyrical prose provide young children with an opportunity to develop multicultural perspectives and an appreciation for the richness of diversity. Through picture books, the mirror and window analogies proposed by Bernice Cullinan are introduced to young readers. Through multicultural picture books, children are provided with either a mirror that reflects a cultural experience familiar to them or a window that offers a view of a cultural experience that is not their own. In both analogies, cultural experiences are validated and broadened for young people.

By introducing multicultural perspectives through picture books, we, as teachers, offer young people the opportunity to learn about and value the diversity of the people with whom they will interact throughout their lives.

Picture books cross all genres and include a multiplicity of media techniques—all of which expand a child's understanding of literature and the visual arts. While this chapter provides the criteria and elements used in evaluating multicultural picture books, it also provides a focus on quality examples of the genres, the categories, and media techniques used by authors and illustrators of multicultural picture books.

CRITERIA FOR SELECTING
HIGH-QUALITY PICTURE BOOKS

To evaluate multicultural picture books requires a broad understanding of the literary and artistic qualities that go into the creation of a picture book. Although many books for young people contain illustrations, a picture book incorporates the illustrations as part of the storytelling. Whether it is a wordless picture book in which the story is dependent on the illustrations, or whether it is a combination of text and illustrations, the book's illustrator artistically and visually captures the nuances of the story for readers. In general, the evaluation criteria presented in this chapter can be used in selecting any picture books. The expanded criteria are specific to multicultural literature and are intended to highlight the need for authentic and accurate cultural representations.

To begin the evaluation process, it is helpful to identify the genre under which the book is classified. Lengthy criteria for specific genres are detailed in later chapters; however, some general genre headings and examples of books in those genres are given. A fuller discussion of the individual books listed is provided in the context of specific categories and characteristics of picture books.

Historical Fiction is a fictionalized story based on actual events. This is an excellent way to introduce students to the historical context of the struggles faced by the diverse cultural groups in the United States. Some examples include *Sweet Clara and the Freedom Quilt* by Deborah Hopkinson, *Baseball Saved Us* by Ken Mochizuki illustrated by Dom Lee, and *Encounter* by Jane Yolen.

Nonfiction (for example, biography, autobiography, and informational) books provide young students with a personal connection to the people who have made major contributions to society through their personal, professional, or political commitments. Some examples are *Duke Ellington* by Andrea Davis Pinkney, *Sadaka* by Eleanor Coerr, *Roberto Clemente: Young Baseball Hero* by Louis Sabin, and *A Boy Called Slow* by Joseph Bruchac.

Realistic or Contemporary Fiction helps us to see the real world with all its richness of diversity and in all its social dimensions of human nature. There are many excellent examples of realistic or contemporary fiction. Titles such as *Storm in the Night* by Mary Stolz and illustrated by Pat Cummings, *Angel Child, Dragon Child* by Michele Surat and illustrated by Mai Vo-Dinh, *Radio Man* by Arthur Dorros, and *Mother's Lap* by Ann Herbert Scott and illustrated by Glo Coalson all examine the role of relationships in the life of a child.

Folktales, Fairy, and Tall Tales provide us with the magic and imagination of a culture and its people. Some delightful titles to share with children include *Mirandy and Brother Wind* by Patricia McKissack, *Yeh Shen* written by Ai-Ling Louie and illustrated by Ed Young, *The Legend of the Hummingbird* by Michael Rose Ramirez and illustrated by Margaret Sanfilippo, and *Ma'ii and Cousin Horned Toad* by Shonto Begay.

Fantasy is the genre that provides us with the opportunity to exercise our imaginations through stories of dragons, ghosts, and mermaids. It challenges us to enter into a world not bound by our realities, yet one in which good and evil abound. Some examples of fantasy literature to be discussed more fully in this chapter include *Sukey and the Mermaid* by Robert San Souci and illustrated by Brian Pinkney, *Stranger in the Mirror* by Allen Say, *Abuela* by Arthur Dorros and illustrated by Elisa Kleven, and *The Mud Pony* by Caron Lee Cohen.

Poetry is the music of language, and through it we are able to listen to the voices of another's experiences. There are many poetry collections that have been illustrated for young people and some excellent examples are *In for Winter, Out for Spring* written by Arnold Adoff and illustrated by Jerry Pinkney, *Red Dragonfly on My Shoulder* translated by Sylvia Cassedy and Kunihiro Suetake and illustrated by Molly Bang, *Latino Rainbow: Poems about Latino Americans* by Carlos Cumpian and illustrated by Richard Leonard, and *The Earth Under Sky Bear's Feet* written by Joseph Bruchac and illustrated by Thomas Locker.

CATEGORIES AND TYPES OF
MULTICULTURAL PICTURE BOOKS

In addition to identifying the genre under which a particular multicultural picture book falls, is the identification of the type or category of the book. Since multicultural picture books span a wide age-group among children and are appropriate for various levels of reading, these categories help teachers to determine the book's usefulness for the group of children with whom they work. For instance, while cloth and board books are most appropriate for the infant-to-toddler age-group, their content will actually overlap with one or more of the other categories such as information books, concept books, informational story books, story books, photo essay books, or illustrated books. Another reason for their appropriateness is their durability. Some identifying features and examples of these categories are found below.

Cloth and Board Books are books whose design is durable and often washable. *Purrrrr* by Pat Cummings explores a young boy's relationship with his cat through a repetitive lyrical verse, and the rhyming verse of *Baby Dance* written by Ann Taylor and illustrated by Marjorie van Heerden shares the playfulness of a father and his young daughter. These books present the concepts of pets, families, language play, and the joy of relationships. The bold and colorful illustrations provide young children and very young readers the ability to see the actions of the text displayed clearly through vivid artistic representations.

Concept Books are books that include concepts such as the alphabet, numbers, colors, relationships, or other basic information. The illustrations often colorfully represent the written concept. These books are generally intended for early childhood reading and can be designed for infants and toddlers to use. Some examples of ABC books are *City Seen from A to Z* by Rachel Isadora, *Ashanti to Zula* written by Margaret Musgrove and illustrated by Leo and Diane Dillon, and *Navajo ABC: A Diné Alphabet Book* by Luci Tapahonso and illustrated by Eleanor Schick.

At the Beach by Huy Voun Lee introduces young readers to the concept of Chinese characters that represent such words as sand, mountains, mother, and child. The conceptual connections between the object and the character are visually demonstrated, thus helping young people to become more aware of the written language. While some concept books teach children about their letters and numbers facts, other books such as *At the Beach* and *Tortillas and Lullabies* written by Lynn Reiser and illustrated by Corazones Valientes focus on elements of language and family relationships. While reading the text and relating it to the illustrations, young children become more aware of cultural influences and are given the opportunity to develop as appreciation of the literary and artistic contributions cross culturally.

Nonfiction or Information Books are books that provide factual information in age-appropriate ways. The illustrations supplement the text and are done as photo-essay books or graphically rendered through an artistic technique such as drawing, painting, collage, or scratchboard. There are a number of information books that help students to understand about people and cultures. From biographies to explanations of cultural celebrations, this genre is the source material that many young readers use to form early impressions about people and cultures. It is essential, then, that these books be accurate and unbiased in their approach. Some examples of nonfiction picture books are discussed below.

Photo Essay Books are nonfiction texts that use photographs to document the written text. Several illustrators use this method to help young people understand the contemporary lifestyles from a specific cultural perspective. George Ancona has captured the faces and lifestyles of the Latino population of the southwest. In his 1998 publication titled *Barrio*, we meet Jose Luis and enter his neighborhood to learn about the people and the traditions that make this barrio and its people special. Ancona's photographs seize our interest with the colorful murals, celebrations, and activities of this community that is part of the mission district of San Francisco.

Cultural celebrations are often the focus of photo-essay books for young people. Written by Diane Hoyt-Goldsmith and featuring the photography of Lawrence Migdale, this duo has researched and created several books about cultural celebrations such as *Las Posadas, Celebrating Chinese New Year, Celebrating Kwanzaa, Celebrating Hanukkah, Day of the Dead,* and *Mardi Gras: A Cajon Celebration.* By explaining the particular cultural celebration through the help of an individual, families, and communities, their work is grounded in the real people and present-day celebrations. Young readers gain insight to cultural celebrations through the eyes of those who share their traditions with Hoyt-Goldsmith and Migdale.

Informational Story Books are books that present authentic information within a story format with characters, plot, and setting. The illustrations in these books enhance and help us to interpret the written text. Books that fall under this category may relate information about cultural traditions or historical facts, but they are situated in the context of a story with characters and often a sense of plot as it relates to revealing the event. Perhaps one of the most interesting examples of this type of multicultural picture book is *The People Shall Continue* written by Simon Ortiz and illustrated by Sharol Graves. Within the framework of this story told from the perspective of an oral tradition, we learn about the history of Native Americans and their struggle to protect themselves and the land (Ortiz 1988, 12). A real strength to this book is the power of the story—handed down—through language and illustrations that are simple in detail while complex in value.

Illustrated Books are books that rely primarily on an extensive written text with some illustrations serving to add detail or visual enhancement. *Coming to America: The Mexican-American Experience*, by Elizabeth Coonrod Martinez, is a good example of an illustrated book. In her book that is full of information about the Mexican American experience, Martinez gives her readers a view of historical and contemporary perspectives. Primarily written text, the narrative is supported by photographs, maps, and paintings to illustrate a particular discussion.

Story Books are fictional or nonfictional stories that have a well-developed sense of plot, setting, characters, theme, and style, tone, and mood. The illustrations complement the written text and enhance the readers' understanding of the story. Books in this category can include biographies and autobiographies, as well as fictional stories. Biographies such as *Duke Ellington* by Andrea Davis Pinkney and illustrated by Brian Pinkney provide young readers with a glimpse of this outstanding jazz musician's life while fictionalized stories such as Rudolfo Anaya's *Farolitos for Abuelo* provide readers with cultural information set in story form. Realistic fiction is a popular genre to introduce young readers to contemporary settings and issues from a multicultural perspective. *Too Many Tamales* by Gary Soto and *Tonio's Cat* by Mary Calhoun, both of which were illustrated by Ed Martinez, provide a look at contemporary experiences of two families. In these stories, we see Martinez capturing the richness of ethnicity visually while Soto and Calhoun weave the language and cultural influences through interspersed Spanish words and phrases. The culture nuances are imbedded into the story of family, friends, and responsible behavior.

THE ART OF MULTICULTURAL PICTURE BOOKS

Specific to the study of picture books is the criteria used to evaluate the elements of the art. Illustrators of picture books are highly skilled artists who create works of art that extend, enhance, and complement narrative texts for young people. Their works are becoming highly sought after by collectors. The ability to apply the elements and principles of design in ways that interpret, extend, and enhance the written text is evidenced through the many awards received by high-quality picture books. Although a more detailed discussion of the characteristics can be found in most comprehensive texts of children's literature, the following information is provided to refresh or reinforce your knowledge as it applies to our discussion of multicultural picture books.

To understand the elements and principles of the artistic characteristics found in picture books in general and in multicultural picture book in particular, let's discuss the characteristics in relation to the artwork of specific books.

Elements of Design refer to the use of line, shape, form, color, texture, and space to create images. An illustrator uses these elements to draw you into the action of the picture in much the same way that a writer uses letters, words, and phrases to create images of language. Board books for the youngest readers often employ bright and colorful images to engage toddlers visually. Pat Cummings's board book *Purrrrr* uses double-page illustrations to create a full view of the activity described, thus allowing a young child to focus on a single event for each two-page illustration.

Principles of Design refers to things such as balance, the sense of rhythm or movement, specific proportions and emphasis, the patterns, and the unity or variety found in individual illustrations as well as in the collection of illustrations that create the picture book itself. In thinking about the importance of these principles, we might compare them to literary story elements such as plot, setting, characterization, theme, and mood, tone, or style. For instance, in Pat Cummings's *Purrrrr*, the colors are bold and bright and the repetition of the sleepy, docile cat brings a level of expectation from the character to the young reader.

Media Choices and Graphic Techniques are the methods by which visual images are created. Drawing with inks, pastels, crayons, or charcoal will create a very different visual experience from illustrations created by painting with watercolor, gouache, tempera, or oil paints. Some illustrators choose photography to present a contemporary or realistic display, while others will choose the intricate techniques of woodcuts or scratchboard to provide a sense of detail and texture. Two very popular illustrators of picture books with very different styles are Jerry Pinkney and his son Brian Pinkney. The elder Mr. Pinkney has illustrated over seventy-five of his picture books using his own artistic style of pencil and watercolor. Whether it be *Drylongso* (Hamilton), *In for Winter, Out for Spring* (Adoff), *Mirandy and Brother Wind* (McKissack), *The Talking Eggs* (San Souci), or *Sam and the Tigers* (Lester), Jerry Pinkney's illustrations are colorful representations with a style all of his own.

Brian Pinkney also has established an illustration style that is distinctly his own. His signature technique is his use of scratchboard. With this medium, he covers a specially treated white board with black and then scratches or scrapes the surface to provide shape and texture. He then uses watercolors, rubbed-in oil paints, or acrylics to add color to his illustrations. Some of his books that use this technique include *Cendrillon* (San Souci), *Cosmo and the Robot* (Brian Pinkney), *Duke Ellington* (Andrea Davis Pinkney), *In the Time of the Drums* (Siegelson), *Seven Candles for Kwanza* (Andrea Davis Pinkney), *Sukey and the Mermaid* (San Souci), *Where Does the Trail End* (Albert), and *Wiley and the Hairy Man* (Sierra).

Another illustrator with a distinctive technique is Floyd Cooper. Using a technique called oil wash on board, he first uses oil paint to cover an illustration board and then with a stretchy or kneading eraser, he erases the paint to

form a picture (www.eduplace.com). In such books as *Coming Home*
(Cooper), *Granddaddy's Street Songs* (DeGross), and *Grandpa's Face*
(Greenfield)—just three of the more than two dozen he has illustrated—his
technique provides a sense of warmth to his illustrations that are rich and
glowing.

GUIDELINES FOR SELECTING
MULTICULTURAL PICTURE BOOKS

In evaluating multicultural picture books, it becomes important for us to
examine the artistic elements and the principles of design in relation to the
cultural representations presented. To avoid stereotypes or the potential for
stereotypes in the illustrations requires a level of knowledge about the culture
as well as a degree of sensitivity to the implications for potential stereotypes—both positive and negative. (Please refer to the section on stereotypes
in chapter 2.) As with all multicultural literature selections, the burden of
finding and presenting authentic or accurate information falls to the classroom teacher. We are expected to provide the best literary selections possible
for our students—selections that will inform, enlighten, and engage our students in ways that promote understanding and respect for the cultural themes
and issues presented. That is not to imply that we should engage in censor-
ship; rather, it means that we know the books that our students are reading
well enough to engage them in informed discussions about the strengths and
weaknesses of each book. To be able to discuss potential weaknesses such as
explicit or implicit stereotypes provides students with an opportunity to begin
to realize and understand the effect of stereotyping groups of people on society. By helping students to ask the following questions about stereotypes in
illustrations will facilitate an awareness and sensitivity often lacking in our
understanding of visual arts—picture book illustrations.

Stereotypes to Avoid in Picture Books. When evaluating picture books
for the possibility of stereotypes, we can begin by asking the following questions about their illustrations. Although we might not have all the right
answers, by asking the questions, we begin to look for and inquire about the
possibilities of implicit or explicit stereotyped images.

- Do illustrations of people appear to be generic rather than culturally specific? In other words, do the characters reveal individuality; do they have
  a variety of facial and physical features and attributes rather than similar
  ones, with everyone looking the same?
- Are the people portrayed in roles or jobs that are labor intensive only?

Does the work of female characters consist only of cleaning houses, cooking, caring for other people's children, or other types of unskilled labor positions or do the female characters hold a variety of jobs that imply educational accomplishments and training?

- Are males viewed primarily as nonexistent in family settings or are they portrayed as active fathers and family role models?
- Are hairstyles and clothing representative of the period; or are characters dressed in styles true to the period?
- Are cultural artifacts, ceremonies, or regalia used appropriately; or are they misappropriated?

Embedded in these questions is the expectation that we will help our students discern what it is we mean by the words *appropriate*, *authentic*, and *misappropriated* in terms of language, character depictions, and for our present discussion, picture book illustrations. This expectation can seem daunting to novice teachers whose experiences in the teaching of literature in general is limited. Without intending to do so, avoiding discussions of stereotypes can be construed as discounting or dismissing the importance of accurate cultural representations. How do we assure ourselves and our students that we are providing quality literature choices that contain no negative stereotyping? The best answer to that question is to employ a variety of evaluative criteria as we will discuss.

Do Awards Guarantee the Lack of Stereotypes? Often as teachers, we lean on those we consider to be the experts in the field to help us make decisions about appropriate literary choices. Awards such as the Newbery, Caldecott, or International Reading Association's Book of the Year or features such as The Reading Rainbow promote and endorse what is said to be the best literary representations for children. Since these books are reviewed by experts in the fields of literature and reading, we assume that the chosen few must be without fault or problems. It is important for us to remember, however, that awards are given for different reasons. Literary or artistic quality, as well as readability and age appropriateness are key criteria for many awards. If cultural representations are used within the text or illustration, it becomes essential that those representations be accurate and authentic in the nature of the presentation. Many award-winning books have been thought to include good cultural representations only to be called into question later by cultural experts. Therefore, it becomes important for us, as teachers, to evaluate soundly the literary selections we use in our classrooms, taking into account the appropriateness for the community within which we teach.

To understand better the types of questionable artistic representations present in some award-winning multicultural picture books, let us review two books that are sometimes used in classrooms. Two award-winning books that have been cited by experts as having problematic cultural representations are *Ten Little Rabbits* written by Virginia Grossman and illustrated by Sylvia Long and *Brother Eagle, Sister Sky* by Susan Jeffers. Both of these books are beautifully illustrated and are often praised in terms of artistic appeal. Artistic appeal, however, is not a sufficient reason to use books that are culturally insensitive—despite the awards they carry—as evidenced by the following vignette.

A couple of years after the publication of *Ten Little Rabbits*, I had the opportunity to be teaching a graduate-level seminar in children's literature. One of my graduate students taught preschool-age children at the Montessori school on the Saginaw Chippewa Reservation, adjacent to our university community. One evening she brought the picture book *Ten Little Rabbits* to class for discussion to illustrate the insensitivity of the book. Her discussion centered on a primary question: Why would an author or illustrator of the 1990s choose to mimic the offensive Ten Little Indians chant by placing rabbits in native dress? She expressed her own displeasure with the book on several different points that related directly to the use of the book with young children.

First of all, she acknowledged that the preschool children with whom she worked loved picture books with animals as characters—that animal fantasy was very important with young children. However, the problem with portraying *Ten Little Rabbits* as animal fantasy was that it carried conceptual knowledge—one of numbers and counting and the other, embedded, of anyone or anything that donned "Indian clothing" was a Native American. Her concern extended to the text, which perpetuated the idea that Native Americans dress in fringed buckskin, blankets, and loin cloths and do things such as send smoke signals, hunt with bows and arrows, and sleep in tepees. Her frustration with the level of misappropriation of cultural traditions in the text was expressed in ways that helped her peers understand the need to read closely written and visual elements of picture books that will be shared with children. The awareness deepened as we discussed the controversy surrounding such books as Susan Jeffers's *Brother Eagle, Sister Sky*. Although Jeffers's illustrations are beautiful, they have come under attack by some who question why the child on the cover and the children at the end of the text are not Native American.

Since not all of the graduate students in the seminar were practicing teachers, the question generated a class discussion that prompted other students to begin a search of other books that they considered insensitive to cultural traditions; contained stereotypes, inaccurate information, or language or illustrations that were offensive or uncomfortable to them. The discussion and exercise proved to be productive for all. We have highlighted some of the books that continue to raise questions among my students, but many are discussed at length by cultural experts in journal articles and book chapters found in the professional references at the end of this chapter.

CONCLUSIONS

Although picture books are effective ways to introduce a variety of cultures to young children, it is important to be alert to the stereotypes that can exist, whether they are intentional or not on the part of the author or illustrator. When one thinks about *The Ten Little Rabbits*, for example, there appears to be no reason to have incorporated a cultural context, such as the Ten Little Indians chant so often used two generations ago, that would instill stereotypes in the minds of new readers.

There are many wonderful selections of picture books that tell the folktales, the historical struggles, and the contemporary lives of all cultural groups in the United States. It is essential that as teachers we read and evaluate each text carefully before we share it with our students so we and the students can be assured that the very best of cultural representations are being shared. Throughout the rest of this text, you will be provided with a set of evaluation criteria for each of the genres covered and a discussion of some of our favorite texts in both picture books and novel formats. While our list is by no means complete, it does provide a sampling of texts that we and many of our teacher friends have used in the classroom. We hope you find the discussions useful. We conclude this chapter with a unit plan provided to us by one of our teacher advisers, Pamela Harris. Her intent and ours is to share some teaching tools that have been used successfully in a classroom so you might take from it some useful ideas and adapt them to your own classroom experience.

UNIT PLAN: BLACK HISTORY
by Pam Harris

Pamela Harris is a third-grade teacher at Pierce Elementary School in Flint, Mich. She has taught in the Flint School System for ten years. She earned a bachelor degree from Marygrove College. She is part of a very large and extended family and has one daughter.

Her philosophy in teaching multicultural education is based on a philosophy of teaching which is that it is imperative that all children obtain information that will help them become good, productive citizens in society. One way to reach that goal is to incorporate multicultural literature into the curriculum.

Multicultural literature encourages children to think and to look at others from a broad perspective. Also, it helps students to realize that although people are different culturally, in many ways people are alike. As children learn about their own heritage, it helps them feel connected to their cultural background and helps to raise their self-esteem. When children feel good about themselves, they are more accepting and understanding of others.

Rationale

Teaching black history is intended to help students learn about the contributions and achievements of African Americans. Teaching black history helps students become more aware and more understanding of the cultural diversity in society. Finally, teaching black history is a way to discover ourselves and others.

Overview

This unit plan is designed for first-grade students. This plan may be taught in one month. Each submitted plan is designed to be taught in a sixty-to-ninety-minute timeframe over a one-week period using a related extension from other core subjects. The four black Americans who will be studied are as follows:

1. Harriet Tubman: The Underground Railroad and the North Star
2. The Underground Railroad: *Sweet Clara and the Freedom Quilt*
3. George Washington Carver: Plant Doctor and Inventor
4. Martin Luther King Jr.: Marcher, Speaker, Leader, and Organizer

The key concepts to be learned are as follows:

- understanding oppression and linking it to heritage;
- understanding contributions and achievements; and
- understanding change.

There will be four key questions:

- What type of oppression did each of the studied African Americans experience?
- What contribution(s) did each African American make to the United States and U.S. history?
- Why did their contributions or achievements make them famous?
- What changes occurred in society or in the United States as a result of each contribution?

Lesson 1

Harriet Tubman: The Underground Railroad and the North Star

Subject: Social Studies
Objectives

1. The student will be able to compare and contrast the lives of African Americans before and after slavery.
2. The student will be able to illustrate a method that Harriet Tubman used to find freedom.

Materials

1. The book *MINTY: A Story of Young Harriet Tubman* by Alan Schroeder
2. A large star

Description of Lesson/Activity

1. Have all the children, but one (the leader), sit under their desks for two to three minutes. Tell them to sit quietly until the leader comes to get them. Have the leader go quietly around the room and have him or her take the students in groups to the north end of the room under a large star. Give each student who makes it to the north end of the room a sticker.
2. Questions:
   a. How did you feel when the leader came to get you?
   b. Did it seem to take a long time?
   c. How did it feel when you received a sticker for making it to the north end of the room?
   d. Why do you think there is a star hanging in the north end of the room?
3. Tell the children that as part of their black history unit, they will be

learning about a woman named Harriet Tubman who helped many people go north to freedom. They will also learn about why the North Star was important.

4. Read *MINTY: A Story of Young Harriet Tubman*
5. Discuss the book and the following questions:
   a. Why would people want to be free?
   b. How would you feel if you were a slave?
   c. Is there anything you can compare slavery to?
   d. What would have happened if Tubman had gotten caught helping the slaves?
6. As a class, compare and contrast the lives of slaves before and after slavery.
7. In their black history journals, have students write or illustrate how Tubman used the North Star to help others find freedom.

Assessment

1. The student clearly writes or illustrates and explains how Tubman used the North Star to help others find freedom.
2. The teacher observes and notes the student's understanding as he or she contributes to the compare/contrast chart.

Enrichment and Extensions

1. Take students to a museum of African American history.
2. Have students learn and discuss Negro spirituals (for example, *Swing Low, Sweet Chariot*; *Steal Away*; and *Go Down Moses*).
3. Students can act out an escape from slavery.
4. Science/Art—Read *The Night Sky* by June English, and complete the experiment to make a drinking gourd or alter the experiment and make the North Star.
5. Using a map, trace different routes that slaves may have used to find freedom.
6. Make a journal from a slave's point of view.

Lesson 2

The Underground Railroad

Subject: Social Studies
Objectives

1. The student will develop an appreciation for the struggle of slave children.

2. The student will describe how various people helped slaves find freedom using the Underground Railroad.

Materials

1. The book *Sweet Clara and the Freedom Quilt* by Deborah Hopkinson
2. A cloth quilt (preferably one in which some of the squares have personal meaning, like part of a father's shirt or grandmother's dress)
3. White cloth squares and fabric crayons (A parent volunteer can sew a quilt.)

Description of Lesson/Activity

1. Display the quilt in front of the students and discuss the patterning of the quilt.
2. Questions:
   a. What are quilts used for?
   b. Do you have quilts at home?
   c. Do you know where they came from?
   d. Do you know anyone who makes quilts? If so, how do they make them? What is used to make them?
3. Tell the students that people used to sew and make quilts a long time ago and that often quilts not only kept people warm but also told a story or were a way for people to remember others. Tell students about the displayed quilt (for example, this was my father's shirt. He used to wear it to work in the automobile factory where he worked. When I see it, it reminds me of . . .).
4. Quickly review with the students how Harriet Tubman helped other slaves find freedom. Tell the children they will be learning about others who helped on the Underground Railroad and how they helped.
5. Read the book *Sweet Clara and the Freedom Quilt*.
6. Discuss the book and the following questions:
   a. How did Clara help people find freedom?
   b. How did others help Clara make her quilt?
   c. How are Clara and Harriet Tubman alike?
   d. Although Clara did not get to freedom, what made her a conductor on the Underground Railroad?
7. In their black history journals, have students write or illustrate how Clara helped others find freedom.
8. Discuss the work slave children performed and have students illustrate something a slave child might have done on their quilt squares.

Assessment

1. The student clearly writes or illustrates and explains how Clara helped others find freedom.
2. The student shows his or her understanding of the work slave children did through the student's illustration on quilt squares.

Enrichment and Extensions

1. Take students to a museum of African American history.
2. Complete a map of the school playground.
3. Invite a quilter to come in to show students how quilting by hand is done and to display completed quilts.
4. Read the book *The Patchwork Quilt* by Valerie Flourney.
5. Math/Science—In small groups of three or four, decide how to make a square quilt using twenty-five square quilt pieces.

Lesson 3

George Washington Carver: Plant Doctor and Inventor

Subject: Social Studies
Objectives

1. The student will be able to list some of the things George Washington Carver made from peanuts.
2. The student will be able to illustrate and explain and/or write a statement explaining how Carver helped the cotton farmers.

Materials

1. The book *George Washington Carver: Plant Doctor* by Miena Benitz
2. Assorted items: ribbons, glue, markers, flour, bowls, cans, labels, sugar, peanuts in their shells, spoons, sugar, and so on

Description of Lesson/Activity

1. Have students sit in groups of four at several tables with assorted items at each table. Tell students to work in cooperative groups (using their group rubric) to make something that might be used by others. Also, each group must use peanuts in or with whatever is made.
2. Questions:

a. Was it hard to think of something to make?
b What made it easy or hard to think of something to make?
c. What did you make and how can it be used?
3. Tell the children they will be learning about George Washington Carver. They will learn about some of the things he made with peanuts. They will learn why he was called the "plant doctor." They will learn why he used peanuts to make different things. They will complete an experiment using peanuts.
4. Read the book *George Washington Carver: Plant Doctor*.
5. Discuss the book and the following questions:
   a. Why was planting peanuts good for growing cotton?
   b. Predict what might have happened if Carver had not invented so many uses for the peanut.
   c. Name some of the things Carver made from peanuts.
6. Have students work in pairs to complete the peanut chart illustrating at least three things Carver made from peanuts.
7. In their black history journals, have students write or illustrate and explain how Carver helped the cotton farmers.

Assessment

1. The student clearly writes or illustrates and explains how Carver helped the cotton farmers.
2. The student contributes ideas to completing the peanut chart showing at least three items Carver made from peanuts.

Enrichment and Extensions

1. Take students to a museum of African American history.
2. Show a video depicting the life of George Washington Carver.
3. Science—Have the class make peanut butter.
4. Set up a display showing items that Carver made using peanuts.

Lesson 4

Martin Luther King Jr.: Marcher, Speaker, Leader, and Organizer

Subject: Social Studies
Objectives

1. The student will be able to explain why there was a need for a leader such as Martin Luther King Jr.

2. The student will be able to explain how King helped others.
3. The student will be able to compare and contrast changes before and after segregation.

Materials

1. The book *A Picture Book of Martin Luther King, Jr.* by David A. Adler
2. Dated and modern pictures of segregation and integration

Description of Lesson/Activity

1. Whole group completes a KWHL chart (what you Know; what you Want/need to learn; How will you learn it; what you Learned) about King.
2. Tell students they will be learning more about Martin Luther King Jr. and how he became the leader of many blacks.
3. Read the book *A Picture Book of Martin Luther King, Jr.*
4. Discuss the book and complete the KWHL chart.
5. In cooperative groups of three, have students complete the before-and-after integration chart using pictures.
6. With completed charts, have each group explain why they chose to place their pictures on one side of the chart over the other.
7. In their black history journals, have students write or illustrate and explain how King helped others.

Assessment

1. The student participates in discussion to complete KWHL
2. The student works cooperatively in a group (using group rubric).
3. The student clearly writes or illustrates and explains how King helped others.

Enrichment and Extensions

1. Take students to a museum of African American history.
2. Write and publish an Affirmation of Peace as a whole group.

WORKS CITED

Adoff, Arnold. *In for Winter, Out for Spring.* Illustrated by Jerry Pinkney. New York: Trumpet, 1991.

Albert, Burton. *Where Does the Trail End.* Illustrated by Brian Pinkney. New York: Simon & Schuster Books for Young Readers, 1991.

Anaya, Rudolfo. *Farolitos for Abuelo.* Illustrated by Edward Gonzales. New York: Hyperion Books for Children, 1998.

Ancona, George. *Barrio: Jose's Neighborhood.* New York: Harcourt Brace, 1998.

Begay, Shonto. *Ma'ii and Cousin Horned Toad.* New York: Scholastic, 1992.

Bruchac, Joseph. *A Boy Called Slow.* Illustrated by Rocco Baviera. New York: Putnam, 1994.

———. *The Earth Under Sky Bear's Feet: Native American Poems of the Land.* New York: Philomel Books, 1995.

Calhoun, Mary. *Tonio's Cat.* Illustrated by Ed Martinez. New York: Morrow Junior Books, 1996.

Cassedy, Sylvia, and Kunihiro Suetake (translators). *Red Dragonfly on My Shoulder.* Illustrated by Molly Bang. New York: HarperCollins, 1992.

Coerr, Eleanor. *Sadako.* Illustrated by Ed Young. New York: Putnam, 1993.

Cohen, Caron Lee. *The Mud Pony.* Illustrated by Shonto Begay. New York: Scholastic, 1988.

Cooper, Floyd. *Coming Home.* New York: Putnam, 1994.

Cullinan, Bernice. *Literature and the Child.* 3rd ed. New York: Harcourt Brace, 1994.

Cummings, Pat. *Purrrr.* New York: HarperFestival, 1999.

Cumpian, Carlos. *Latino Rainbow: Poems about Latino Americans.* Chicago: Childrens Press, 1994.

DeGross, Monalisa. *Granddaddy's Street Songs.* Illustrated by Floyd Cooper. New York: Hyperion, 1999.

Dorros, Arthur. *Abuela.* Illustrated by Elisa Kleven. New York: Dutton, 1991.

———. *Radio Man.* Translated by Sandra Marulanda Dorros. New York: HarperCollins, 1993.

Flournoy, Valerie. *Patchwork Quilt.* Illustrated by Jerry Pinkney. New York: Dial Books for Young Readers, 1985.

Greenfield, Eloise. *Grandpa's Face.* Illustrated by Floyd Cooper. New York: Philomel Books, 1988.

Grossman, Virginia. *Ten Little Rabbits.* Illustrated by Sylvia Long. New York: Chronicle, 1998.

Hamilton, Virginia. *Drylongso.* Illustrated by Jerry Pinkney. New York: Harcourt Brace, 1992.

Hopkinson, Deborah. *Sweet Clara and the Freedom Quilt.* New York: Knopf, 1993.

Hoyt-Goldsmith, Diane. *Celebrating Chinese New Year.* Illustrated by Lawrence Migdale. New York: Holiday House, 1998.

———. *Celebrating Hanukkah.* Illustrated by Lawrence Migdale. New York: Holiday House, 1996.

———. *Celebrating Kwanza.* Illustrated by Lawrence Migdale. New York: Holiday House, 1994.

———. *Day of the Dead.* Illustrated by Lawrence Migdale. New York: Holiday House, 1994.

———. *Las Posadas.* Illustrated by Lawrence Migdale. New York: Holiday House, 1999.

———. *Mardi Gras: A Cajun Celebration.* Illustrated by Lawrence Migdale. New York: Holiday House, 1995.

Isadora, Rachel. *City Seen from A to Z.* New York: Greenwillow, 1983.

Jeffers, Susan. *Brother Eagle, Sister Sky.* New York: Dial, 1991.

Lee, Huy Voun. *At the Beach.* New York: Henry Holt, 1994.

Lester, Julius. *Sam and the Tigers.* Illustrated by Jerry Pinkney. New York: Puffin, 1996.

Louie, Ai-Ling. *Yeh Shen.* Illustrated by Ed Young. New York: Philomel Books, 1982.

Martinez, Elizabeth Coonrod. *Coming to America: The Mexican-American Experience.* Brookfield, Conn.: 1995.

McKissack, Patricia. *Mirandy and Brother Wind.* Illustrated by Jerry Pinkney. New York: Knopf, 1988.

Mochizuki, Ken. *Baseball Saved Us.* New York: Scholastic, 1993.

Musgrove, Margaret. *Ashanti to Zulu.* New York: Puffin, 1980.

Ortiz, Simon. *The People Shall Continue.* Illustrated by Sharol Graves. San Francisco: Children's Book Press, 1988.

Pinkney, Andrea Davis. *Duke Ellington.* Illustrated by Brian Pinkney. New York: Scholastic, 1998.

———. *Seven Candles for Kwanza.* New York: Puffin, 1993.

Pinkney, Brian. *Cosmo and the Robot.* New York: HarperCollins, 2000.

Ramirez, Michael Rose. *The Legend of the Hummingbird.* Illustrated by Margaret Sanfilippo. New York: Mondo, 1998.

Reiser, Lynn. *Tortillas and Lullabies.* Illustrated by Corazones Valientes. New York: Greenwillow, 1998.

Sabin, Louis. *Roberto Clemente: Young Baseball Hero.* Illustrated by Marie Dejohn. New York: Troll, 1997.

San Souci, Robert. *Cendrillon.* Illustrated by Brian Pinkney. New York: Simon & Schuster Books for Young Readers, 1998.

———. *Sukey and the Mermaid.* Illustrated by Brian Pinkney. New York: Four Winds Press, 1992.

———. *The Talking Eggs.* Illustrated by Jerry Pinkney. New York: Dial Books, 1989.

Say, Allen. *Stranger in the Mirror.* Boston: Houghton Mifflin, 1995.

Scott, Ann Herbert. *Mother's Lap.* Illustrated by Glo Coalson. New York: Clarion, 2000.

Siegelson, Kim. *In the Time of the Drums.* Illustrated by Brian Pinkney. New York: Hyperion, 1999.

Sierra, Judy. *Wiley and the Hairy Man.* Illustrated by Brian Pinkney. New York: Lodestar, 1996.

Soto, Gary. *Too Many Tamales.* Illustrated by Ed Martinez. New York: Putnam, 1993.

Stolz, Mary. *Storm in the Night.* Illustrated by Pat Cummings. New York: Harper & Row, 1988.

Surat, Michele Marie. *Angel Child, Dragon Child.* Illustrated by Mai Vo-Dinh. New York: Scholastic, 1989.

Tapahonso, Luci. *Navajo ABC: A Diné Alphabet Book.* Las Vegas: Sagebrush Press, 1999.

Taylor, Ann. *Baby Dance.* New York: HarperFestival, 1999.

Yolen, Jane. *Encounter.* Illustrated by David Shannon. New York: Harcourt, 1993.

Chapter Four

Folktales, Fairy Tales, and Tall Tales

While there is often a special relationship between fairy tales and children, parents and educators agree that fairy tales, when used thoughtfully, can both entertain and be useful in contributing to the education and socialization of young people. In *Fantasy Literature for Children and Young Adults*, authors and educators Gates, Steffel, and Molson state that the most common way of explaining the benefits is to note that, because they are highly imaginative, fairy tales can help cultivate young imaginations. In addition, they argue that fairy tales allow children, by facilitating self-imaging and self-identification, to gain entry into their own emotions as well as into others, thus enriching their emotional and psychological experiences. Furthermore, Gates, Steffel, and Molson believe that by introducing or reinforcing wonder, beauty, and mystery, fairy tales widen mental horizons and, in doing so, become invaluable in preparing the groundwork for children to acquire literary taste and gain access to their literary heritage. Finally, they point out that fairy tales can be used efficaciously to teach without overt sermonizing (Gates, Steffel, and Molson 2003).

A close and special association between fairy tales and children is not always universally applauded or accepted. Some critics believe that the aspect of escapism, the physical violence, and the elaboration of violence and terror in text and illustrations found in many fairy tales may have harmful or negative effects on young minds and imaginations. With regard to multicultural folktales and fairy tales, other concerns are raised, but for significantly different reasons. While folktales and fairy tales are based on culture and provide bridges of understanding that link us all to the human experience, there are many who believe that exposure only to folktales and fairy tales of cultural groups may severely limit the development of accurate information about the cultures. A great fear is that students whose literary experiences are confined to cultural folktales or fairy tales may not recognize the contributions a particular cultural group has played and continues to play in society today. Without explicit data that demonstrate convincingly one way or the other, it is not possible to dismiss completely these concerns or to ignore possible harmful effects, especially on impressionable children. At the same time, concerned adults should not underestimate the power and benefits of sharing a story. The affectionate and supportive environment that very often accompanies fairy tale telling is as much a part of the experience as the story itself.

According to Gates, Steffel, and Molson, fairy tales are short narratives composed or written in prose. Common to virtually all fairy tales are the ordinary qualities that include a blend of clarity, terseness, and being down-to-earth. This, combined with little ornamentation and a fondness for repetition and generic description (for example, an old man, an old hag, the youngest son, the oldest princess), provides fairy tales with their distinctive sound, look, and style. Part of the distinctive style is the highly oral quality, which is understandable, given the history of fairy tales. Fairy tales not only sound as if they are being recited but also hint at the presence of speakers addressing their stories to audiences (Gates, Steffel, and Molson 2003).

With the emphasis on action, fairy tales expend relatively little time and energy in setting up scenes, describing locales, and portraying characters. Avoiding detailed descriptions of all kinds and often omitting proper names, fairy tales focus on essentials and not extraneous details. Therefore, the details provided are not filler but instead are significant elements to the action.

The well-known introductory formula "Once upon a time" aptly indicates that the fairy tale's disregard for detailed characterization extends also to locale and time. In other words, the world of fairy tales is "placeless" and "timeless." Yet, oddly enough, events within this world reflect the same concern for weighty matters, such as survival, rebirth, growth, and maturation. Within the world of fairy tales, one finds also that miracles (the result of divine intervention in the affairs of human beings) and magic are not the object of surprise or admiration. Their appearances are a matter of course; their existence is so much taken for granted that miracles and magic must be acknowledged as pervasive in fairy tales. Further, it can be argued that, regardless of the beliefs of listeners or storytellers, miracle (which presupposes divinity) and luck (which does not) function similarly in stories as far as the requirements of plot are concerned.

Protagonists in fairy tales come from all social classes and are of both sexes. Generally speaking, they enjoy similar fortunes or misfortunes; having fallen from a relatively high social status to a lower one or already being situated there when the tale begins, the protagonists by the end of the stories are either returned to their high social status or substantially elevated. The rags-to-riches feature of fairy tales, along with the prominence of miracles and luck as the means by which protagonists achieve success, strongly suggests that the origin of fairy tales and their historical capacity to sustain interest owe much to individual or group wish-fulfillment on the part of listeners.

Two important features of fairy tales prevail. One is that the protagonists are frequently challenged explicitly to meet goals or fulfill purposes that involve taking journeys, undergoing physical ordeals, or enduring some kind of testing. Often obstacles block the quest or restrict the purpose, and they must be overcome or circumvented in order to achieve the goal. The other feature is the prevalence of the number three: three sons or daughters, three tasks, three obstacles, three helpers, three wishes, and so on. While some people believe that the fondness for three in fairy tales reflects the mystery and power associated with the Christian belief in the trinity, others suggest that the prevalence of the number three needs no other explanation than that it is part of the abstract style that is characteristic of fairy tales. These features cross all cultural boundaries, and it is the very archetype or motif that often provides teachers the literary tools by which to study multiple versions of the same tale as is discussed in this chapter's classroom unit.

TYPES OF FAIRY TALES

Fairy tales are easily divided into two categories, folk and art. Folk fairy tales tend to be old; some of them (or at least, parts of them) can be traced back to the dawn of recorded history. They are an oral literature, created by storytellers, told to audiences who, there is reason to believe, were active collaborators in the shaping of the tales. These tales were passed on from one generation to another by storytellers who likely retained, added, or embellished the tales to fit the needs and preferences of their audiences. The term *folk* is an indicator that these tales are indebted to folk or ordinary people. Although the exact nature of this debt is open to dispute, in general what is meant by debt is that the attitudes, values, aspirations, and needs of the common people are reflected and articulated in folk fairy tales. Not surprisingly, the tellers of folk fairy tales were anonymous, and only in the eighteenth and nineteenth centuries, when tales first began to be collected, most notably by the Grimm brothers, did information about the storytellers and their remarkable feats of memorization and narration become available. The Grimm brothers' collection of folk fairy tales may be the most famous and arguably the most influential of all collections, but by the end of the nineteenth century, virtually every European country and other countries throughout the world had their folk fairy tales systematically collected and edited, out of the conviction that their tales required preservation because they constituted an important part of a people's cultural and historical heritage.

The debate on the origin of folk fairy tales remains unsettled. Some experts champion monogenesis—the theory that a particular tale originated in one place and then, as people came to like it and wanted to share their enjoyment with others, spread gradually over a large area. Other experts, however, contend that polygenesis is a more likely explanation; because folk fairy tales represent universal situations or natural relationships, similar tales originated in different lands at different times as the people needed to express, articulate, or find value in a particular concern or situation. Regardless of which explanation is ultimately vindicated, it is clear that various versions of a number of tales exist in many countries and cultures. For example, according to one recent count, seven hundred variants of the Cinderella story have been collected (Opie 1974, 121). In addition, folklorists have discovered that, when a folk fairy tale is analyzed, various story elements or motifs can be isolated and shown to appear in tales from around the world. The phenomenon of motifs has deepened the understanding of the universality of folk fairy tales and their structure.

Art fairy tales are deliberately crafted by individual, known artists who either incorporate into their tales elements actually borrowed from folk fairy tales or imitate their form and spirit. Although often having an oral quality, art fairy tales are primarily literary, composed to be read as well as heard. As for their being preserved for subsequent generations, the survival chances of art fairy tales depend, as in the instances of other literary works, upon the talent of their creators and the degree to which they successfully incorporate or imitate fairy tale form.

Because art fairy tales are composed by individual authors, often they have a distinctive flavor reflecting the style of those writers, which is particularly important in our study of multicultural literature. Art fairy tales are often much longer than folk fairy tales, sometimes novel-length, and yet they retain most of the essential characteristics of the latter: a matter-of-fact acceptance of magic and miracle; a tendency to types of and extremes in characterization; a close relationship between characters and nature; emphasis on action rather than introspection and description; a relatively clear style; and the presence of goals, quests, and obstacles both internal and external.

CRITERIA FOR EVALUATING MULTICULTURAL FOLKTALES, FAIRY TALES, AND TALL TALES

Similar to poetry, the essence of evaluating multicultural folktales, fairy tales, and tall tales revolves around the language used, the cultural richness, and the active participation of the reader. The language sounds natural, with authentic sounding dialogue and melodious rhythms. For example, *The People Could Fly: American Black Folktales*, by Virginia Hamilton, has a collection of stories written about historic events in the lives of African Americans, from their enslavement through to the civil rights era. The dialogue is authentic, and it changes as you are taken from decade to decade in her stories. In *Uncle Remus Tales*, Lester and Pinkney use "a modified contemporary southern Black English, a combination of Standard English and Black English where sound is as important as meaning" (1999, x). Although language is probably the primary criterion for evaluating multicultural folktales, fairy tales, and tall tales, a second criterion is that the story is able to maintain the cultural richness of early retellings.

Because these tales have stood the test of time, so to speak, they will not lose the essence of the original message. They are timeless. A collection that exemplifies this is *Aesop: Tales of Aethiop the African*, by Jamal Koram and Demba Mbengue. This collection of stories speaks through the history and experiences of African Americans, and each of the twenty-nine stories are moral laden. In "The Fox and the Goat," the moral is "every smiling face don't mean you no good." And in "The Ostrich and the Farmer," the lesson is somewhat familiar: "People are known by the company they keep."

Another timeless tale that captures exquisite artwork is Marilee Heyer's *The Weaving of a Dream*. This Chinese folktale is retold and illustrated by Heyer and is about the journey that three sons make to retrieve their mother's magnificent tapestry. The two eldest sons decide that the task of returning their mother's tapestry is too much of an effort, and they take the money offered by the witch and do not return home. When the youngest son goes in search of the tapestry and his brothers, he is able to follow the rules the witch provides, find the mountain where the tapestry is located, and retrieve it for his mother.

SELECTIONS OF MULTICULTURAL FOLKTALES, FAIRY, AND TALL TALES

The previous chapters have situated culture within a specific time or place or both, whereas in this chapter, folktales, fairy tales, and tall tales reach outside the normal boundaries of time and place. This genre is also more expansive in that it includes stories that are not necessarily situated within the American culture and authors and illustrators who are not necessarily from the cultural backgrounds of the stories they tell. Generally speaking, these tales have been handed down through generations by many storytellers. And, with each retelling, the tale changes just a bit. These tales usually attempt to explain what the world was like long ago, and they provide a way for children and young adults to have a better understanding of how earlier generations tried to make sense of their world.

African

Oh, Kojo! How Could You! by Verna Aardema is an Ashanti folktale that brings to life the River That Gurgles, a magic river that grants wishes. When Tutuola, a lonely woman who wanted a child, goes to the river, she is granted her wish to have a son, Kojo. Because Kojo was born through magic, he grew at an astonishing rate and was a young man by the end of the first day. The river had told Tutuola that her son would not be perfect, but that it would all work out in the end. Believing this, she gave in to Kojo's foolish requests, but warned him to stay away from the trickster Anansi. Kojo, however, is foolish and was deceived three times by Anansi, before he finally outwits him, making his mother very happy. The illustrations in this book are by Marc Brown and are created with lead pencil, colored pencils, and watercolors detailing Kojo's adventures.

Aardema, who is not African American, has written many picture books that were inspired by African traditions. In 1976, *Why Mosquitoes Buzz in People's Ears*, written by Aardema and illustrated by Leo and Diane Dillon, won the Caldecott Medal. In this humorous West African tale, Aardema tells the story of how mosquitoes' gossiping gets him into trouble. The illustrations are bright and colorful extensions of the text.

Diane Wolkstein presents a comical tale from Haiti titled *Bouki Dances the Kokioko*. The illustrations by Jesse Sweetwater were done with liquid acrylics, watercolors, and gouache on watercolor paper. The story was inspired by Wolkstein's trip to Haiti in 1974, where this story was told to her by a young Haitian who performed it. The story tells of Bouki who was the friend of Malice, a servant and trickster who worked in the king's garden. The king enjoyed dancing but did not want to pay for dancers in his court so he made up a dance and called it the Kokioko; he issued a challenge and promised to pay five thousand gourdes to the first person who could dance this dance. Dancers, young and old, from all over came to show their "stuff" to the king so they could win the gourdes; however, no one was successful. Malice saw the king dancing one night and convinced Bouki that he could surely win with his help. After much coaching from Malice, Bouki did dance the Kokioko and was able to win the gourdes, only to lose it all later to the trickster, Malice. While the illustrations are colorful representations of the island setting, the facial features have been criticized for being stereotyped, too reminiscent of picture books such as Helen Bannerman's *Little Black Sambo*.

Readers will often hear about spider stories throughout this chapter. In *A Story, A Story*, Gail E. Haley writes a tale about how the spider stories began, and how they are associated with the name "Anansi." Haley tells her readers that the spider is meant to represent small or defenseless animals or people who happen to discover clever ways to succeed in challenging tasks. She begins her tale by saying that long ago there were no stories to share and that all the stories were kept by Nyame, the Sky God. When Anansi, the spider man, asked for the stories, Nyame gave him three enormous tasks to complete before he would be willing to hand over the box that held all the stories. Anansi had to bring to the god a leopard, a swarm of bees, and a fairy. Because of his cleverness, Anansi completed all three tasks, and the king gave him the box and proclaimed that his "stories belong to Anansi and shall be called 'Spider Stories'."

An Anansi story from Jamaica is retold and illustrated by Frances Temple in her book *Tiger Soup*. If you ever wonder why monkeys hang out in trees and tigers are no longer vegetarians, then this is a tale for you. The legendary Brother Anansi is a spider who wants to find a way to get Tiger away from his delicious sweet-smelling soup. The spider offers to teach Tiger to swim, but Tiger can only think about eating his soup. Finally, just to get Anansi off his back, he agrees to take a swimming lesson while his soup cools off. Anansi tricks the tiger by telling him that they both will close their eyes before jumping in the water. Of course, the spider does not go for a swim but heads back to Tiger's soup pot. After he eats all the soup, he crawls over to where a group of monkeys are playing and teaches them a song about eating tiger's soup. Thinking the monkeys are the ones who ate his soup, he seeks revenge—but to no avail as they swing away through the branches of a tree. Anansi, of course, gets away with his trickery.

Anansi, the spider, appears again in *Anansi and the Talking Melon*. This African folktale is retold by Eric Kimmel and illustrated by Janet Stevens. This time we see the trickster spider making his way into one of Elephant's melons. After getting himself into the melon, the spider enjoys the treat until he can hardly eat another bite. However, when he tries to leave the melon from the small opening, he discovers that he is too fat. Knowing that he would not be leaving for a while, he decides to trick Elephant into thinking that the melon can talk. Once he heard the melon talk, Elephant decides to take it to the king so that he could also hear the talking melon. On the road to the king, Elephant meets several other animals: a hippopotamus, a warthog, an ostrich, a rhinoceros, and a turtle. They are all excited about a talking melon and accompany the elephant to see the king. However, Anansi would not speak for the king at first, and this disturbed the king very much. Finally, when Anansi did speak, the king was very angry and hurled the melon away, splattering the melon and freeing Anansi.

Another trickster tale is a traditional African tale that Francesca Martin illustrates and retells in her book *Clever Tortoise*. It is set at a time when both the elephant and the hippopotamus are considered bullies. They brag about how they could trample all the smaller animals. The smaller animals get together to brainstorm about what they could do to protect themselves because they are afraid of these two large animals. The tortoise has a brilliant idea: he challenges both the elephant and the hippopotamus to a tug-of-war. By tricking them both, the tortoise is able to convince each of them that each one is stronger than the other.

From an Asante tale, a clever turtle appears in Jessica Souhami's book *The Leopard's Drum*, which she illustrates as well. Her illustrations were adapted from her own shadow puppets. This tale from West Africa is about Osebo, a leopard that was very stingy with his drum. He bragged to all the other animals about how huge his drum was, but he would not let anyone borrow it, including Nyame, the Sky God. Nyame summoned all the animals and promised a reward to the animal who could bring him the drum. The snake, the elephant, and even the monkey tried but without success. Finally, Arch-cheri, the turtle, tried and was able to trick Osebo and take the drum to Nyame. For his reward, the turtle asked that his shell be hard instead of soft; Nyame granted his wish.

When Lion Could Fly is the title of and one of the thirty-six stories in Nick Greaves's book about tales from Africa. Illustrated by Rod Clement, this volume combines animal tales from African folklore with interesting facts about animals that are native to Africa's grasslands and rain forests. "When Lion Could Fly and Why Vulture Scavenges" is an ancient Hottentot tale that tells about a time when lions flew and vultures couldn't. Another vulture story "Why There Are Cracks in Tortoise's Shell," from the Barotse, tells a story about a vulture and a tortoise who are the best of friends. At the end of these two stories, Greaves provides the reader with facts about vultures. This includes information about sizes, life span, habitat, diet habits, and breeding. Facts about the African animals featured in this collection are included in a glossary and add an informational element not generally found in folktale collections.

Another collection of African folktales was inspired by the Bantu tales of Southern and Central Africa and retold by Diana Pitcher and illustrated by Meg Rutherford. Although each story is about a specific event or person who contributed to the creation of the earth or parts of it, the entire book reads as a chapter book. In the first chapter, for example, we are introduced to First

Woman and First Man who, while working, meet Tokoloshi who, in the second chapter, provides them with the first flocks and herds. In the third chapter, The Calabash Child, Tokoloshi sends them a son. The book continues with other stories about fire, why apes have no tails, and why mosquitoes buzz.

In *The Origin of Life on Earth*, a Coretta Scott King Award book, author David Anderson and illustrator Kathleen Atkins Wilson retell an ancient African creation myth that describes a time when there were only two regions: the sky above and the water below. In this tale, Olorun, the supreme god of Yoruba, decides to send down an *orisha*, a powerful messenger (synonymous with angel). Obatala was the *orisha* who was sent down because he was concerned about the "watery waste" of the domain below them. He wanted to be able to use his powers to create a world with people who would take care of it. With only a chain of gold, sand, palm nuts, maize (corn), and "the egg," he left for his journey. After Obatala had molded clay into an image of himself through a reflection in a pond, the mighty Olorun blew the breath of life into them and set what is now called Earth on its axis.

The Magic Tree written by T. Obinkaram Echewa and illustrated by E. B. Lewis is a Nigerian folktale that is a combination of a Cinderella, Rudolph the red-nosed reindeer, and Moses on Mt. Sinai. What began as a very difficult time for the story's main character, Mbi, eventually turned into a time of celebration that is beautifully detailed through watercolor illustrations. Mbi's first challenge was with a family who made him work more and harder than all the other children. Also, the family starved him, giving him only scraps to eat. A second challenge he faced was that the other children would never play with him. They only tolerated Mbi when they needed someone to pick on and ridicule. He faced a third challenge when he heard a voice from nowhere, giving him instructions on the planting of a magic tree. This tree grew at an extraordinary speed, producing flowers and ripened fruit in less than a day. With this tree, Mbi could eat as much fruit as he wanted, and it "bowed" to his every command. Despite the wonderful tree, the villagers were still mean to Mbi. Only through an act of heroism was Mbi finally able to change the actions of the people in his village and find his place as part of the community.

If you ever wanted to know why cats and rats are arch enemies or why cats purr, then you should read the African tale by Ashley Bryan titled *The Cat's Purr*. According to this tale, Cat and Rat were best of friends once upon a time. They did almost everything together around the house and in the field. Cat shared his flute with rat and they had a great friendship. However, one day Cat's uncle brought him a drum that had been passed down from generation to generation. This very special drum could only be stroked in order to hear its melodious sound. You could not tap it, rap it, beat it, or poke it. In fact, Cat was not to let anyone else use it. This caused a big problem for Rat who was used to Cat's generosity and friendship. Since Cat would not share his drum with Rat, Rat devised a plan, a trick to play on Cat. The trick worked for a while, but when Cat found out what was going on, he became furious with Rat and threatened to eat him. The tale states that the events that happened that day caused cats and rats to hate one another from that day forward.

The book *When Birds Could Talk and Bats Could Sing* by Virginia Hamilton and illustrated by Barry Moser consists of a series of short stories about a mythical time when our feathered friends could communicate like humans. The stories are based on African American folktales that began in the South during the enslavement of Africans. Each of the eight stories tells a tale about Bruh Sparrow, Sis Wren, Bruh Buzzard, or Miss Bat. Each story concludes with a lesson from which children can learn. The stories themselves are inspiring and make the reader ponder and even wonder if there could be some truth to the scenario.

Another folktale by Hamilton is a version of the German story Rumpelstiltskin titled *The Girl Who Spun Gold*. This story highlights an ultimatum a young woman receives from her husband, the king, which is to spin gold. With the help of a funny, little ugly man, the young woman was able to have the gold for the king. All that the little man asked in return was that she guess his name or that she leave with him and live in the woods. Hamilton's version is from the West Indies and is illustrated by Leo and Diane Dillon. The artwork was done with acrylic paint on acetate, painted over with gold paint.

In another collection by Hamilton titled *Her Stories* is a spirited celebration of the strength and dreams of women and their precious gift of life and love from generation to generation. The book includes nineteen stories, organized into the following five categories: (1) Her Animal Trees; (2) Her Fairy Tales; (3) Her Supernatural; (4) Her Folkways and Legends; and (5) Her True Tales. Each story ends with special comments by the author regarding specific information about how the story originated. This Laura Ingalls Wilder Medal Award winner was also illustrated by Leo and Diane Dillon.

Virginia Hamilton's *In the Beginning: Creation Stories from around the World*, illustrated by Barry Moser, won the Newbery Honor Book Award. Similarly to *Her Stories*, each creation story in this collection is followed by the author's comments that tell of its origin. The stories are set in Guinea, China, Australia, and Iceland.

Julius Lester and Jerry Pinkney have teamed up and worked on several books, including *Uncle Remus: The Complete Tales* and *John Henry*. I remember growing up singing a ballad about John Henry and his competition with the steam drill. As the story goes, when John Henry was born, he grew up literally overnight. He was able to help his father rebuild the porch that he had broken the day before—the day of his birth. As a child, John Henry was exceptionally strong and miraculously quick. He was also very competitive and once raced against a horse and beat the horse and his rider. According to the tale, he was so fast, that during that race, "the wind was out of breath trying to keep up with him." Finally, he went up against a steam drill that was making its way through a mountain, while he made his way with only a hammer and a rainbow. And as the story ends, he died with a hammer in his hand.

Another joint effort by Lester and Pinkney is *Sam and the Tigers*, which is a revised version of the controversial story Little Black Sambo. The colorful artwork was prepared using pencil and watercolors. In this story, people and animals live in a town called Sam-sam-sa-mara where all the people are named Sam, including the women. Although it may be confusing at first, you soon realize which Sam was being discussed. As the story unfolds, young Sam is shopping with his parents for school clothes. He decides that he is old enough to select his own clothes and chooses the brightest array of clothes. His pants were purple, his shirt was yellow, his jacket was red, and his shoes were silver, and he carried a green umbrella. On his way to school for the first day, he encountered five tigers that vowed that they would devour him. On each occasion, he was able to spare his life for a piece of clothing. While down to his underwear, the tigers began to remove the items that they got from Sam and fought over who was the best-dressed feline. Not only was Sam able to get his new clothes back, but he brought home enough butter to share with the neighbors as they ate homemade pancakes.

In *Uncle Remus*, Lester retells the stories of Brer Rabbit, while Jerry Pinkney illustrates the story with richly detailed drawings. This six-hundred-page volume contains stories about the trickery of Brer Rabbit.

Other stories about Brer Rabbit can be found in *Jump* and *Jump Again!* by Van Dyke Parks and Malcolm Jones. Both books were illustrated by Barry Moser.

The Ethiopian tale *Fire on the Mountain* written by Jane Kurtz and illustrated by E. B. Lewis is about a clever boy, Alemaya, and his dream to be rich. Challenged by a rich and boastful man, Alemaya wins a wager but soon discovers that he will need the help of his sister and the rich man's servants to collect his due. Kurtz grew up in a small village near Ethiopia and was inspired by many of the stories she heard before coming to the United States.

Angela Shelf Medearis's very humorous book *Too Much Talk* is a cumulative story about a yam, a dog, a fish, a piece of cloth, and a river—all of whom startle the humans they encounter with their gift of speech. After the king hears their fantastic story, he becomes annoyed with them and dismisses them. The king, however, is taught quite a lesson when his own throne speaks its mind to the king. This West African tale is illustrated by Stefano Vitale in oil paints on wood.

Patricia McKissack, who has written many children's books, including poems, has also written several folktales and tall tales. *The Dark-Thirty* refers to the half hour before the sun sets. This is supposedly the time when supernatural tales would be the most convincing and believable. This collection of ten ghost stories was a result of stories McKissack heard as a child while she lived in the South. Her grandmother would tell stories about runaway slaves who became ghosts or about a woman who became insane when the members of her family died in a tragic fire. McKissack's tales were also inspired by African American history, and they range from the time of slavery to the civil rights movement. The illustrations were done by Brian Pinkney in his highly acclaimed scratchboard technique that enhances the mystical aspects of the tales.

In another book, McKissack writes about a tradition that has been rooted in African American culture called the *cakewalk*. The cakewalk is a dance in which the winning couple, as determined by their performance, takes home a cake. In *Mirandy and Brother Wind*, Mirandy is determined to win the prize in her first junior cakewalk contest with Brother Wind as her partner. Her first quest, however, is to catch him. She had been told that if she could catch Brother Wind that he would grant her wishes. The illustrations were done in exquisite watercolors by Jerry Pinkney, and the book received a Caldecott Honor Book Award.

In *A Million Fish . . . More or Less* (McKissack 1992), Hugh Thomas had heard many stories from Papa-Daddy and Elder Abbojon about a number of events that happened in Boyou Clapateaux. Some of these stories were just unbelievable, such as the five-hundred-pound wild turkey they caught and the largest snake ever seen that had legs! Hugh Thomas was amazed, yet skeptical of some of these tales. However, one day after he caught a million fish, he was so excited that he could hardly wait to get home and share the news. On his way, he had to overcome many obstacles, from alligators, to raccoons, to birds. By the time he got home, all he had left were three small fish and a big story of his own to tell. The illustrations were done in bright, expressionistic paintings by Dena Schutzer.

Wiley and the Hairy Man (Sierra, 1996) is a folktale from Alabama retold by Judy Sierra and illustrated in vibrant oil paints over scratchboard by Brian Pinkney. This tale warns readers of a hairy beast that captures people who are not cautious, such as Wiley's dad. As the legend goes, Wiley needed to outwit the Hairy Man three times before he would be free of him forever.

Through an array of humorous adventures, Wiley and his mother were finally able to outsmart the monster.

In *Cendrillon,* a Cinderella story with a Caribbean twist, Robert San Souci and Brian Pinkney collaborate on this timeless tale. Set on the island of Martinique, Cendrillon's mother died soon after her birth. Her father remarried and so the story unfolds. As Cendrillon grows up, her stepmother and stepsister are very cruel to her, making her do all the housework, including washing the laundry at the river. Her godmother, Nannin, always kept an eye on her after her mother had passed and stayed in touch with her as she grew up. As the story unfolds, Cendrillon wanted to go to the ball; with the help of her godmother, a fruit a' pain (breadfruit), six agoutis (rodents), a manicou (an opossum), and a little magic, Cendrillon was on her way. This story incorporates elements from West Indian culture and costumes. A glossary of French Creole words and phrases is also provided.

Robert San Souci and Brian Pinkney team up again to give readers another magical story with *Sukey and the Mermaid.* The illustrations were done on scratchboard and in oil pastels. The main character, Sukey, lived with her mother and stepfather, a man she referred to as "Mr. Hard-Times." Once, while she sat in the sand on a beach, a "beautiful, brown-skinned" mermaid appeared. They became friends and the mermaid gave Sukey a precious gold coin each day they were together. Her parents became suspicious of this new-found wealth and eventually discovered the mermaid. After her mother and stepfather tried to capture her, the mermaid disappeared for a long time only to appear to Sukey in a dream promising to take her away. Years later, Sukey returns a wealthy woman in search of the man the mermaid told her to marry. But once again, greed rears its head in the form of Sukey's stepfather, and he kills the man she is to marry. Broken-hearted, Sukey returns to the sea to share her sad story with the mermaid. She is given a magic pearl to place on the lips of the man she loves, and he awakens from the dead to identify his murderer and to live happily ever after with Sukey. The mystic and magic of this story will delight the young and the young at heart.

In *The Talking Eggs,* another rendition of the Cinderella-like tale, San Souci weaves the story about a mean-spirited mother who favors one daughter over the other. Blanche, the rejected daughter, is summoned to do all the chores while her sister and mother sit around being lazy and vindictive. When Blanche befriends a witch, she is brought into a world of magic, which includes a two-headed cow, rainbow colored chickens, and talking eggs. Her mother sends her spiteful sister to find this witch and to trick the witch into giving her some of the riches that she gave Blanche. However, because of the nastiness of this sister, the trick backfires on her and her mother. This southern folktale with watercolor illustrations by Jerry Pinkney is a Caldecott Honor and Coretta Scott King Award Honor book.

"[It] takes a mighty strength not to forget . . ." is what Mentu finally understood when his grandmother told him there would come a time when he needed to be "strong-strong." In the book *In the Time of the Drums* Kim Siegleson tells of a slave, Twi, who came from the Ibo tribe. She worked on a plantation in Georgia near Teakettle Creek, but like most slaves, she longed for her home in Africa. She kept hold of many of her traditions by sharing stories and teaching Mentu to beat the drums. Most people thought that Twi possessed magical powers, and so she was both feared and respected by young and old. When a ship landed with a cargo of slaves from Twi's homeland, magical powers were revealed and the legend begins. Illustrated by well-known artist Brian Pinkney, the books' illustrations depict many of the drums from his own private collection.

The African tale *Mufaro's Beautiful Daughters* was first published in 1895 and was retold and illustrated by John Steptoe in 1987. His illustrations were inspired by the ruins of an ancient city found in Zimbabwe. In this Cinderella story, Mufaro has two daughters, Manyana and Nyasha. Manyana, the ill-tempered sibling, always teased and taunted her sister. When the Great King announced that he was looking for a bride, the girls began their journey to the city. Along the way, many mystical events happened to the sisters and their reactions lead the king to make one of them his bride. This book received the Caldecott Honor Book Award.

Remembering that most folktales are based on some truths, no matter how small that truth may be, does not seem to fit the tale *Casey Jones's Fireman: The Story of Sim Webb* by Nancy Farmer. According to Farmer, Casey Jones and Sim Webb were real people who worked for the railroad, and an accident took the life of Casey Jones in 1900. As the story goes, Casey was lured into using a seven-quill whistle, direct from the trumpet of the angel Gabriel. Sim was suspicious of this whistle and its previous owner. Because train whistles were powered by the steam, it was apparent to Sim that this seven-quill whistle was a disaster waiting to happen. And sure enough, a disaster did happen as the train reached maximum speeds in order for Casey to be able to blow the seventh pipe. Sim stopped shoveling coal into the fire when he noticed another train coming straight toward them and Casey jammed on the brakes for dear life. Unfortunately, it wasn't enough to save his life. Sim, however, jumped off the train on Casey orders and survived to be able to tell the story.

Asian American

Illustrated by Ju-Hong Chen with ink and watercolors on handmade rice paper, *The Jade Stone* is a Chinese folktale adapted by Caryn Yacowitz. In her first picture book, Yacowitz provides a pictorial index of the characters, from Chan Lo, the stone carver, to Imperial Ambassador. This tale is about Chan Lo and his request from the Imperial Ambassador to carve him a dragon from a jade stone. Chan Lo, who can only carve what he hears from the stone, had a serious dilemma. When he could not hear the dragon in the stone, he carved what he heard and was thrown into a dungeon. However, after three days, the ambassador begins to hear what Chan Lo heard, and he was released and returned to his "village in a way befitting the Master Carver to the Great Emperor of All China."

Ed Young, a renowned illustrator, has provided graphics for many books for children, including folktales. His book *Lon Po Po*, a Caldecott Medal winner, is a Chinese version of Little Red Riding Hood. Young uses a style that combines ancient Chinese panel art and contemporary palette of watercolors and pastels.

In *Yeh-Shen*, by Ai-Ling Louie, Young again uses pastels and shimmering watercolors to illustrate this Chinese version of Cinderella.

Another book written and illustrated by Ed Young is *Night Visitors*, which is a retelling of a Chinese folktale that was inspired by stories told during the T'ang Dynasty and during 6 BC. This story tells about a very kind-hearted boy who had to find a way to keep ants out of his family grain. Through a dream, he was able to figure out how to seal the grain shed to keep the ants out so that his father would not need to drown all the ants.

In another ancient tale, Young with author Feenie Ziner portray the story of a boy, his father, and a cricket. *Cricket Boy* is a tale about the poor man Scholar Hu who was raising his son Hu Sing. Hu Sing was not interested in many of the important things that his father thought he should be interested in. His son's joy came from crickets, and he had a nice collection. On the day that the emperor requested that his cricket fight Hu Sing's best cricket, Hu Sing accidentally broke the jar that held his fighting cricket. Because of the shame he felt, Hu Sing plunged into the river and was presumed dead. But because of certain Chinese traditions, Hu Sing's body had to rest for seven days before he could be buried. During that time, his father found another cricket that had been given to him in a vision, and this was the cricket that fought and defeated the emperor's cricket. What happens next is truly amazing, but readers soon discover how Hu Sing came by the name of Cricket Boy.

Another version of this tale can be found in *The Cricket Warrior* retold by Margaret and Raymond Chang. In this version, Wei Nan seeks the help of a mysterious old man to turn him into a cricket, which saves his family.

In *Mysterious Tales of Japan*, Rafe Martin provides the reader with ten stories of a somewhat cryptic and puzzling nature. "Black Hair" is about a warrior who was not satisfied with his life. He was used to having status in his society, but now with his lord dead, he had lost his position in the community. His wife, who had long, silky black hair was bringing in money by weaving. Since this was not enough for the warrior, he left his wife to remarry—his new lord's daughter. With his new bride, he has riches and status, but eventually he longed for the love of his first wife. He finally left to find his house and yard in turmoil and all that was left of his wife was her beautiful black hair.

In "The Frog's Gift," a man saves the life of a frog from a snake and promises the snake one of his daughters in return for the life of the frog. The youngest daughter agrees to marry the snake but needed 1,000 gourdes and needles. Using the gourdes and needles as distractions for the snakes, she escapes to a hut in the woods. The next day, the old woman in the hut convinces her that she is the chosen one to wed the lord. How ironic that a girl who was sentenced to marry a snake ends up marrying royalty, but only with the help of a frog.

Another frog tale has to do with the frogs in Sheila Hamanaka's *Screen of Frogs*. This Japanese tale is about the life of a lazy, wealthy boy who grows up to be a lazy man. Instead of working, which he had promised that he would never do, when he needed money he would sell off his possessions, which included his property. At a time when he barely had anything left to sell except his house and a mountain, he received a visit from a frog. This frog begged him not to sell the mountain because it was the animal's source of survival. Although the man first thought he was dreaming, he did not sell the mountain. Then when his screen, which had been blank, is covered with frogs, he becomes a changed man and begins to work.

Three Strong Women, another tall tale from Japan, was originally written by Claus Stamm and Kazue Miurmura in 1962 and was an ALA Notable Book. Its copyright was renewed in 1990 with pictures by Jean and Mou-sien Tseng. This humorous tale finds Forever-Mountain, a strong and conceited man, being strong-armed by Maru-me, a woman. After finding out that Maru-me was strong, he also found out that her mother and grandmother could carry cattle and pull up trees from out of the ground. It was decided that the women would help him prepare for the wrestling match that would be in three months. During that three-month period, Forever-Mountain became very, very strong. He even managed to pin grandmother down for a short time. When the time came for the wrestling match, he prepared to leave, but not before he asked for Maru-me's hand in marriage.

The team of Jean and Mou-sien Tseng have illustrated over thirty books for children, including some written by well-known author Laurence Yep. In *The Ghost Fox*, a boy, Little Lee, has to fight a demon who invaded his mother's body. His father is out at sea and Lee has to rely on his own wits to help his mother. This story is adapted from a seventeenth-century Chinese ghost story.

Also illustrated by the Tsengs and retold by Yep is *The Khan's Daughter: A Mongolian Folktale*. This story centers on a sheep herder who had been told by his dying father that he would one day marry the Khan's daughter. When he went to seek her hand in marriage, the Khan and his wife gave him three dangerous tasks to solve. After he was victorious with the first two, he felt confident about the last request: to conquer Bagatur the Clever and Mighty.

Another Chinese tale that has the main character needing to fulfill three impossible tasks is *The Shell Woman and the King* by Yep. This tale is illustrated by Yang Min-Yi in fluid watercolor paintings. In the story, Shell can transform herself into a giant seashell and the king is so overwhelmed with her that he wants her to leave her husband and become his queen. When she refuses, the king threatens her by threatening to take her husband's life if she does not successfully complete the three tasks. Through her cleverness, she is able to outwit the king and get away from him, leaving nothing but ashes in the place where the king resides.

An additional mythical tale by Yep and magnificently illustrated by Kam Mak, can be found in *The Dragon Prince: A Chinese Beauty and the Beast Tale*. The beast in this story is a dragon that lived beneath the sea. Out of the seven daughters that the farmer had, his youngest daughter was the only one who would make the sacrifice to save her father. And as it turns out, the beast is a handsome prince in disguise, and the daughter falls in love with him and they marry. A jealous sister tries to kill the youngest sister and replace her. However, the prince knew something was very wrong and would not rest until he found his true love.

Another ghost story by Yep is *The Man Who Tricked a Ghost*, which is about Sung, a brave man who was not afraid of anything. Based upon a story from the third century, this story basically tells readers how Sung was able to outwit a ghost who was determined to scare him or kill him. Once Sung found out the one thing that all ghosts must stay away from, he was able to keep the ghost from transforming into various forms.

Finally, in *Junior Thunder Lord*, Yep gives us a Chinese fable about how a little kindness can go a long way. Because Yue was able to help the big hairy man, he was repaid in a big way that helped his entire community.

In *Tongues of Jade*, Yep provides the reader with seventeen Chinese American folktales from a variety of Chinese communities across the United States. This book was illustrated by David Wiesner and divided into five sections: Roots, Family Ties, The Wild Heart, Face, and Beyond the Grave.

These sections deal with both mythical and miraculous Chinese tales. Another Yep and Wiesner collaboration was *The Rainbow People*, which included twenty Chinese folktales and was also divided into five sections: Tricksters, Fools, Virtues and Vices, In Chinese America, and Love.

Yoshiko Uchida wrote several folktales for children and young adults during her lifetime. The first two books, *The Magic Listening Cap* and *The Sea of Gold* were written nearly four decades ago. These stories provide readers with many folktales about Japan.

The Magic Listening Cap was the sequel to *The Dancing Kettle*, written in 1949, and follows its style of humor and wisdom. *The Dancing Kettle* includes fourteen stories about Japan. One story, "The Rabbit and the Crocodile," tells about a somewhat clever rabbit who played a trick on a crocodile to get a ride across the river. When the crocodile realized that he had been tricked, he pulled the fur off of rabbit's body. Although the rabbit was tricked by a group of mean gods, a good god eventually came to his rescue and helped him to get his fur back.

Many of these stories were new for American children several decades ago, but may be more popular in the twenty-first century. "The Rice Cake That Rolled Away" is very similar to *The Talking Eggs* (San Souci 1989). Instead of two sisters, there is a set of neighbors. Instead of a witch, there is Ojizo-sama (the guardian god of children). But like *The Talking Eggs*, in the end, the greedy person loses out. Other stories in *The Magic Listening Cap* include "Three Tests for the Prince," "The Fox and the Bear," and eleven other short stories. Uchida was also the illustrator for this book.

Uchida also wrote *The Sea of Gold*, which was illustrated by Marianne Yamaguchi. This collection of Japanese folktales is formatted similarly to the previous book in that it consists of twelve tales and a glossary of terms at the end. One of the stories titled "The Two Foolish Cats" was later published as a picture book and illustrated in watercolors by Margot Zemach. This story tells of two cats who had been quarrelling over rice cakes. They decided to go to the old monkey to have him settle the dispute. In the end, the dispute was settled but not to the satisfaction of the cats.

The Magic Purse, written by Uchida and illustrated by Keiko Narahashi, is a Japanese folktale about a farmer who helped a young woman. This young woman lived in a magical swamp. The young woman needed the farmer to take a letter to her parents who resided in a very dangerous area. In return for his help, she gave the farmer a purse that was filled with gold coins and told him that as long as he left at least one coin in the purse every night, it would magically fill up every morning with gold coins.

In her book *The Wise Old Woman*, Uchida tells of a farmer who had the unfortunate task of carrying his aging mother to the mountain to live out the rest of her life. The ruler of this region saw elderly people as a nuisance, with no worth. So at the age of seventy, elderly people were forced to live their remaining lives on the mountain. But being the kind of son he was, the farmer brought his mother back to his home and hid her in a secret room for two years. When Lord Higa declared war on their village, the farmer was forced to reveal his mother's presence. As it turned out, because of her cleverness, she was the person who was able to keep the village safe. As a result, she was granted her freedom to live in the village. Martin Springett is the illustrator for this brightly colored book.

Tales from the Bamboo Grove, by Yoko Kawashima Watkins, is based on stories that she heard while growing up in Japan. Watkins's mother would introduce different tales to her daughter as they related to events in her life. One example comes from when Watkins questioned her beauty. Her mother proceeded to tell her about a girl who was so obsessed with her beauty that she wished for eternal beauty. Her wish was granted by drinking from a magic spring. The problem, however, was that she was never able to return home because she was no longer human.

Another tale from *Tales from the Bamboo Grove*, "The Grandmother Who Became an Island," describes the sacrifices that a woman makes for her grandson after his father had been assassinated. After her grandson could not be found, she prayed that she would become an island—a place her grandson could always come to. The illustrations are done in watercolors using brush and ink on Bristol board and were created by Jean and Mou-sien Tseng.

Because Cambodian farmers and villagers often felt like the underdogs, they often enjoyed stories where the little animal, or underdog, was clever enough to outwit the larger animal, or those representing power. In Minfong Ho's and Saphan Ros's *Brother Rabbit*, the little rabbit not only outwits a human and a large elephant but also fools a crocodile three times. In order to get a ride across the river, the little rabbit told the crocodile that he had a remedy for his scaly skin. Then he tricked the crocodile into revealing himself when the crocodile was trying to fool the rabbit. Finally, when the crocodile thought that he was going to have rabbit as a meal, the rabbit literally talked his way out of the belly of the crocodile. Jennifer Hewitson uses watercolor paints and ink to illustrate the pictures.

The Legend of the Li River, written and illustrated by Jeanne M. Lee, is a Chinese folktale that explains how the river's beauty was created. In this tale, the princess of the Dragon King of the South China Sea had felt compassion as she watched the men working to build the Great Wall of China. They had to carry enormous rocks for very long distances and some died in the process. The princess sought help from the goddess of mercy, who offered help by creating these magical animals to do the work. The princess had to agree, however, not to speak a word to anyone that she might encounter on her journey. Everything was going fine until she tried to get the attention of an elderly man and spoke. All the animals that had been helping and the elderly man instantly disappeared. In their place, great rocks formed along the riverbanks. The goddess told the princess that she did not fail her quest because the rocks not only beautified the river but also gave poor people a place to rest.

Another book illustrated by Lee and retold by Linda Fang is *The Ch'i-lin Purse: A Collection of Ancient Chinese Stories.* Among the nine tales in this book is the story "Mr. Yeh's New Year." Mr. Yeh is a schoolteacher who gave the last of his money to a friend's wife who had planned on killing herself because she thought that her husband had died or had abandoned her. This left Mr. Yeh and his wife in a financial bind, not having money to buy food for the New Year. As a last resort and at the insistence of his wife, Mr. Yeh went to a neighbor's home to steal sweet potatoes. However, the neighbor's son actually aided him in getting the sweet potatoes by giving him a "sign" from the gods.

Author-illustrator Demi has written many children's books. Included in her collection of folktales are *The Magic Boat, The Empty Pot,* and *The Greatest Treasure.* In *The Magic Boat,* Chang rescues an old man after he had fallen off a log into the water. To show his gratitude, the old man gives Chang a boat that changes from small to large by just saying the magic words. When a flood threatens his home, he and his mother use the boat for safety. During the flood, they also rescue an ant, a crane, a cat, and a very tricky and lazy man named Ying. When Ying discovers the magic of the boat, Ying misleads Chang into letting him use it to purchase materials to rebuild their home. With the help of the ant, the cat, the crane, and a special friend, Chang was able to get his boat returned.

Ping, in *The Empty Pot,* is a boy with a green thumb, except when it came to growing a plant from the seed given to him by the emperor. As the story goes, the emperor, who is very old, is looking for a successor to the throne. He announces that he will choose his successor from the children of the village on the basis of the beauty of their plants. All the children received a seed, and they had a year in which to grow their plants. At the end of that year, Ping's pot was empty. With the encouragement of his father, however, he took the empty pot to show the emperor. As it turned out, the emperor had given the children seeds that were not supposed to produce anything, and Ping was the only one who was honest enough to come forth. And because of his honesty, he was pronounced the new emperor.

In Demi's third book, *The Greatest Treasure,* Pang spent all day counting and recounting his riches. He never had time to spend with his children, was just grumpy all the time, and wanted nothing but quiet as he counted his money. Li, a nearby neighbor, was poor and spent much time with his family playing the flute, dancing, and having fun. In order to keep Li and his family quiet, Pang gave Li a bag of gold coins. And for three days, Li did not play his flute or play with his family. He first counted and recounted his coins. Then he took a day to figure out where to hide the coins, and then he spent another day trying to decide what to buy with the coins. Finally he decided that he needed to return the coins to Pang, feeling very sorry for him. The next day he not only returned the coins but also gave Pang the "greatest treasure of all."

A very heartwarming story appears in *The Mountains of Tibet*, written and illustrated by Mordicai Gerstein. In the story, a young boy is born in a tiny village in Tibet. He loves flying kites and always talks about going out to explore other worlds and other countries. However, he grew old and never got a chance to explore beyond his little village in Tibet. One day a voice told him that he had a choice of either going to heaven or living another life. When he chose to live another life, he had to decide on the following choices: In what galaxy? On what planet? As what creature? As what race? In what country? From what parents? And finally, as what gender? It was very difficult for him to decide on all these choices, but he did make the choices, and readers learn the value of each of his choices.

How the Rooster Got His Crown is a Western Chinese tale retold and illustrated by Amy Lowry Poole. This tale recounts how a long time ago, China had six suns and all was well until a drought came and the suns refused to set. Yao, the emperor of China, called on ten wise elders to help him decide what to do about the problem. After much thought, it was decided that an archer would shoot down the suns. When the first five suns were shot down, the sixth sun hid and stayed out of sight for fear of being shot down. Now this created a new problem—with no daylight, the crops began to die. Again the ten elders were summoned, but they were not able to solve this new problem. Therefore, a tiger was summoned to call out the sun, but his low roar did not get the attention of the sun. After that, they tried to have a cow "moo" the sun out. That did not work either, so they tried a rooster who gave out a sound that brought out the sun. The sun was so grateful that he rewarded the rooster with a red crown.

Latino and Hispanic American

Nicholasa Mohr grew up in Spanish Harlem in New York with six older brothers. Graduating from a trade school, Mohr studied art in New York and Mexico. Eventually, she began writing "about the ongoing struggles of

Puerto Rican People on the Mainland . . . often incorporating a strong social statement . . ." that reflected Puerto Rican people (Day 1999, 169). She has written many children's books, including biographies, short stories, screenplays, and folklore. *Old Letivia and the Mountain of Sorrows* is an original folktale that was conceived when she spent a summer in the rain forest (el Yunque) of Puerto Rico. The story makes you think of the old saying, "be careful of what you ask for, you just might get it." The tale revolves around a woman who possessed enchanted powers, a turtle who performed magic tricks and could fly, and a boy who was only inches tall and was unable to talk. After a fierce storm damaged the town, the people who ordinarily did not socialize with the woman, pleaded with her to stop the storm. In her quest to accommodate the townspeople, she also had to help the wind, which was trapped in the Mountain of Sorrows. If freed from the mountain, the wind offered to grant her four wishes, which she hastily accepted. In her haste, she could not foresee the repercussions of these wishes. Beautifully illustrated by Rudy Gutierrez, the book includes sprinklings of Spanish words and phrases.

Brother Anansi and the Cattle Ranch, told by James De Sauza and adapted by Harriet Rohmer, is a bilingual folktale about the Anansi and how he tricked the tiger. Brother Anansi is a folk hero from the Ashanti people of West Africa. This legendary character has been cast as a spider and a man, and although he may be a bad or a good character, the Anansi is always a trickster. In this book, the trick is for Brother Anansi to find a way to get Tiger's winnings from a lottery. After Tiger invests in a cattle ranch with Brother Anansi, they work well as partners for several years and end up with a large herd of animals. Now, Brother Anansi, not being satisfied, wants to find a way to get all the cattle. The illustrations are by Stephen Von Mason, a first-time illustrator for a picture book. He uses acrylic paints and colored pencils on rag paper.

The Legend of Food Mountain is another bilingual folktale, adapted by Harriet Rohmer from a creation story that has survived over the centuries. The tale was originally adapted from one of several picture-writing manuscripts recorded by a native priest after the Spanish conquest of Mexico. This legend has to do with the importance of rain and food. The illustrations are by Graciela Carrillo.

Tony Johnston writes *The Tale of Rabbit and Coyote*, which is illustrated by Tomie dePaola. This tale originates from Oaxaca, Mexico, and weaves together traditional threads of stories (such as Brer Rabbit, the story of Coyote swallowing the moon, and the rabbit in the moon). Because Rabbit had gotten into the farmer's chili field and eaten the "biggest, glossiest, greenest" one, the farmer decided to put a beeswax doll in the field to catch the rabbit. The rabbit got stuck, and the farmer caught him and started to boil water to make rabbit stew. Rabbit quickly had to decide how he was going to get out of this predicament. With the help of an unsuspecting coyote, he got free but then had to suffer the consequence of Coyote capturing him.

The women who are portrayed in Mexican folktales are often seen as extremely powerful. In both *The Woman Who Outshone the Sun* (Cruz 1991) and *Fiesta Femenina* (Gerson 2001), you see this strength and assertiveness in Lucia and other females represented. *Fiesta Femenina* was retold by Mary-Joan Gerson and illustrated with the acrylic artwork by Maya Christina Gonzalez. The seven folktales focus on female characters and their tenacity to do the undoable. In "The Hungry Goddess," La Diosa Hambrienta became Mother Earth and gave us our mountains and valleys, rivers and streams, and fish and frogs. The stories come from a variety of cultural traditions, including the Maya, Aztec, and Yaqui cultures.

Based upon a poem written by Alejandro Cruz Martinez, *The Woman Who Outshone the Sun* is a bilingual story that retells the Zapotec legend of Lucia Zenteno. The Zapotec legend is also part of the oral history of the Zapotec Indians of Oaxaca, Mexico. The book is brilliantly illustrated by Fernando Olivera who also resides in Oaxaca. In this book, Lucia is the magical woman who mysteriously appears one day in a village. The villagers were amazed at her beauty and grace, comparing her to the brilliance of the sun. Others, however, were cautious and behaved disrespectfully toward her because they saw her as being different. Eventually, the entire village bands together and forces Lucia to leave the village, unaware that the river and all its inhabitants would leave with her. In their quest to have her return, she taught them a lesson about love and understanding that they would never forget.

Another creation story set in Puerto Rico is *The Golden Flower* written by Nina Jaffee. According to Jaffee, a long time ago, before Columbus arrived, Puerto Rico was called Boriquen by the Taino people who resided there. As the story goes, the land was barren with the exception of a huge mountain. While playing, a young boy found a seed floating in the wind. He took it and put it in a pouch. He then found another one, then another one, until eventually his pouch became full. He decided to plant the seeds at the top of the mountain and with that, creation begins. First the forest unfolds, followed by plants and vegetables, including an enormous, brightly colored ball with rumblings inside. This ball turned out to be a pumpkin that was accidentally cracked opened when two men were fighting over it. Inside were waves of water with whales, dolphins, crabs, and sunfish. The water covered the earth and rose to the edge of the magic forest that the young boy planted. Sprinkled throughout the book are Spanish words. The book was illustrated by artist and musician Enrique O. Sanchez.

The Legend of the Hummingbird, retold by Michael Rose Ramirez and illustrated by Margaret Sanfilippo, is a magical tale also from Puerto Rico. The story begins like a Romeo and Juliet scenario. Alida and Taroo belong to opposing tribes, but they fall in love anyway. Once Alida's father hears of this relationship, he forbids her to see Taroo and soon arranges a marriage for her to someone else. Alida is heartbroken and prays to the stars for help. The stars were so touched by her sadness that they changed her to a red flower. When Taroo learns what Alida's father had arranged for her, he asks the stars to help him find this red flower. The stars change him into a hummingbird so he can fly and find his love. The book also contains some factual information about hummingbirds and Puerto Rico.

Written by Juliet Piggott and illustrated by John Spencer, *Mexican Folk Tales* comprises eleven tales about Mexico. Some deal with creation and evolution, and others are about traditions, culture, and legends of Spanish and native peoples. One such legend is about Tepoztecal, who is either a god or a human possessed of magical powers. He is considered by most to be a hero of sorts. Raised by an elderly couple ("grandparents") who had no children of their own, Tepoztecal appeared early to be very smart and clever. He was able to design and make things at an extremely young age. He also had a special fascination with bows and arrows. After it was directed that his "grandfather" was to be eaten by Xochialcatl, the great giant, Tepoztecal decided to take his place instead. Because Tepoztecal was still just a child, the great giant swallowed him whole, which allowed Tepoztecal to cut his way out using one of his arrows. He escaped and made his way back to his grandparents.

Paco and the Witch is a Puerto Rican version of Rumpelstiltskin and is retold by Felix Pitre. In this version, Paco is captured by an old witch as he travels through the forest one day. In order to gain freedom from her, he is given three chances to guess the witch's name. The story takes place in Puerto Rico and the colors of the scenery are brilliantly illustrated by Christy Hale. Because Spanish words are used throughout the book, the book comes with a glossary.

Native American

A widely told Native American tale about how the chipmunk got stripes is retold by Joseph and James Bruchac, a father-and-son team, in *How Chipmunk Got His Stripes*. The story evolves around a very young squirrel who teased a bear when the bear was unable to stop the sun from rising. The bear was so embarrassed when the sun rose the next day partly because all the animals in the forest were there to witness his defeat. But his embarrassment soon turned to anger as the squirrel continued to tease him because he had not come to terms that he was not in control of everything. The bear decided that he had had enough from squirrel and was going to eat him. Squirrel barely escaped with the skin on his back; in fact, the bear's scratches caused squirrel to look like a chipmunk—the striped one. Illustrations are by Jose Aruego and Ariane Dewey.

Another book by Bruchac deals with earth, wind, fire, and air. *Four Ancestors: Stories, Songs, and Poems from Native North America* comprises thirty-one stories about Native Americans who represent various tribes. Some of the tribes include Pawnee, Colville, Nisqually, as well as Mohawk, Chippewa, and Navajo. The elements, earth, wind, fire, and air, represent the four ancestors. The illustrations are magnificent as four artists display their talents in this book. The illustrators are S. S. Burrus (Cherokee artist), Jeffrey Chapman (Ojibwa artist), Duke Sine (Yavapai Apache artist), and Murv Jacob (Cherokee painter).

Jacob also was the illustrator for *The Boy Who Lived with the Bears* by Joseph Bruchac. This book includes the story about the chipmunk and the bear and has five other Iroquois tales.

In a creation-type, love story by Joseph Bruchac, *The First Strawberries*, we read about the first man and woman on earth. The Cherokee couple lived together in harmony and peace for a long time. One day, however, the man was upset with his wife because she was picking flowers instead of preparing him dinner. The woman was very displeased by his behavior and left him. He followed her, but it seemed impossible for him to catch up with her. The sun tried to slow her down by placing various obstacles in her path. First it was raspberries, then blueberries, and then blackberries. None of these fruit could entice her to stop. Then the sun placed the strawberries before her, and as she tasted them, she thought of the love and kindness between her and her husband, who was finally able to catch up with her.

The Earth Under Sky Bear's Feet is a book of poetry by Joseph Bruchac and Thomas Locker (for more on this book, see chapter 8). The thirteen poems are based on Native American tales about the Big Dipper from various cultures. Also by Bruchac and Locker, is *Between Earth and Sky*. The book is written as a conversation between Little Turtle and his Uncle Old Bear. The conversation begins when Little Turtle asks about sacred places. Old Bear shares with him that there are seven sacred places between the earth and sky. Throughout the book, he explains each of those places as they relate to a specific tribe. The seven sacred places are as follows: East (Wampanoag), North (Seneca), West (Navajo and Papago), South (Cherokee), Center (Hopewell), Above (Cheyenne), and Below (Hopi). Old Bear also tells his nephew that all of these places should give us balance, and then he gives an example of when balance is lost (Walapai) and when balance is held (Abenaki). The pictures are done in oils on canvas and are magnificent. The book ends with a map of the United States, depicting locations of Native Americans.

Although copyrighted in 1976, *The Red Swan*, edited by John Bierhorst, provides a plethora of myths and tales about Native Americans. Within the fifteen sections and 386 pages, there are over sixty stories about dozens of tribes. Some of the tribes included are Yuki (Northern California), Okanagon (Washington and British Columbia), Central Eskimo (Canada), Menominee, and Navajo. These myths can basically be categorized into the following four areas: (1) setting the world in order, (2) the family drama, (3) fair and foul, and (4) crossing the threshold. The drawings throughout the book are by various artists and are intended for young adults.

Inspired by her Norwegian husband, Virginia Driving Hawk Sneve writes a sixteen-chapter book about tricksters (Iktomi) and trolls in *The Trickster and the Troll*. The troll represented the trickster figure in the Norwegian culture. In the book, the troll and the trickster are initially very competitive. They later learn to help each other and eventually trust each other as they explore ways to maintain their respective cultures and traditions. The book includes both a Sioux and a Norwegian glossary.

In *The Twelve Moons*, Sneve teams up with illustrator Marc Brown. In this classic tale, Carmen is sharing with her mother what she is learning in school about Sioux names for the months of the year. Because calendars were not available during that time, Sioux Indians named each month according to what was happening in nature. For example, January was called Moon of the Terrible because of the bitter cold and snow. April was called Moon When the Geese Returned because that was the time when the birds would begin to return from the South. And August was referred to as Moon When All Things Ripened, relating to the harvest.

Iktomi has been credited with the natural mistakes and disasters of the world (for example, earthquakes, floods, diseases, flies, and mosquitoes). This can be seen in Paul Goble's *Iktomi and the Boulder*, another Iktomi trickster story. Common in Iktomi stories is the first line, "Iktomi was walking along," which gives the reader the impression that Iktomi was just kind of chillin' with not much to do. In this story, Iktomi was full of himself about how good he looked in his clothes. During his walk, however, he lied three times. First he lied to the boulder about the use of his blanket. Then he lied to the buffaloes about how the rock ended up pinning him down. And finally, he lied to the bats, saying that the boulder said very rude things about them. At this point the bats were furious with the boulder and begin attacking it. The results of that attack explain why bats have flat faces and why the Great Plains have rocks scattered all around.

An author and an illustrator, Goble has written several other Native American folktales, both before and after the publication of *Iktomi and the Boulder.* *Buffalo Woman*, published in 1984, is about the mystic powers of animals turning into humans and vice versa. In this love story, a young Indian male, who also holds claim to being a great hunter, married a woman who had transformed herself into a buffalo. After a while, they had a son, but since the young man's tribe was so mean and bitter to his wife, she left with their son. When her husband tried to follow them, she warned him that if he did that, he would die. But he loved them so much that he was willing to take a chance to be with them. In the end, because of his perseverance, a ceremony was performed and he, too, was transformed.

In this next love story, imagine yourself being the grandchild of the sun and the moon! That was exactly the case in *Star Boy*. However, it seems that Star Boy was not too excited about this, at first. Instead of living in Sky World with his grandparents and his father, he and his mother were banished to earth. His mother had disobeyed the rules of Sky World, and she had to leave. Some might say that she died of a broken heart because she could not be with her husband Morning Sun in life. But in death she became Evening Star and the two are always together. But Star Boy, their son, was left with the "scar of disobedience" and grew up being called Scarface. However, after he decided to marry, he found his way back to Sky World where he asked his grandparents for forgiveness. From that day on, he lived a great life and was united in death with his parents: Evening Star and Morning Sun.

In Goble's book, *The Gift of the Sacred Dog*, the people were looking for buffaloes to hunt because they were so hungry. But the buffaloes were too fast to be caught. A young boy decided to go in the mountain and ask the Great Spirit for help. The spirit sent the people colorful horses, which they called "sacred dogs." These horses would be used to aid the people in their hunt for buffaloes. From that day on, every time a buffalo was killed, they would give thanks to "the spirit of the buffalo who died."

Goble also wrote another book about animals in *The Great Race*. The race was between humans, which included all two-legged animals, and four-legged animals. The reason for the race was to determine who would have the power—man or buffalo. Also, it provided an explanation of why buffaloes have long hair on the chins. In determining who had the power, man and birds were on one team and the buffaloes and all other four-legged animals were on the other. As the race progressed, the human that represented the two-legged species was very good, but his speed could not beat that of the buffalo. The magpie, however, was still in the race. He had been sitting on the back of the buffalo for the entire race. As the buffalo neared the finish line, the magpie flew off his back and was the first to cross the finish line.

And that is how the two-legged creatures gained power over the four-legged ones—a race.

Adopted by the Eagle, written by Goble and based on the Lakota Indian tradition, puts birds in the role of hero again and two brothers with the other two-legged creatures. White Hawk and Tall Bear were best of friends. They did everything together, and they were always there for one another. They even liked the same girl, Red Leaf. On a trip to find wild horses, White Hawk tricked Tall Bear into being lowered down the side of a mountain to collect eagle feathers for their tribe. However, after he was lowered, White Hawk snatched up the rope, leaving his friend to die. But he didn't die. Instead, he made friends with the young eagles, and the eagles' parents adopted Tall Bear. He stayed on the side of the mountain for a long time. Then once the young eagles were strong enough, he took hold of their legs and they flew him down safely to land. Tall Bear returned to his camp, but White Hawk had fled once he had heard of his return. Tall Bear and Red Leaf married and vowed to honor the eagles by providing dried meats and berries.

Lastly, *Remaking the Earth* is a creation story written and illustrated by Goble and includes animals from some of his other stories. This tale explains how earth was created. Beginning only with fish and animals that could survive in water, Earth Maker (The Creator) decided to add to this wetland. He needed mud to begin his building. He first made land so the birds and animals had a place to rest. Then he made mountains with trees, rocks, and snow. Next he made four-legged animals, including many, many buffaloes, and two-legged humans. He gave permission to the humans to hunt and kill buffaloes because they needed their meat and skin for survival and he had made an abundance of them.

In Tomie dePaola's *The Legend of the Bluebonnet*, after the death of her parents, a Comanche girl is left as an orphan to be raised by villagers. Her name was She-Who-Is-Alone, and all she had left in the world was her doll, which she took with her all the time. A drought that had lasted for an extremely long time had caused many older adults (including her parents) and young children to die. After much praying to the Great Spirit, the Comanche people were told that in order for their prayers to be answered, they must sacrifice their most worthy possession. This sacrifice represented a token of giving back to the land. When no one had offered to sacrifice a possession, She-Who-Is-Alone sacrificed her doll as a burnt offering. Into the wind, she threw the ashes in four directions—east, north, west, south. What she and the other villagers found the next morning was a hillside of blue flowers, which became known as bluebonnets. The Great Spirit also answered their prayers with rain. Tomie dePaola illustrated this book as well.

The story *The Boy Who Lived with the Seals*, retold by Rafe Martin and illustrated by David Shannon, is about a Native American boy who disappeared one day near the water where his father was working. After searching extensively for the boy, his parents ended the search and left the area. Some time had passed when his parents heard of a place where seals lay in the sun on a large rock. What made the story so interesting was that a boy could also be seen laying around with the seals on the rock. The parents knew that it had to be their son and immediately left to find him. They found him and brought him back to live among his people. After some time, the boy began to behave more like a human, less like a seal; but he was sad and longed for his other home with the seals.

Also by Martin and Shannon, *The Rough-Face Girl* is an Algonquin version of Cinderella. Living with her father and two sisters, the Rough-Face Girl acquired her name because of the amount of scars and burns on her hands and face that she had received from keeping the fire lit in their wigwam. Also in this village was an Invisible Being who was an eligible bachelor who had a lot of power. All the women wanted to marry him, but his sister as gatekeeper was able to tell who was pure, honest, and sincere. No one had measured up, including Rough-Face Girl's two sisters. One day Rough-Face Girl decided that it was time to go to the Invisible Being's wigwam and become his bride. The Invisible Being asked Rough-Face Girl the same two questions that all the other women had been asked. And because she was able to correctly reply and could truly see him, they were married and all the scars disappeared from her hands and face.

Similar to *The Rough-Face Girl* is Robert San Souci's version of *Sootface*. In the story, again, a father is left with three daughters after his wife dies. Although the daughters were to equally share the responsibilities of the chores, the two older sisters made the youngest one do all the work. Because the father was away hunting frequently, the older sisters were able to get away with being mean and cruel to Sootface, a name she acquired because her sisters would beat her and smear ashes on her face. In the village there was a great warrior, who was also invisible and whose sister was a gatekeeper. One day it was announced that this great warrior was seeking a bride and would marry the girl who could see him. Sootface's sisters went to the hut of the great warrior and pretended that they could see him. They were dismissed by the warrior's sister. When Sootface journeyed to his hut, the villagers laughed at her presence because her hair was tangled and her clothes were raggedy. However, the warrior's sister could see the good inside her and Sootface could see the warrior.

Daniel San Souci illustrated *Ceremony—In the Circle of Life*, written by White Deer of Autumn. In this story, Little Turtle, a teenage Native American youth, is feeling sad and alone in his new environment. His classmates make fun of him, and his teacher appears very unfriendly toward him. Also, he is very distressed and upset with the fact that the park, his favorite place, is being torn down and destroyed. During this sorrowful time, a vision appears to him in the form of a wise old man named Star Spirit. Star Spirit takes him on a magical journey that teaches him about the connection between the earth and all living things. In essence, Little Turtle learns about the Circle of Life and how it represents the four directions: East, North, West, and South. The Circle of Life, which is a sacred symbol among Native Americans, helped Little Turtle understand that he is truly never alone and that he has relatives all over the universe.

A Caldecott Award book by Gerald McDermott, *Arrow to the Sun* is an adaptation of how the Spirit of the Lord of the Sun was brought to earth. A boy who was born by the sun rays and lived a life on earth without a father, in the physical sense, always felt alone, and the other children in the village did not welcome him because his father was not present. As the boy grew older, he became very curious about his father, the Sun, and sought ways to get to him. After asking advice from a corn planter and a pot maker, who were both unable to help, he finally sought the help of an arrow maker. The arrow maker was able to help him by physically making the boy into an arrow and shooting him up to the sun. Once he reached the sun, his father did not accept him at first. He was required to pass a series of tests to prove himself. When he passed the final test, he was transformed and "filled with the power of the sun." His father now accepted him and sent him back to take his spirit to the people of earth.

In another tale, we are told that a long time ago, in a Native American village, people lived well. Everyone was happy, and the people had no worries. One day a bright star appeared in the sky. It did not hang high but close to the earth. Braves were sent to investigate this spectacular star but left frightened. However, as one brave slept, he dreamt of a silver maiden who spoke to him. The maiden told him that she wanted to live among the people but did not know what form she should take. She wanted the brave to talk to the wise men of the village so that they could inform her. Everyone was so excited to hear about the star that they wanted to prepare a special greeting for her. They also told the brave to let her know that she could come in any form she wanted. At first she came as a flower on a hillside but decided that it was too far from the people. Next she came as a flower on the prairie but decided that there was too much noise. Finally, she hung over a lake and saw her reflection. She was so excited about the radiant glow that she called upon her sister stars to come join her. *The Star Maiden* was retold by Barbara Juster Esbensen and illustrated by Helen K. Davie in pastels.

Transformations are common in many Native American folktales, as in *The*

Legend of Mackinac Island retold by Kathy-jo Wargin and illustrated by Gijsbert van Frankenhuyzen. A great turtle named Makinauk was considered the oldest and wisest animal around. He was also a storyteller, and animals would gather around him to hear his wonderful tales. Makinauk was also a very kind and generous turtle. When the animals were too tired to swim, he allowed them to rest on his enormous back. One day, he informed his friends that he had been directed by the Great Spirit to become the foundation for an island. But in order to build this island he would need some soil from the bottom of the lake. The loon, beaver, and otter all tried to retrieve the soil, but were unsuccessful in reaching the bottom of the lake. While they rested on the back of Makinauk, the muskrat came along and volunteered to retrieve the soil. All the animals, except Makinauk, laughed at the possibility of this small creature succeeding in something that they were all unable to accomplish. But the muskrat brought up the soil and placed it on the back of the turtle. Amazingly rocks, trees and flowers began to grow. And in remembrance of the turtle, the name Makinauk was given to the island.

Another book by Wargin and van Frankenhuyzen is *The Legend of Sleeping Bear*. This legend explains how The Sleeping Bear Dunes and North Manitou and South Manitou Islands were formed. According to the legend, a mother bear with two cubs lived in a forest located in a part of what is now Wisconsin. This was a great life for the bear family and everyone was happy. When a forest fire sparked, all the animals scurried for safety. The mother bear and her cubs immersed themselves into the waters of Lake Michigan, where they would swim safely to the other side. Because the lake was so large, however, the cubs were not able to finish the journey. When Mother Bear reached land, she planted herself on a nearby hill where she vowed to stay and wait for her cubs. Days became months and months became seasons, as Mother Bear remained unmoved from her hill. The Great Spirit of the Land sympathized with Mother Bear and transformed the cubs into islands: North and South Manitou. They were placed near the hill where Mother Bear had so diligently remained. The hill which overlooks the island is called Sleeping Bear Dunes.

In many of the legends and folktales, readers are told that long ago, animals were always friends to one another. For example, in Harriet Peck Taylor's retelling of *Brother Wolf*, the wolf was so kind and helpful to the birds that they referred to him as a brother. The wolf and the raccoon were also good friends. They enjoyed teasing each other for fun. But one day, the raccoon went too far when he put a mixture of red clay and sticky tar over the eyes of wolf while he was asleep. When the wolf woke up, he was unable to remove the mixture from his eyes and was unable to see anything. In anguish he howled, which summoned the birds to his rescue. The birds—Bluejay,

Cardinal, Oriole, Hummingbird, Goldfinch, Owl, Woodpecker, and Wood Duck—all came to his rescue. After the wolf regained his sight, he sought revenge on the raccoon for his prank and because the birds had helped him, he rewarded them by granting them each a wish.

CONCLUSIONS

Folktales and fairy tales have always been used to explain the unexplainable. Across cultures, these wonderful tales have delighted children and adults alike. With the attention to broadening cultural understandings, we have been blessed with an abundance of cultural tales, which help young students become acquainted and familiar with cultural motifs and symbols. Many teachers encourage students to examine a single tale, such as Cinderella or Little Red Riding Hood, for the cultural influences that are present in the text and illustrations. With an examination of particular motifs, students are able to discuss the similarities and differences with clarity and a deeper understanding of what elements are important and consistent to the tale across cultures. The ability to read and examine texts deeply is an important tool for analyzing texts and one that can be incorporated into literature discussions at an early age. That said, it is important to note that while we have included a broad selection of tales in this chapter, it is not meant to be seen as either a complete or exclusive list. It is important to note as well that while most of the selections are recognized as culturally appropriate and sensitive, not all of the tales discussed in this chapter receive a blanket acceptance by all cultural experts. For the most part, the books included in this chapter represent what we have found in many of the school libraries and classrooms that we have visited as well as a few others that have not been seen as often.

While it is easy to introduce students to cultural folktales and fairy tales, it is important not to limit students' cultural development to this genre only; to do so would provide a very limited window into understanding any culture. Since picture books are prime media by which folktales are told, they also provide wonderful windows and mirrors into cultural experiences for the very young child. It is our hope that you will provide both breadth and depth for your students by using folktales and fairy tales, legends, and myths to introduce archival elements and motifs that span the boundaries of cultures while recognizing that this is but one genre important to the development of cultural understandings. As with some of our other chapters, one of our many teacher friends has provided a unit for you to explore with your students. We hope you will find it both educational and useful for your classroom.

UNIT PLAN: CINDERELLA
By Pamela Petty

Pamela Petty is an assistant professor of literacy at Western Kentucky University in Bowling Green, Ky. She serves as codirector of the Kentucky Adult Educators Literacy Institute at Western Kentucky and is the university coordinator for e-train express, a federally funded technology grant focused on the integration of technology in university courses. Her professional interests and research agendas include technology as a teaching and learning tool, early literacy, multicultural education, children's literature, and the use of technology in adult literacy education. Her Internet presence includes over 600 web pages located at www.pampetty.com.

Rationale

Traditional literature including fairy tales and folktales are woven into our American culture in print media, musical lyrics, images, political cartoons, and the entertainment industry (Disney). It is imperative that all children be familiar with these tales. Tales that originate in multiple cultures provide for a world view that values all people. This unit also challenges students to view events from different perspectives, to be alert to stereotyping and false representation of a culture, and to become more active and critical readers.

Goals and Objectives (NCTE/IRA)

- Students read a wide range of print and non-print texts to build an understanding of texts, of themselves, and of the cultures of the United States and the world; to acquire new information; to respond to the needs and demands of society and the workplace; and for personal fulfillment. Among these texts are fiction and nonfiction, classic, and contemporary works.
- Students conduct research on issues and interests by generating ideas and questions and by posing problems. They gather, evaluate, and synthesize data from a variety of sources (for example, print and non-print texts, artifacts, people) to communicate their discoveries in ways that suit their purpose and audience.
- Students develop an understanding of and respect for diversity in lan-

guage use, patterns, and dialects across cultures, ethnic groups, geographic regions, and social roles.

Materials Needed

- The following publications:

  Climo, Shirley. *The Egyptian Cinderella.* New York: HarperCollins, 1989.

  ————. *The Irish Cinderlad.* New York: HarperCollins, 1996.

  ————. *The Korean Cinderella.* New York: HarperCollins, 1993.

  ————. *The Persian Cinderella.* New York: HarperCollins, 1999.

  Hickox, Rebecca. *The Golden Sandal: A Middle Eastern Cinderella Story.* Illustrated by Will Hillenbrand. New York: Holiday House, 1999.

  San Souci, Robert D. *Cendrillon: A Caribbean Cinderella.* Illustrated by Jerry Pinkney. New York: Simon & Schuster Books for Young Readers, 1998.

  San Souci, Robert D. *The Little Gold Star: A Spanish American Cinderella Tale.* New York: HarperCollins, 2000.

  Steptoe, John. *Mufaro's Beautiful Daughters: An African Tale.* New York: Scholastic, 1987.

  Winthrop, E. *Vasillissa the Beautiful.* New York: HarperCollins, 1991.

- Thematic literature: Other versions of Cinderella (holidays, traditional European versions, spoofs, regional versions, and so on)
- Internet access
- Information books on Egypt, Ireland, Korea, Africa, the Caribbean, the Spanish American Southwest, Zuni Native Americans, Persia, and Russia

The following learning modules should be used for approximately nine months, thirty minutes per day.

Module One: Foundation

- Set the tone for the unit of study by doing a teacher read aloud from the book *If the World Were a Village* by David Smith.
- Prior to reading aloud, ask students to respond to an anticipation guide that provides true and untrue facts about topics in the book. For example: I agree/disagree that there are over 200 billion people in the world today.
- After reading aloud, revisit the anticipation guide asking students to

adjust their responses on the basis of what they just learned from the book. The teacher should prompt for discussions on the various topics addressed in the book (nationalities, languages, ages, religions, food, air/water, schooling/literacy, money/possessions, electricity, past, future).

- Introduce Cinderella by displaying items one at a time from a "book box" reflecting story elements from the fairy tale. The book box might include a pumpkin, a mouse, a magic wand, an apron, a piece of coal, a glass slipper, and a watch set to 12:00.

- Prompt students to guess the fairy tale in which these items appear and then to take turns retelling parts of the story until a chart reveals the entire traditional version of the tale. Students should go onto the Internet to investigate and record some fascinating details of this tale, which will then be used to update or enhance the chart:

    www.geocities.com/Athens/Academy/6064/cinderella.html
    www.lib.usm.edu/~degrum/html/research/FAQS/FAQS-Cinderella.htm
    www.surlalunefairytales.com/cinderella/history.html

- Ask students to complete a KWHL chart (what you Know; What you want/need to learn; How will you learn it; what you Learned?) on each of the following, prior to the introduction of each Cinderella version from that country or culture: Caribbean, Russia, Africa, Ireland, Korea, Egypt, Zuni Native Americans, Spanish American Southwest, and Persia.

- Explain to students that over the course of the school year they will be reading many different versions of Cinderella. These versions reflect different cultures, and students are to view the books as "artifacts" from those cultures. Using the artifacts, students are to be investigative reporters as they gather information about the cultures from the text and the images, categorize and synthesize that information, and then compare what they find with factual information sources (print and electronic) to determine how reliable each piece of literature is in reflecting a particular culture.

Module Two: The Tales

Note: Modules Two, Three, and Four should be followed consecutively for each book before introducing the next book.

Students should read each book outlined for this unit. The teacher should vary the organization of this reading by whole group, small group, and partner reading. The initial readings should focus on the enjoyment and comprehension of the literature and should include the following:

- Prereading strategies/activities
- During reading strategies/activities
- Postreading strategies/activities

The following are possible resources:

- www.somers.k12.ny.us/intranet/reading/prereading.html
- www.ncrel.org/sdrs/areas/issues/students/learning/lr1grorg.htm
- www.somers.k12.ny.us/intranet/skills/thinkmaps.html
- Yopp, R. H., and H. K. Yopp. (2001). *Literature-based reading activities.* 3rd ed. Boston: Allyn and Bacon.

After the initial reading students should reread (partners or small groups) the books while providing certain types of information (characters, troublemakers, helpers, why chosen, magical events, and ending) for the following books:

- *The Egyptian Cinderella*
- *The Irish Cinderlad*
- *The Korean Cinderella*
- *The Persian Cinderella*
- *Cendrillon*
- *Little Gold Star*
- *Mufaro's Beautiful Daughters*
- *Vasilissa the Beautiful*
- *The Golden Sandal: A Middle Eastern Cinderella Story*

Module Three: Cultures

Surface Culture: Ask students to read the author's notes at the end of each book to list the particular ways the authors tried to present a true reflection of each culture. Ask students to evaluate each version of Cinderella on the basis of the following criteria:

- Food
- Dress
- Music
- Language
- Celebrations
- Architecture

Deep Culture

Ask students to evaluate each version of Cinderella on the basis of the following criteria:

- Concept of beauty
- Family structure
- Courtship practices
- Work ethic
- Expressions of humor
- Body language
- Societal roles as determined by age, sex, and class

Module Four: Accurate Reflection of Culture

Ask students to work together in pairs or teams to determine the following regarding each book: Is this version of Cinderella truly reflective of the culture in which the tale originates? Use the information gathered in the grids to brainstorm a list of key words to search for (either electronically through a search engine or in print form in the library), and locate trustworthy information regarding each culture. The following resources might be helpful for students:

- www.teachervision.com/lesson-plans/lesson-6293.html?s19& detoured = 1
- www.broward.k12.fl.us/ci/whatsnew/strategies_and_such/ thinking_skills.ht ml

Ask students to prepare a presentation, in the venue of their choice, to share with others what they have discovered about the literature, the cultures, and the accurate depiction of cultures within the fairy tales.

Assessments and Evaluations

Teachers should devise rubrics for each of the four modules. The rubrics should be provided to students prior to each module to allow for self-evaluation. An individual reflective paper at the end of the unit could be used to assess student understanding of various cultures and how accurately those cultural attributes were depicted within the Cinderella literature.

WORKS CITED

Aardema, Verna. *Oh, Kojo! How Could You!* Illustrated by Marc Brown. New York: Dial Books for Young Readers, 1984.

————. *Why Mosquitoes Buzz in People's Ears.* Illustrated by Leo and Diane Dillon. New York: Dial Books, 1975.

Anderson, David A. *The Origin of Life on Earth: An African Creation Myth.* Illustrated by Kathleen Atkins Wilson. Mt. Airy, Md.: Sights Productions, 1991.

Bannerman, Helen. *Little Black Sambo.* New York: Buccaneer Books, 1976. (Orig. pub. 1899.)

Bierhorst, John, ed. *The Red Swan.* New York: Farrar, Straus and Giroux, 1976.

Browne, Maggie. *Wanted—A King.* London: Cassell & Co., 1890.

Bruchac, Joseph. *The Boy Who Lived with the Bears.* Illustrated by Murv Jacob. New York: HarperCollins Publishers, 1995.

————. *The First Strawberries: A Cherokee Story.* Illustrated by Anna Vojtech. New York: Puffin, 1993.

————. *Four Ancestors: Stories, Songs, and Poems from Native North America.* Illustrated by S. S. Burrus, Jeffrey Chapman, Duke Sine, and Murv Jacob. Mahwah, N.J.: Bridgewater Books, 1996.

————. *Fox Song.* Illustrated by Paul Morin. New York: Paper Star Book, 1993.

Bruchac, Joseph, and James Bruchac. *How Chipmunk Got His Stripes.* Illustrated by Jose Aruego and Ariane Dewey. New York: Dial Books for Young Readers, 2001.

Bruchac, Joseph, and Thomas Locker. *Between Earth and Sky: Legends of Native American Sacred Places.* New York: Harcourt Brace, 1996.

————. *The Earth under Sky Bear's Feet: Native American Poems of the Land.* New York: Putnam & Grosset Group, 1995.

Bryan, Ashley. *The Cat's Purr.* New York: Atheneum, 1985.

Caduto, Michael J., and Joseph Bruchac. *Keepers of Life: Discovering Plants through Native American Stories and Earth Activities for Children.* Golden, Colo.: Fulcrum Publishing, 1994.

Calvino, Italo. *Italian Folktales.* Translated by George Martin. New York: Pantheon, 1981.

Chang, Margaret, Raymond Chang. *The Cricket Warrior: A Chinese Tale.* Illustrated by Warwick Hutton. New York: McElderry Books, 1994.

Climo, Shirley. *The Egyptian Cinderella.* New York: HarperCollins, 1989.

————. *The Irish Cinderlad.* New York: HarperCollins, 1996.

————. *The Korean Cinderella.* New York: HarperCollins, 1993.

————. *The Persian Cinderella.* New York: HarperCollins, 1999.

Cole, Judith. *The Moon, the Sun, and the Coyote.* Illustrated by Cecile Schoberle. New York: Simon & Schuster, 1991.

Cruz Martinez, Alejandro. *The Woman Who Outshone the Sun.* Illustrated by Fernando Olivera. San Francisco: Children's Book Press, 1991.

Day, Frances. *Multicultural Voices in Contemporary Literature.* Portsmouth, N.H.: Heinemann, 1999.

Demi. *The Empty Pot.* New York: Henry Holt, 1990.

————. *The Greatest Treasure.* New York: Scholastic Press, 1998.

————. *The Magic Boat.* New York: Henry Holt, 1990.

dePaola, Tomie. *The Legend of the Bluebonnet: An Old Tale of Texas.* New York: G. P. Putnam's Sons, 1983.

De Sauza, James. *Brother Anansi and the Cattle Ranch.* Adapted by Harriet Rohmer. Illustrated by Stephen Von Mason. San Francisco: Children's Book Press, 1989.

Echewa, T. Obinkaram. *The Magic Tree: A Folktale from Nigeria.* Illustrated by E. B. Lewis. New York: Morrow Junior Books, 1999.

Esbensen, Barbara Juster. *The Star Maiden.* Illustrated by Helen K. Davie. Boston: Little, Brown, 1988.

Fang, Linda. *The Ch'i-lin Purse: A Collection of Ancient Chinese Stories.* Illustrated by Jeanne M. Lee. New York: Farrar, Straus and Giroux, 1995.

Farmer, Nancy. *Casey Jones's Fireman: The Story of Sim Webb.* Illustrated by James Bernardin. New York: Phyllis Fogelman Books, 1999.

Gates, Pamela S., Susan B. Steffel, and Francis J. Molson. *Fantasy Literature for Children and Young Adults.* Lanham, Md.: Scarecrow Press, 2003.

Gerson, Mary-Joan. *Fiesta Femenina: Celebrating Women in Mexican Folktale.* Illustrated by Maya Christina Gonzalez. New York: Barefoot Books, 2001.

Gerstein, Mordicai. *The Mountains of Tibet.* New York: Trumpet Club, 1987.

Goble, Paul. *Adopted by the Eagles.* New York: Aladdin Books, 1994.

———. *Buffalo Woman.* New York: Aladdin Books, 1984.

———. *The Gift of the Sacred Dog.* New York: Bradbury Press, 1985.

———. *The Great Race of the Birds and Animals.* New York: Aladdin Books, 1985.

———. *Iktomi and the Boulder.* New York: Orchard Books, 1988.

———. *Remaking the Earth: A Creation Story from the Great Plains of North America.* New York: Orchard Books, 1996.

———. *Star Boy.* New York: Aladdin Books, 1983.

Greaves, Nick. *When Lion Could Fly and Other Tales from Africa.* Illustrated by Rod Clement. Hauppauge, N.Y.: Barron Educational Series, 1993.

Haley, Gail E. *A Story, A Story: An African Tale.* New York: Aladdin Books, 1970.

———. *Two Bad Boys: A Very Old Cherokee Tale.* New York: Dutton Children's Books, 1996.

Hamanaka, Sheila. *Screen of Frogs.* New York: Orchard Books, 1993.

Hamilton, Virginia. *The Dark Way: Stories from the Spirit World.* Illustrated by Lambert Davis. San Diego: Harcourt Brace Jovanovich, 1990.

———. *The Girl Who Spun Gold.* Illustrated by Leo and Diane Dillon. New York: Blue Sky Press, 2000.

———. *Her Stories: African American Folktales, Fairy Tales, and True Tale.* New York: Blue Sky Press, 1995.

———. *In the Beginning: Creation Stories from around the World.* Illustrated by Barry Moser. San Diego: Harcourt Brace Jovanovich, 1988.

———. *The Magical Adventures of Pretty Pearl.* New York: Harper & Row, 1983.

———. *The People Could Fly: American Black Folktales.* Illustrated by Leo and Diane Dillon. New York: Knopf, 1985.

———. *When Birds Could Talk and Bats Could Sing.* Illustrated by Barry Moser. New York: Blue Sky Press, 1996.

Han, Oki S. *Kongi and Potgi: A Cinderella Story from Korea.* New York: Dial Books for Young Readers, 1996.

Heyer, Marilee. *The Weaving of a Dream.* New York: Puffin, 1986.

Hickox, Rebecca. *The Golden Sandal: A Middle Eastern Cinderella Story.* Illustrated by Will Hillenbrand. New York: Holiday House, 1999.

Ho, Minfong, and Saphan Ros. *Brother Rabbit: A Cambodian Tale.* Illustrated by Jennifer Hewitson. New York: Lothrop, Lee & Shepard Books, 1997.

Jaffe, Nina. *The Golden Flower: A Taino Myth from Puerto Rico.* Illustrated by Enrique O. Sanchez. New York: Simon & Schuster Books for Young Readers, 1996.

Johnston, Tony. *The Tale of Rabbit and Coyote.* Illustrated by Tomie dePaola. New York: G. P. Putnam's Sons, 1994.

Kimmel, Eric A. *Anansi and the Talking Melon.* Illustrated by Janet Stevens. New York: Holiday House, 1994.

Koram, Jamal, and Demba Mbengue. *Aesop: Tales of Aethiop the African*, vol. 1. Silver Spring, Md.: Sea Island Information Group, 1989.

Kurtz, Jane. *Fire on the Mountain.* Illustrated by E. B. Lewis. New York: Simon & Schuster Books for Young Readers, 1994.

Lee, Jeanne M. *The Legend of the Li River: An Ancient Chinese Tale.* New York: Holt, Rinehart and Winston, 1983.

Lester, Julius. *John Henry.* Illustrated by Jerry Pinkney. New York: Dial, 1994.

———. *Sam and the Tigers: A New Telling of Little Black Sambo.* Illustrated by Jerry Pinkney. New York: Puffin, 1996.

———. *Uncle Remus: The Complete Tales.* Illustrated by Jerry Pinkney. New York: Dial Books for Young Readers, 1999.

Louie, Ai-Ling. *Yeh-Shen: A Cinderella Story from China.* Illustrated by Ed Young. New York: Philomel Books, 1982.

Lunge-Larsen, Lise, and Margi Preus. *The Legend of the Lady Slipper: An Ojibwe Tale.* Illustrated by Andrea Arroyo. Boston: Houghton Mifflin, 1999.

Malotki, Ekkehart. *The Mouse Couple.* Illustrated by Michael Lacapa. Flagstaff, Ariz.: Northland Press, 1988.

Martin, Francesca. *Clever Tortoise: A Traditional African Tale.* Cambridge, Mass.: Candlewick Press, 2000.

Martin, Rafe. *The Boy Who Lived with the Seals.* Illustrated by David Shannon. New York: G. P. Putnam's Sons, 1993.

———. *Mysterious Tales of Japan.* Illustrated by Tatsuro Kiuchi. New York: G. P. Putnam's Sons, 1996.

———. *The Rough-Face Girl.* Illustrated by David Shannon. New York: Scholastic, 1992.

McDermott, Gerald. *Arrow to the Sun: A Pueblo Indian Tale.* New York: Puffin, 1974.

———. *Coyote: Trickster Tale from the American Southwest.* San Diego: Harcourt Brace, 1994.

———. *Raven: Trickster Tale from the Pacific Northwest.* San Diego: Harcourt Brace, 1993.

———. *Zomo, The Rabbit: Trickster Tale from West Africa.* San Diego: Harcourt Brace, 1993.

McKissack, Patricia C. *The Dark-Thirty: Southern Tales of the Supernatural.* Illustrated by Brian Pinkney. New York: Knopf, 1992.

———. *A Million Fish . . . More or Less.* Illustrated by Dena Schutzer. New York: Knopf, 1992.

———. *Mirandy and Brother Wind.* Illustrated by Jerry Pinkney. New York: Knopf, 1988.

Medearis, Angela Shelf. *Too Much Talk.* Illustrated by Stefano Vitale. Cambridge, Mass.: Candlewick Press, 1995.

Mohr, Nicholasa. *Old Letivia and the Mountain of Sorrows.* Illustrated by Rudy Gutierrez. New York: Penguin Books, 1996.

Opie, Iona, and Peter Opie. *The Classic Fairy Tales*. London: Oxford University Press, 1974.

Osofsky, Audrey. *Dreamcatcher*. Illustrated by Ed Young. New York: Orchard Books, 1992.

Oughton, Jerrie. *How the Stars Fell into the Sky*. Illustrated by Lisa Desmini. Boston: Houghton Mifflin, 1992.

Parks, Van Dyke. *Jump Again! More Adventures of Brer Rabbit*. Illustrated by Barry Moser. San Diego: Harcourt Brace Jovanovich, 1987.

Parks, Van Dyke, and Malcolm Jones. *Jump!* Illustrated by Barry Moser. San Diego: Harcourt Brace Jovanovich, 1986.

Piggott, Juliet. *Mexican Folk Tales*. Illustrated by John Spencer. New York: Crane Russak, 1976.

Pitcher, Diana. *Tokoloshi: African Folk Tales*. Illustrated by Meg Rutherford. Millbrae, Calif.: A Dawne-Leigh Book, 1980.

Pitre, Felix. *Paco and the Witch*. Illustrated by Christy Hale. New York: Lodestar Books, 1995.

Poole, Amy Lowry. *How the Rooster Got His Crown*. New York: Holiday House, 1999.

Ramirez, Michael Rose. *The Legend of the Hummingbird: A Tale from Puerto Rico*. Illustrated by Margaret Sanfilippo. Greenvale, N.Y.: Mondo Publishing, 1998.

Rohmer, Harriet. *The Legend of Food Mountain*. Illustrated by Graciela Carrillo. San Francisco: Children's Book Press, 1982.

———. *Uncle Nacho's Hat*. Illustrated by Mira Reisberg. San Francisco: Children's Book Press, 1989.

San Souci, Robert D. *Cendrillon: A Caribbean Cinderella*. Illustrated by Jerry Pinkney. New York: Simon & Schuster Books for Young Readers, 1998.

———. *Sootface: An Ojibwa Cinderella Story*. Illustrated by Daniel San Souci. New York: Bantam Doubleday Dell Books for Young Readers, 1994.

———. *Sukey and the Mermaid*. Illustrated by Brian Pinkney. New York: Four Winds Press, 1992.

———. *The Talking Eggs*. Illustrated by Jerry Pinkney. New York: Dial Books for Young Readers, 1989.

Schroeder, Alan. *Lily and the Wooden Bowl*. Illustrated by Yoriko Ito. New York: Bantam Doubleday Dell Books for Young Readers, 1994.

Shepard, Aaron. *Master Man: A Tall Tale of Nigeria*. Illustrated by David Wisniewski. New York: HarperCollins, 2001.

Siegelson, Kim L. *In the Time of the Drums*. Illustrated by Brian Pinkney. New York: Hyperion Books for Children, 1999.

Sierra, Judy. *Wiley and the Hairy Man*. Illustrated by Jerry Pinkney. New York: Lodestar Books, 1996.

Sloat, Teri. *The Eye of the Needle*. New York: Dutton Children's Books, 1990.

Smith, David. *If the World Were a Village*. Illustrations by Shelagh Armstrong. Toronto: Kids Can Press, 2002.

Sneve, Virginia Driving Hawk. *The Trickster and the Troll*. Lincoln: University of Nebraska Press, 1997.

———. *The Twelve Moons*. Illustrated by Marc Brown. New York: Houghton Mifflin, 1977.

Snyder, Dianne. *The Boy of the Three-Year Nap.* Illustrated by Allen Say. Boston: Houghton Mifflin, 1988.

Souhami, Jessica. *The Leopard's Drum: An Asante Tale from West Africa.* Hong Kong: Little, Brown, 1995.

Stamm, Claus. *Three Strong Women: A Tall Tale from Japan.* Illustrated by Jean Tseng, Mou-sien Tseng, and Kazue Mizumura. New York: Viking, 1990.

Steptoe, John. *Mufaro's Beautiful Daughters: An African Tale.* New York: Lothrop, Lee & Shepard Books, 1987.

———. *The Story of Jumping Mouse: A Native American Legend.* New York: Lothrop, Lee & Shepard Books, 1972.

Stevens, Janet. *Coyote Steals the Blanket: A Ute Tale.* New York: Holiday House, 1993.

Taylor, Harriet Peck. *Brother Wolf: A Seneca Tale.* New York: Farrar, Straus and Giroux, 1996.

Temple, Frances. *Tiger Soup: An Anansi Story from Jamaica.* New York: Orchard Books, 1994.

Uchida, Yoshiko. *The Magic Listening Cap: More Folk Tales from Japan.* New York: Harcourt Brace, 1955.

———. *The Dancing Kettle and Other Japanese Folk Tales.* Illustrated by Richard C. Jones. New York: Harcourt, Brace & World, 1949.

———. *The Magic Purse.* Illustrated by Keiko Narahashi. New York: McElderry Books, 1993.

———. *The Wise Old Woman.* Illustrated by Martin Springett. New York: McElderry Books, 1994.

———. *The Sea of Gold and Other Tales from Japan.* Illustrated by Marianne Yamaguchi. New York: Charles Scribner's Sons, 1965.

———. *The Two Foolish Cats: Suggested by a Japanese Folktale.* Illustrated by Margot Zemach. New York: McElderry Books, 1987.

Wargin, Kathy-jo. *The Legend of Mackinac Island.* Illustrated by Gijsbert van Frankenhuyzen. Chelsea, Mich.: Sleeping Bear Press, 1999.

———. *The Legend of Sleeping Bear.* Illustrated by Gijsbert van Frankenhuyzen. Chelsea, Mich.: Sleeping Bear Press, 1998.

Watkins, Yoko Kawashima. *Tales from the Bamboo Grove.* Illustrated by Jean Tseng and Mou-sien Tseng. New York: Bradbury Press, 1992.

White Deer of Autumn. *Ceremony—In the Circle of Life.* Illustrated by Daniel San Souci. Hillsboro, Ore.: Beyond Words Publishing, 1983.

Wolkstein, Diane. *Bouki Dances the Kokioko: A Comical Tale from Haiti.* Illustrated by Jesse Sweetwater. New York: Gulliver Books, Harcourt Brace, 1997.

Yacowitz, Caryn. *The Jade Stone: A Chinese Folktale.* Illustrated by Ju-Hong Chen. New York: Holiday House, 1992.

Yep, Laurence. *The Dragon Prince: A Chinese Beauty and the Beast Tale.* Illustrated by Kam Mak. New York: HarperCollins, 1997.

———. *The Man Who Tricked a Ghost.* Illustrated by Isadore Seltzer. Mahwah, N.J.: Bridgewater Books, 1993.

———. *The Ghost Fox.* Illustrated by Jean Tseng and Mou-sien Tseng. New York: Scholastic, 1994.

———. *The Khan's Daughter: A Mongolian Folktale.* Illustrated by Mou-sien Tseng. New York: Scholastic Press, 1997.

————. *The Junior Thunder Lord*. Illustrated by Robert Van Nutt. Mahwah, N.J.: Bridge-water Books, 1994.

————. *The Rainbow People*. Illustrated by David Wiesner. New York: Harper & Row, 1989.

————. *Tongues of Jade*. Illustrated by David Wiesner. New York: HarperCollins, 1991.

————. *The Shell Woman and the King*. Illustrated by Yang Ming-Yi . New York: Dial Books for Young Readers, 1993.

Yopp, Ruth, and Hallie K. Yopp. *Literature-Based Reading Activities*. 3rd ed. Boston: Allyn and Bacon, 2001.

Young, Ed. *Night Visitors*. New York: Philomel Books, 1995.

————. *Lon Po Po: A Red-Riding Hood Story from China*. New York: Philomel Books, 1989.

Ziner, Feenie, and Ed Young. *Cricket Boy: A Chinese Tale*. Garden City, N.Y.: Doubleday, 1977.

Chapter Five

Historical Fiction

Understanding Our Past
to Learn for the Future

George Santayana, a twentieth-century poet and philosopher, once stated that "those who do not remember the past are condemned to repeat it." That quotation guides me as I begin each new semester of teaching about multicultural literature for children and young adults because we must know and fully understand the historical mistreatment of individuals before we can be assured that we will not help to perpetuate the evil. The power of its implications for us as teachers is daunting, yet I believe it is key if there is to be a promise for change. We must understand the history of racism and prejudice in our country if we are to change the practices that still permeate our society.

Beginning the study of multicultural literature each semester with historical fiction—rather than, say, biography—has proven to be a successful way to engage my students at the clearly emotional level that I believe is an essential part of learning. Furthermore, by beginning with historical fiction, we can feel the anger, the pain, the shame, and ultimately the hope of the people of the stories; we can be engaged with the events; and we can come to understand the past so we will not repeat or perpetuate its negative aspects. Authors of historical fiction allow us to do that when they make us laugh and cry with the characters whose stories they tell. On the other hand, authors of history textbooks, though they report facts, seldom are able to engage us in the lives of the people who made history. Therefore, historical fiction provides a rent or portal by which to enter into periods and people's lives that are otherwise limited to a series of dates and names to be memorized.

By engaging students in the lives of the people from the past, we provide them with an opportunity to feel a part of a culture that may not be theirs, to feel a part of a time that is not theirs, and to witness the pain and horrors of discrimination that African Americans, Asian Americans, Latino Americans, and Native Americans experienced. Anyone who has read *Ajeemah and His Son* by James Berry will never again be able to think about slavery without feeling the pain of Ajeemah and Atu, separated from family, from each other, and from their life in Africa. Those who have read Laurence Yep's *Dragon's Gate* will be forever changed by the power of discrimination and hatred experienced by Otter and his Chinese coworkers as they build the transcontinental railroad in America. Other books, such as Shirley Sterling's *My Name is Seepeetza*, provide us with information about the racism and hardships of Native American boarding school experiences. Sherry Garland's *Indio* shows us the horrors that native people experienced at the hands of the Spanish conquistadors in areas now known as Mexico and the southwest regions of the United States.

You might ask how we find such books that will move our students into deeper levels of understanding that is appropriate for them developmentally. This is a struggle that each of us will need to address. There are, however, some general criteria for choosing historical fiction that can guide us as we begin to evaluate the books for children and young adults, but before we discuss these criteria, we need an understanding of the concept "historical fiction." Here are definitions of *history* and *fiction* in the *American Heritage Dictionary* (1982, 614, 500):

> **History** 1. A narrative of events; story. 2. A chronological record of events, as of the life or development of a people or institution, often including a commentary on those events . . . 7. A drama based on historical events.
>
> **Fiction** 1. An imaginative creation or a pretense that does not represent actuality but has been invented . . . 4a. A literary work whose content is produced by the imagination and is not necessarily based on fact. 4b. The category of literature comprising works of this kind including novels, short stories, and plays.

On the basis of the definitions above, *historical fiction* might be defined as any creative work with imaginary characters or events that is an account of what has happened in the life of a country or people. In other words, historical fiction is a blend of the historical and imaginary stories of people, places, and events. For the purposes of this text, we would like to employ the following definition: *multicultural historical fiction is a blend of the historical and imaginary stories about people, places, and events that reflect the diversity in terms of class, culture, gender, religion, and sexuality as they specifically relate to the issues of race and ethnicity.*

EVALUATION CRITERIA FOR MULTICULTURAL HISTORICAL FICTION

From chapter 2, we saw how using story elements can help us frame our evaluation of the literature we seek to use in the classroom. Within the study of historical fiction, it is essential that the elements of story—plot, setting, characterization, theme, style, tone, and mood—be congruent and authentic on the basis of the period in which the story is set. To examine the structure of story requires a basic understanding of the elements themselves and the appropriate discernment in relation to the genre in which the story is written. Although the basic definitions of plot, setting, characterization, theme, style, tone, and mood are consistent across genres, the particular nuances affiliated with each genre in relation to multicultural literature vary. These nuances will be the focus of defining and redefining how we evaluate multicultural literature for children and young adults in our classrooms.

Plot

Plot structure provides us with the framework of the story. It is the element within which conflicts or problems are introduced, where rising action, climax, and resolution to these problems occur, and in which the order of all of the above happen—chronological, in medias res, or flashback. When we evaluate multicultural literature, we need to know if *the experiences, conflicts, and ultimate resolutions are consistent with what is known about the period in which the story is set.* To do that, we must have some historical understanding and knowledge of the occurrences and events of the period. Although this requires that the teacher know about the specific periods, there are many sources from which to gain that knowledge. For instance, the Internet provides teachers and students with easy access to historical information through a variety of educational sites such as www.americanhistory.com or www.ya-hooligans.com.

Setting

Setting is the second element that we must consider when evaluating multicultural historical fiction. While setting is basically the time and place of the events in a story, we must ask the question, *Is the setting authentic on the basis of our knowledge of time and place within this particular period?* Again, resources abound to validate or refute the accuracy of the story's setting. That the events in the story be true to the events and geography of the period assigned is essential because references to historical events or landmarks that were not a part of the actual period and place are disastrous as they undermine the credibility of the entire text.

Characterization

Evaluating the element of characterization can require an even closer reading and application of historical knowledge. In evaluating characterization, we must concern ourselves with how accurately *primary and secondary characters reflect and express values and beliefs appropriate for and authentic to the period and region, including levels of class structure.* One of the clearest ways to understand how people of a particular period behaved and responded to events is to read diaries and journals from that particular period. Words from the people who lived during a specific era provide an authentic voice from the past. This level of period research may seem too detailed and is sometimes time intensive; however, it is worth the work. Again, Internet sites often provide quotations and excerpts from journals of the period that you are researching. One particularly handy site for quotations is found at www.Bartleby.com, where literary quotations can be identified and cited for future classroom use.

Theme

In evaluating the element of theme, we are called to determine if it is *worthwhile and consistent on the basis of our knowledge of the period.* We cannot expect themes of historical fiction to be representative of themes of the twenty-first century. Ideas and practices that were part of our history might be offensive or even against the law today. That said, one must determine if the theme or themes presented in a piece of historical fiction are worthwhile. In other words, is there a universality that crosses the boundaries of time and allows us to become observers? Themes of man's inhumanity to man, human dignity, and freedom cross all periods and can help us to understand Santayana's plea.

Style, Tone, and Mood

We often find the elements of style, tone, and mood lumped together into a single category. Although many texts do this, it is important to understand how they differ from one another in context while complementing one another in actuality. *Style* is often concerned with the language—word choices—the way in which the author arranges words to create a certain effect—how the author uses language to tell the story. By arranging words in particular ways, an author creates the *tone* of the story. Characters can appear formal or informal; events can seem mundane or intense. The tone of the story allows us to *feel* what the characters *feel*—liberation, oppression, boredom, or engagement. Tone is one of those emotional barometers in a story. *Mood* is the result of the style and tone—how we, as readers, interpret the other combined elements of plot, setting, characterization, and theme. The element of mood provides us with another type of emotional connection to the story events—joy, sadness, hope, or despair as we reflect on the story as a whole and its close ties to the intended theme.

Refer to the following criteria when evaluating multicultural historical fiction:

- The experiences, conflicts, and ultimate resolutions must be consistent with what is known about the period in which they are set with respect to the people and culture represented.
- The setting must be authentic on the basis of our knowledge of the period and geographical regions depicted.
- Primary and secondary characters must reflect and express values and beliefs that are appropriate for and authentic to the period and region, including levels of class structure.
- Explicit and implicit themes of the story must be deemed worthy and consistent with the period and region.
- The language must authentically represent the characters, the period, and the region depicted.
- Illustrations should complement the text and accurately represent what is known about the period and region.
- The language, illustrations, theme, or characters should accurately portray authentic ethnic or cultural representations without stereotypes.

SELECTIONS OF MULTICULTURAL HISTORICAL FICTION

The intent of this section is to provide several selections of historical fiction organized by historical periods for particular cultural groups. By examining the history of racism and prejudice toward cultural groups through the eyes of strong characters who face incredible challenges, we and those we teach may be able to understand better how racism and prejudice continue to influence us as a society. Although it is my intent to offer authentically representative selections of historical fiction, I have not limited these selections only to authors of the culture as I have done in other genre chapters such as the poetry chapter. I believe that history and historical fiction, in particular, *must* be researched extensively and thoroughly if it is to represent the people and events of the period. Therefore, although it might seem most appropriate, to limit the selections to authors of the culture would exclude some excellent voices that resonate the truths of our past. As teachers, we must tell everyone's history in ways that are authentic and that supplement the texts we are required to use. The selections are intended to provide accurate and sometimes new information for young readers without the stereotypes that have often misrepresented groups of people. I do not suggest that the selections provided are the only representations or even the best representations available as it is impossible to know every published text or source. I have chosen texts that I have used and discussed with my students and ones which have provided excellent discussions about historical events and periods— discussions that have promoted an open examination of the history, the underlying forces of racism and prejudice, and the hope and dignity of people. The order in which I have reviewed the selections offers a historical perspective of the events that have affected each cultural group the most, and it provides a foundation on which to build understanding.

African American Historical Fiction

Stories of the Slave Trade

To begin the section of African American historical fiction is to begin with the horrors of the slave trade. One very powerful example of this time is found in *Ajeemah and his Son* by James Berry. The author draws us into the lives of a father and son who were ripped from their homeland in Africa and sold into slavery in what is now Jamaica. Kidnapped on the way to the home of his bride to be, Atu and his father Ajeemah find themselves on the other side of the world—a world where they are separated and sold. Neither man speaks English or understands the strange world into which he is thrust. Atu, a young man of eighteen, struggles to survive the beatings he receives to try to break his spirit when he is sold into slavery. As readers, our hope and his spirit are renewed for a short time when he obtains an orphaned foal and cares for him—finding joy in raising the colt. However, the joy is short-lived, and Atu's world is once again shattered when the horse is taken away from him. Refusing to let the plantation head man take his horse and ride it, Atu breaks the legs of the horse and is severely beaten for his insolence. In a final act of defiance that has characterized his captivity, Atu takes his own life by choosing to die at the front gate of the plantation where the owner and his wife are forced to see his broken body. His tragic life events shatter us as readers, and we experience some of Atu's emotional pain through James Berry's unadorned descriptions.

By creating a parallel story, Berry gives readers the opportunity to also experience Ajeemah's plantation reality. Though Ajeemah is unhappy and yearns for his family and the freedom to return home, he does not bring the rage of the plantation owner down upon himself as does his son Atu. However, he does plan an uprising, but when suspicion occurs, he abandons his plans—taking what some would think is the easy way out. Whether his spirit is broken, or whether he has learned how to endure a terrible situation, Ajeemah survives. Eventually, he meets Bela, a house slave, and they begin a life together on the plantation. In 1838, thirty years after his kidnapping, slavery is abolished in Jamaica, and Ajeemah, Bela, and their daughter are all finally free.

James Berry depicts the tragedy and horror of the slave trade with a simple and clear description of what it meant to people like Ajeemah and Atu. Kidnapped from their homes and families, stripped of their freedom, and forced to endure incredible cruelty at the hands of their captors, Ajeemah and Atu make real—through historical fiction—the horrors of this period.

The Captive by Joyce Hansen is another story of slavery and is based on the story of Olaudah Equiano, an Ashanti prince who was captured and sold into slavery in 1755. Hansen names her character Kofi and sets the story in Massachusetts rather than in the West Indies where the real Equiano was enslaved. Like Equiano though, Kofi learns to read, gains his freedom, and ultimately writes his own story. Kofi displays an incredible level of personal fortitude, refusing to acknowledge any bondage to those who would own him. His strong-willed personality helps readers to appreciate his courage and struggle to become literate and free.

Other books about life as a slave during the pre–Civil War years offer fascinating opportunities for young people to experience the daily challenges faced by African Americans during the mid-1800s. With *Christmas in the Big House, Christmas in the Quarters*, Patricia and Fredrick McKissack offer readers a window into the lives of slaves and slave owners who prepare for Christmas. In the story, the plantation slaves tend to the needs of the household, while they attempt to learn more about John Brown's raid on Harper's Ferry. The McKissacks give readers a sense of urgency and tension as they observe the work behind the scenes—the abolitionist movement in the midst of Christmas preparations.

Gary Paulsen, best known for his work in contemporary survival fiction, has also written two books about the issues of slavery and literacy, *Nightjohn* and *Sarny*. In *Nightjohn*, Paulsen weaves a story of a man who risks everything and receives brutal treatment for teaching slaves to read. The story is told through the character of Sarny, who explicitly describes the cruelty that the master of the plantation delivers to any who challenge him. The whippings, the dogs, the dismemberment, are all depicted in ways that warrant discretionary use with young children. In *Sarny*, Paulsen continues the saga of the young protégé in *Nightjohn* and provides an understanding of the hardships for the newly freed slaves following the Civil War.

Mary Lyons also shows her readers a harsh picture of what life for a slave woman was like in *Letters from a Slave Girl: The Story of Harriet Jacobs*. Like Joyce Hansen in her book *The Captive*, Lyons weaves a story based on the journal excerpts of Harriet Jacobs, a slave woman who hid in an attic crawl space for seven years to escape the attentions of the man who owned her. Unable to bear the thought of leaving her children completely, she hides away and watches them grow. After seven years, Harriet finally escapes to the North, only to live in fear of being hunted down and returned to the South. Her story is emotionally gripping and illustrates the risks some slaves took to free themselves from the indignities thrust upon them by those who sought to hold them captive.

The Underground Railroad

This instrument of escape for slaves is depicted in both picture book format for young readers and novels for older readers. Two picture books that help young students understand the concept of the Underground Railroad are Jeanette Winter's *Follow the Drinking Gourd* and Deborah Hopkinson's *Sweet Clara and the Freedom Quilt*. Both books tell the story of how routes to the North were mapped for those wishing to escape to the North. Jeanette Winter's *Follow the Drinking Gourd* is the tale of Peg Leg Joe, an old sailor who helped slaves escape to freedom. In the story, Peg Leg Joe would hire himself out to plantation owners as a cover to teach a seemingly harmless song to the slaves. The song was about following the drinking gourd—the Big Dipper and the North Star—that secretly told the way to freedom. Through the lyrics, the journey was charted through the fields, woods, and rivers to the Ohio River where Peg Leg Joe waited to ferry the runaways to the North where white sympathizers hid and fed them on their dangerous journey to Canada.

In *Sweet Clara and the Freedom Quilt*, Clara is taken from her mother and placed to work as a field hand. When her adopted aunt teaches her to sew, she moves to the Big House to work and discovers information about the Underground Railroad. With hoarded pieces of fabric scraps, Clara creates a quilt that maps the journey to the North for those willing to risk the trek. Once she finishes the quilt, Clara and Jack, a field hand she loves, decide to run away, leaving the quilt for those who wish to follow. The story itself illuminates young readers to the risks slaves took to be free, and it is done with richly detailed illustrations that depict the importance of Clara's work.

In Katherine Patterson's novel for older readers, *Jip: His Story*, we find Jip as a preteen working on the county farm for the poor. As a toddler, he fell off a wagon and was left behind. Jip's hope is that his family will come back in search of him, but that doesn't happen. The county work farm takes in orphaned children, widows and their children, and people who today would be considered mentally challenged. Although given a place to sleep and eat, the chores are endless, and it becomes quickly obvious to the reader that Jip and the others who live at the farm are treated poorly and without respect. When it is discovered quite by chance that Jip's mother was a run-a-way slave, he suddenly finds himself hunted by the man who owned his mother. Forced into hiding, he is able to escape to Canada with the help of a Quaker family.

Another novel that depicts the work of the Underground Railroad is Kathryn Lasky's *True North*. The protagonists in this novel are two young women—a female slave who is running away and traveling north and a young woman who discovers her, befriends her, and travels with her as they make their way to Canada. This story is fraught with the dangers and restrictions faced by young women during that time and the abolitionist movement.

Other well-written narratives about slavery and the Underground Railroad include such novels as Mary Stolz's *Cezanne Pinto: A Memoir*, Sandra Forrester's *Sound of Jubilee*, and Gloria Houston's *Bright Freedom's Song: A Story of the Underground Railroad*. Each of these novels tells the story of people who risked their lives either to escape or to help others escape to freedom. Both Forrester and Houston present stories that are not often reflected in history texts. Forrester's story examines the historical colonizing of Roanoke Island by freed slaves, while Houston's story presents the lesser known Appalachian route of the Underground Railroad. The characters in all three novels are well developed and provide insights into the turbulent period.

Stories of the Civil War

There are many excellent novels that help young people understand the conflicts that led to the Civil War. Though many deal with events of the war itself, several address the tensions that slaves faced on the plantations. With talk of President Lincoln's plans to issue a proclamation to free the slaves and later with talk of freed slaves fighting for the Union, fears ran deep. A recent addition to these narratives is *Silent Thunder: A Civil War Story* by Andrea Davis Pinkney. This story is told through the alternating chapters of a brother and sister—Rosco and Summer—slaves who were fathered by the plantation owner Gideon Parnell. The story describes their lives and relationships with the household and the lure of learning to read. The fall of 1862 brings news of the impending emancipation proclamation and the plantation is rocked by the hope of freedom. The story is full of rich descriptions that make the characters and events fully believable and engaging to the reader.

One of the finest picture book depictions of the Civil War and its horror is found in Patricia Polacco's *Pink and Say*. This finely illustrated picture book tells the story of two Union soldiers—one black and one white—who become friends. Caught behind enemy lines, the tragic outcome becomes a poignant example of the cruelty of war. Polacco retells the event through the voice of her grandfather—a story passed down from generation to generation.

Historical fiction consistently provides the stories of people, places, and events. Mildred Taylor's work has added a wealth of information about the early years of the twentieth century through her stories about the Logan family. In *The Well*, set in the 1920s, Taylor introduces young readers to David Logan, Big Ma, and the Simms family. We are able to see the foundations of hatred that influence her other novels: *Song of the Trees*; *Roll of Thunder, Hear My Cry*; *Let the Circle Be Unbroken*; *The Mississippi Bridge*; and *Road to Memphis*. Throughout these stories, we are able to see the levels of hatred and prejudice that existed in our country. They tell young readers of life for African Americans after the Civil War and prior to the civil rights movement. These stories help students understand that the end of slavery did not mean the end to discrimination—quite the contrary.

Another addition to this period is the 2000 Newbery Award winner, *Bud, Not Buddy*, by Christopher Paul Curtis. Whereas Taylor's work is set in the South, Curtis's story is set in Michigan. Beginning in Flint, Mich., during the early 1930s, we are introduced to Bud, not Buddy, a young boy whose mother died four years earlier, leaving him in the care of orphanages and foster care homes. Although his mother has told him nothing of his father, Bud is certain that his father is one of the men featured on the five handbills found in his mother's things that advertise a band. He is determined to find his father when he escapes the clutches of his final foster care experience. Curtis provides a poignant commentary on the state of poverty during the Depression era through descriptions of food lines and Hooverville shantytowns. With determination, Bud, not Buddy, goes in search of his father—ready to walk across the state if necessary. Curtis weaves a story of hardship, humor, and healing to bring his readers to a deeper understanding of the importance of family.

Another novel set in the era of the Great Depression is Karen English's *Francie*. This story is set in Noble, Ala., where thirteen-year-old Francie

Weaver works day jobs cleaning with her mother while they wait for the return of her father who has gone to Chicago to work as a Pullman porter. The story richly details the daily struggles of dealing with small-town gossips and bullies where the social organization still reflects segregation, even though slavery is abolished. English provides her readers with believable characters and situations that illustrate clearly the racial and class structures of the period.

Civil Rights

The civil rights movement of the 1950s and 1960s is another era that is ripe for student discovery of the continued historical struggle for African Americans. Once again, Christopher Paul Curtis gives his readers an opportunity to understand the dynamics of a family from Flint, Mich., in *The Watsons Go to Birmingham—1963*. Traveling to Birmingham, Ala., in 1963 provides young readers with an emotional connection to Kenny and his family as they travel into the heart of the civil rights movement and ultimately to the site of the church bombing and death of six children. To understand the civil rights movement is to understand the pain of racism and prejudice, which permeates our society. The Watson family helps readers to see all facets of family life in the context of the violence that touched so many lives.

Ossie Davis gives readers another fictionalized account of the civil rights movement and its effect on the young people of the time in *Just Like Martin*. In this story, we see the commitment and personal struggle of a young man to emulate his hero, Martin Luther King Jr. This novel addresses the difficulties that Stone, the fourteen-year-old protagonist, has in trying to live up to his commitment of nonviolence in the face of the bombing deaths of his friends. Set in Alabama in the summer and fall of 1963, Davis's book provides a historical context for the violence of the times—Medgar Evers was killed in June, the children were killed in the church bombing in September, and the president of the United States was assassinated in November. In the midst of these incredible acts of violence, is Martin Luther King Jr.'s "I have a dream" speech and his plea for nonviolence. Davis clearly engages his readers at a level that can't be ignored and helps us understand the importance of our history.

Asian American Historical Fiction

Defining Asian American

To begin an examination of historical fiction depicting the struggles of Asian Americans in North America is to understand first that the term *Asian Ameri-*

can does not represent a singular group of people. Instead, the designation of Asian American includes people whose cultural heritage comes from Cambodia, China, India, Indonesia, Japan, Korea, Laos, Pakistan, Philippines, Taiwan, Thailand, or Vietnam. Our knowing that each of these countries has its own language, culture, religion, ethnic identity, and traditions is important. Some Asian Americans are recent emigrants to the United States or Canada, while other families have been here for generations; therefore, it is impossible to generalize about historical experiences. For that reason, I always suggest that teachers and students research the country and culture of which these groups are part. By doing so, it may be easier to understand the prejudicial problems and stereotypes that individual groups have faced. In reviewing some of the historical fiction available, it becomes quickly evident that the historical stories seem to break into cultural pockets associated with particular U.S. historical events. For instance, the works associated with the 1800s are generally about the Chinese emigrants who came to the United States to help build the transcontinental railroad and who settled in the western regions of the country. The next group of historical narratives is associated primarily with the Japanese people who came under suspicion after the bombing of Pearl Harbor during World War II. Again, the focus is on groups of people located along the West Coast and in Hawaii; these people were the citizens who were imprisoned in the internment camps. Finally, the 1960s and 1970s brought the United States into the Vietnam War, and the stories that ensue are primarily about the people who, following the war, emigrated here from Vietnam, Cambodia, and Laos. An interesting historical fiction void is found in the years following the Korean conflict for which there are few pieces of literature addressing that period.

As in the cases of the other cultures discussed in this book, a significant shortage of texts characterizing Asian Americans' experiences is clearly apparent. According to a committee at the Council for Interracial Books for children, only sixty-six books with Asian characters were published for a thirty-year span between 1945 and 1975. To acknowledge that the sources may be limited is not to suggest that those published since 1980 have not been exemplary. As the discussion will show, there are a number of excellent historical fiction texts that will help students understand aspects of particular cultures as well as the level of prejudice that the people of those cultural heritages endured during specific eras. I do not suggest that particular groups of people felt the wrath of racism only during certain periods, but, rather, I suggest that the hatred of particular groups of people reached new heights during those eras noted in the texts.

Nineteenth-Century Stories

Our introduction to racist behaviors against Asian Americans begins with a discussion of *Dragon's Gate* written by Laurence Yep. Set in the 1860s following the Civil War, Yep begins the tale of Otter with a young boy who wishes to escape the injustices of China and to go with his father and uncle to the land of riches. Otter soon discovers the harsh realities of his choice, however, when he finds himself a virtual slave laborer in the building of the transcontinental railroad. Yep captures his readers through vivid descriptions of intolerable conditions within which the laborers must live and work. Ultimately, Otter must risk everything to survive, and readers are stunned by the brutality of man and nature.

Another book set in the late 1860s is Barbara Goldin's *Red Means Good Fortune: A Story of San Francisco's Chinatown*. The protagonist in this story is a twelve-year-old boy, Chin Jin Mun, who challenges two cultures to take a stand against the injustice of slavery. The slavery in this story involves a young woman, Lew Wai Hing, whom Chin Jin Mun meets in San Francisco; he discovers that she is a *mui tsai*—a slave girl. Young readers will find themselves shocked by this little known form of slavery that is not discussed in many history textbooks.

Other books that help students understand the levels of racism and prejudice that existed historically for Asian Americans include Laurence Yep's *Dragonwings* and *The Star Fisher*. Two other books that, although not set in the United States, provide insight into Korean-American relationships during the early 1950s are Sook-Nyul Choi's *Year of the Impossible Goodbyes* and *Echoes of the White Giraffe*. Choi approaches the topics of discrimination and hatred from a Korean perspective, thus helping young readers understand the complexity and breadth of racism and prejudices across cultures.

Stories of Pearl Harbor and World War II

The next group of texts addressing the epitome of racist behavior in our own country focuses on the Japanese American communities in the 1940s following the bombing of Pearl Harbor. Young readers who are introduced to *Journey to Topaz* by Yoshiko Uchida are often stunned by the incarceration of Japanese Americans—American citizens—during World War II. Within *Journey to Topaz* and later in her sequel *Journey Home*, Uchida weaves the story that incorporates her own experiences and those of others living in the camps. In the story, from the moment Yuki's family is forced to leave their home and belongings to move into makeshift housing made from horse stalls at a former racetrack, readers become bewildered by the actions taken by the U.S. government. Then to be rounded up like cattle and sent to camps where buildings were not much better than shacks—a compound surrounded by barbed wire fences and armed guards—seems impossible to believe, but we must believe it, if we are to remember the past. Over fifty years later, young readers struggle with trying to understand how the fear of war could cause us as a country to automatically assume that our own citizens—Japanese American citizens—would be traitors. What Uchida does, however, is create a positive picture of the Japanese American community. Although many of the Japanese Americans must have been angrier than most of us can imagine at the actions of the government, there seems to be an implicit level of understanding on the part of the characters in the book. One of the most difficult parts of the story for young people to understand is the part in which the military recruiters come to the relocation camp of Topaz to encourage young men—Japanese American young men—to enlist to fight for "their" country to prove their loyalty. Many of my students have been appalled first by the audacity of the recruiters and then by the willingness of the young men to enlist to fight for a country that incarcerated them and their families. Uchida does an excellent job of helping us understand the situation within the contexts of the fear of war, while providing readers with the clear sense of how wrong it was.

While Yoshiko Uchida provides us with a powerful yet accessible story appropriate for upper elementary students, Jeanne Wakatsuki Houston gives older readers a book of life in the internment camps from a teenage perspective. In *Farewell to Manzanar*, Houston tells a story of Manzanar—another Japanese internment camp. Written for older readers, this story describes the issues related to life for high school–age students in the camps. The story is powerful, and the characters are believable albeit somewhat too accepting of the conditions according to many of my readers.

A novel based on this historical time but set in Hawaii is *Under the Blood Red Sun* by Graham Salisbury. Through this story, readers find themselves relating to Tommy and his fears and frustrations about his grandfather's allegiances and loyalties to Japan—his country of birth. Although embarrassed by his grandfather's actions prior to the war, Tommy realizes the danger of his grandfather's actions after Pearl Harbor has been bombed. Tommy's father, a fisherman, is fishing when the attack happens and is taken away and imprisoned with other Japanese American men who are suspected of helping the Japanese. Tommy and his mother realize the danger and bury the Japanese flag and samurai sword owned by his grandfather in hopes of diminishing the risk to the family. An important emotional incident occurs in the story when soldiers come to the house and discover the roost of carrier pigeons that

Tommy has tended to. Immediately recognizing them as a threat, the pigeons are killed while Tommy stands by. By this time, we recognize the level of danger Tommy's grandfather has created for the family by his outspoken loyalty to Japan. The story is filled with tensions, racist attitudes, and fear that illustrate the complexity of issues surrounding the bombing of Pearl Harbor.

During the decade of the 1990s, several picture books have been written to help younger readers better understand this terrible time in U.S. history. Although many are nonfiction texts that will be reviewed in chapter 6, two excellent historical fiction examples are *Baseball Saved Us* and *Heroes*, both written by Ken Mochizuki and illustrated by Dom Lee. *Baseball Saved Us* takes place in the early 1940s when a young boy and his family are relocated to an internment camp. Though the people have been uprooted from their communities and homes and thrust together in a desolate camp setting like those seen in *Journey to Topaz* and *Farewell to Manzanar*, they rally together to build a baseball park where the humiliation and injustices of the situation find an outlet.

The second book written and illustrated by Mochizuki and Lee, *Heroes*, takes place after World War II when a young boy is the brunt of racist remarks and attitudes from his classmates because of his Japanese heritage. The war may have ended, but the distrust and taunts continue. He pleads with his father to help him deal with his classmates who harass him constantly. Finally, the father and uncle show up at school one day in full military dress uniform, complete with medals, in order to show the children that Japanese Americans were not the enemies of America.

Stories of Vietnam

The 1960s and 1970s brought the Vietnam War into the living rooms of America and with it new people to hate. The war itself was a point of dispute with Americans, and what to do with the refugees who fled the wartime destruction of their countries was yet another problem for many people.

Although set in a refugee camp at the border of Cambodia and Thailand, *The Clay Marble* by Minfong Ho provides a harsh picture of what happened to the people of Cambodia immediately following the American withdrawal from Vietnam. With the Communist Khmer Rouge declaring victory, the people of Cambodia became their next victims and suffered incredible atrocities at the hands of their enemies. As a result, thousands of people fled their country and found themselves in the refugee camps along the borders. *The Clay Marble* is the story of one child and her search to find her family—a story that situates itself in the camps where the hope of children is witnessed as they create playthings by rolling clay marbles out of the mud from the riverbanks. Minfong Ho demonstrates that even in the midst of sorrow and the horrors of war hope can and does exist especially in the lives of children.

Two books that present the story of the Vietnamese experiences following the war are *Song of the Buffalo Boy* by Sherry Garland and *Goodbye, Vietnam* by Gloria Whelan. Both books were published in 1992 and tell the stories of families who have been affected by the destructiveness of the war. In *Song of the Buffalo Boy*, we learn of Loi, a young woman and the daughter of an American soldier who left her mother unwed and disowned by her family. Loi has fallen in love with a buffalo herder whose family refuses to let him marry a *con-lai*, a half-breed. When Loi's uncle, however, agrees to a marriage proposal from an older military officer against her wishes, she fakes her own death and flees the village. In Saigon, she finds Americans who will sponsor her move to America to search for her father and becomes friends with Joe, a young Amerasian boy who was abandoned by his mother but dreams of going to America. As the story develops, Loi must finally decide whether to stay in Vietnam or go to America; she must decide where she really belongs.

The second novel, *Goodbye, Vietnam*, is the story about a family who must flee Vietnam. With their lives threatened, Mai and her family escape the Mekong Delta to become boat people, eventually ending up in the refugee camps of Hong Kong. Their struggle to survive and get to America epitomizes the struggle of many of thousands of refugees who left Vietnam following the war.

Both of these books, written for older students, represent the aftermath of the Vietnam War experience—unwed Vietnamese women with children fathered by American soldiers and South Vietnamese officials and professionals who are seen as a threat to the new government. The trauma of staying or fleeing becomes real to the reader as we watch the protagonists wrestle with the decisions and circumstances forced upon them.

To read the literature about the varied historical experiences of Asian Americans is to discover that during the past 140 years, cultural groups have suffered discrimination and threats to their survival—although different groups have suffered through significantly different hardships, the results have been the same.

Latino/Hispanic Historical Fiction

Latino or Hispanic American literature embodies the experiences of people originating from Mexico, Central and South America, Puerto Rico, Dominican Republic, Cuba, and the West Indies. The term *Hispanic* has generally referred to people emanating from a Spanish background and has been used primarily by the census bureau and other government agencies as a designator. Although the term *Hispanic* is used by some people, many others prefer the cultural designator of *Latino* or *Latina* to reflect their heritage. Primarily, *Latino* refers to people with a Latin American history, which includes Mexico, Central and South America, and the West Indies. Spanish is the dominant, shared language among people from Latin America, Cuba, and Puerto Rico, and the dominant religion is Catholicism. As with other cultural groups discussed in this chapter, it is easy to understand that although some similarities in language and religious affiliation across the groups may be shared, there are customs and traditions, including food preparations, that are distinct from one group to the other. For the purposes of this section, the term *Latino* will be used to refer to the group as a whole; but whenever possible, a specific cultural background will be noted such as Mexican American, Puerto Rican American, Cuban American, or El Salvadorian American because many from within these groups refer to their place of origin.

One of the first things that teachers and students notice when we begin a study of Latino American literature is the limited number of books available, especially in the genre of historical fiction. Part of the reason lies in the number of quality books published prior to 1990. Other than folktales or biography, few authors of the culture where publishing fiction for young people. The notable exception is Nicholasa Mohr whose work is primarily contemporary fiction. Although information books were published prior to 1990, too often the text and illustrations reinforced negative stereotypes of a lazy and impoverished people for whom siestas were the rule and migrant labor was the way of life. During the past decade, the number of Latino books has increased; however, it still falls far short of the number of books being published that represent other cultures. That said, the few pieces of historical fiction reviewed here span some four centuries from the late1500s up through the 1960s.

Beginning with *Indio* by Sherry Garland, we are introduced to Ipa-tah-chi who survived an Apache attack at ten only to be captured by Spaniards as a young woman of fourteen and sold into slavery at a silver mine. Ipa is powerless to protect her younger brother from insanity after he witnesses a terrible mining accident or her cousin from rape at the hands of a mining foreman. Ipa strikes out, however, against the brutality of the rape and the enslavement to help her cousin escape; in doing so, she finds her way back to the village of her youth—at least for a short time.

Another book that depicts the Spanish presence in the southwest is Scott O'Dell's *Carlota*. This story takes place in the 1800s in the region of what is now California and is about Carlota, the daughter of Don Saturnino whose ancestors came from Spain. The tensions in this story reflect the resistance of Carlota to take on the traditional feminine roles and expectations of the time. Her unbridled independence is the focus of this social commentary of the times.

The next set of books takes readers into the early 1940s and 1950s with Nicholasa Mohr's *Nilda* and Esmeralda Santiago's *When I Was Puerto Rican.* Both of these books explore the role of women—Puerto Rican, poor, and in charge of taking care of the family. Although men are present, we understand where the strength and determination obviously lie. Both of these stories are of memoir quality and give us strong young girls who grow into their womanhood with a sense of knowledge and independence that epitomizes what it means to be Puerto Rican American.

By understanding the trauma and struggles of the early Latino peoples, young readers may be able to understand better the strength evident in the biographies, nonfiction, and contemporary fiction.

Native American Historical Fiction

To begin a review of literature about Native Americans is to acknowledge first that, in general, publications prior to 1970 have historically been fraught with stereotyped and erroneous information. Like publications about other ethnic groups, the stories published about Native Americans prior to this time were seldom authored by people of the culture. What exists then, are stories that were influenced and told from the perspective of Europeans or European Americans. During the 1970s and 1980s, however, things began to change. With an increased focus on diversity and the need for more authentic selection of multicultural literature, Native American authors and illustrators began to have their works published. This is not to suggest that works by non-Native American authors are not credible or authentic; on the contrary, it is simply to propose that generally more works published about Native Americans during the last two decades of the twentieth century were less fraught with stereotyped or inaccurate information. As the review will show, many books published by nonnative authors contain strong themes of family and survival and a sense of honoring the Native American beliefs; however, these well-intentioned portrayals do not always represent the people or the events realistically or authentically. Therefore, whenever possible, another book choice will be offered as a stronger representation of a similar experience.

The Early Times

Some publications about the earliest encounters between the Europeans and the Native Americans came from author Michael Dorris. During his lifetime,

Dorris published works for adults and children. His three novels for children—*Morning Girl, Guests*, and *Sees Behind Trees*—all present alternative historical understandings of Native American life. In *Morning Girl*, Dorris presents the curiosity and fear that may have surrounded the strangers who arrived on a Bahamian island in 1492. Within this story, Dorris describes life on the island, through the eyes of two siblings, alternately—Morning Girl and her brother Star Boy, and the impending threat of the arrival of the strangers. With detailed descriptions, Dorris presents a portrait of a life and people that is in stark contrast to the image of the "noble savage" that Christopher Columbus presented to Spain and the rest of Europe.

In his second book for children titled *Guests*, Dorris gives his young readers a Native American perspective on the first Thanksgiving celebration. Set in an area that will one day be Massachusetts, a young boy named Moss is curious about the strangers his father has invited to dinner. Once again, Dorris provides readers with a young person's perspective and insights into the possible interaction between the European visitors and their Native American hosts.

In his final book for children, *Sees Behind Trees*, Dorris weaves a story about a young boy who is visually impaired but whose wisdom and inner sight ultimately provide his family and us, as readers, with a better appreciation for the gifts far greater than sight. Set in the sixteenth century, this coming-of-age novel finely details the physical and emotional struggles that Walnut Sees Behind Trees must face on his journey to adulthood.

Other writers such as Velma Wallis (*Bird Girl*), Brian Burks (*Runs with Horses*), and Joseph Bruchac (*Children of the Longhouse*) create dynamic coming-of-age stories for readers. The Native American experiences are historical in nature and illustrate the daily dramas of their characters' settings and challenges. Although both *Runs with Horses* and *Children of the Longhouse* are excellent choices for young readers, I would caution against using Velma Wallis's *Bird Girl* with elementary students. The cruelty and explicit violence described in this story are disturbing to most readers and would need to be discussed at length for readers (young or old) to understand it without creating further negative stereotyping.

Fight against Disease

Two novels of historical fiction that introduce the aspect of disease that Europeans brought to this continent are Jan Hudson's *Sweetgrass* and Louise Erdrich's *The Birchbark House*. Set in the winter of 1837–1838, *Sweetgrass* is a fifteen-year-old member of the Blackfoot tribe. She is considered immature by her father and must prove herself ready to marry. When her father leaves to hunt during that winter, Sweetgrass is to wait for his return with her mother and siblings. Within days of his departure, smallpox strikes the family. Throughout the winter, she cares for her sick mother and brother, buries the two babies, and finds food to feed her mother and brother as they begin to recover. Sweetgrass proves to her father, and more important to herself, that she is indeed strong and able to do the work needed to survive. The story is a mixture of survival, coming of age, and a love story and does fairly well. However, other than the historical existence of the disease itself, it is difficult to determine clearly how Sweetgrass's behavior and that of her family is grounded in authentic Blackfoot customs of the time. Also, the novel presents female characters in a negative light that may cause readers to question the true roles and behaviors of Blackfoot women.

Another book that provides a story of family and survival is *The Birchbark House* by Louise Erdrich. Set in the northern regions of Minnesota, the tale is about Omakayas and her family living on an island in Lake Superior in 1847. Erdrich's descriptions of their birch bark summer home and their cedar log winter home celebrate the diversity of the seasons and their traditional Ojibwa life. As we soon discover, this world of traditional work and family life is destroyed when a winter guest visits their lodge and brings with him the deadly disease of smallpox. Erdrich provides a clear picture of life, death, family, and loss in the rich storytelling fashion for which she is famous. Her characters are well developed and they represent the varied roles that might have been found in tribal communities of that region and era.

Boarding School Stories

Another area of historical fiction that provides harsh insight into the struggles of Native Americans relates to the boarding school experiences. Early in the twentieth century, the Bureau of Indian Affairs (BIA) began a systematic program of removing children from their families, homes, and communities and placing them into what they considered an educational setting of boarding schools. Across the United States and Canada, families were required to send their children to these boarding schools, which were often hundreds of miles from their communities. If parents did not send their children willingly, agents of the BIA would go into the communities and take the children—by force if necessary. The practice split up families and crushed the traditional tribal and cultural training the children traditionally received from the elders. Children taken from their families were not allowed to speak the language of their people and were required to learn English and adopt the ways of the white people. Traditional ceremonies were most often forbidden, and students would be punished if they clung to their cultural ways. The practices of boarding schools were harsh and students were made to feel ashamed of being Native American. How do we know all this? We know it because of the stories told by those who experienced it. Native American boarding schools existed into the late twentieth century, but the forced attendance fortunately ended decades earlier.

One exceptionally fine book about the boarding school experiences of the late 1950s is *My Name Is Seepeetza* by Shirley Sterling. Based on some of her own experiences, Sterling creates the character of Seepeetza, a ten-year-old girl who attends an Indian residential school. The story is in the form of a diary that allows the character to share her frustrations and feelings about being forced to deny her cultural identity and all it means to her. The narrative spans the period of one school year and ends with Seepeetza returning home to her family. Through that year experience, however, we are able to witness the harsh treatment that children endured in the name of education. This story, like Ruby Slipperjack's *Honour the Sun* and Beatrice Culleton's *In search of April Raintree,* may be loosely based on experiences of the author. Nonetheless, all tend to bring to the narrative more of a composite of many young people and their experiences, thus creating novels that speak to a variety of issues adding a concreteness to the universality of the experience.

Whereas *My Name Is Seepeetza* captured a one-year look at the harshness imposed upon young Native American children in boarding school settings, both *Honour the Sun* and *April Raintree* take on more complex and young adult themes and develop a social commentary on the destructive role that alcohol use and foster care homes had on families and communities. Since these two books are meant for young adults rather than children, they provide additional opportunities for older readers to delve into the severe conditions faced by Native Americans in the recent past.

As the following chapter will show, there are several sources of nonfiction found in biographies, memoirs, and informational books that you can use to extend your students' knowledge of the various Native American experiences. In addition, there is a plethora of folktales and traditional stories in the form of picture books that help younger children develop an early appreciation for the richness of Native American storytelling.

Other Cultural Representations in Historical Fiction

There are other cultural and religious groups found in the genre of historical fiction that predominately represent the European Americans who also suffered prejudice at the hands of the dominant society such as the Irish, the Italians, the Shakers, and the Jewish Americans. Throughout different periods, each of these groups has been maligned and mistreated. Probably the greatest body of historical fiction that has been published for children and young adults addresses the Holocaust. Although based in Europe, this body of literature is incredibly powerful and provides insight for teachers and students who intend to research this period in history. Authors such as Lois Lowry, Jane Yolen, Judith Kerr, Uri Orlev, and Johanna Reiss—to name a few—tell of the horrors within the appropriate limits for children.

CONCLUSIONS

Historical fiction allows us to see and feel emotionally connected to events and people of the past. It provides young people with an opportunity to connect the historical data to the human side of history. Authors who engage us in the lives and events of the past through the stories they create weave the fabric of our own freedom quilt. For to understand the landscape of where we've been is to assure that we won't lose our way again.

UNIT PLAN: JAPANESE INTERNMENT
By Nancy Cantrell

Nancy Cantrell is a graduate of Central Michigan University and taught for thirty-four years before she retired in 2004. She spent the last twenty-one years of her career teaching at Mary McGuire elementary—a school that has had a long history of serving the Native American children in the area.

Throughout her teaching career, Nancy is most proud of the work she and her grade mate Susan Horgan did in developing strong integrative units in their sixth-grade classrooms. She is particularly proud of the connections that students were able to make across the areas of social studies, literature, and art. In addition, she believes that the work they did in the development of units that specifically addressed issues of racism and prejudice provided key opportunities for their students to make better sense of the world in which they live.

Rationale

This unit is taught to help students establish their own point of view as they begin to explore the topic of racism and prejudice among different groups of people. Some outcomes for sixth-grade language arts are also met through this study.

Goals and Objectives

- To understand the war in the Pacific and the ramifications of it in the United States
- To understand how Japanese Americans were treated after the bombing of Pearl Harbor
- To understand the danger of stereotyping and judging people based on their physical features
- To understand the power of fear
- To describe and discuss shared human experiences depicted in texts

Materials Needed

- Response journals
- World map

Assessments and Evaluations

RAFT letter (Role, Audience, Format, and Topic)

Extensions

Read additional books by Yoshiko Uchida and others pertaining to the topic. Watch for possible speakers, local exhibits, and appropriate television shows.

Resources for Unit on Internment

Carnes, Jim. "Home Was a Horse Stall." In *Us and Them: A History of Intolerance in America*. Montgomery, Ala.: Teaching Tolerance, The Southern Poverty Law Center, 1995.

Kudlinski, Kathleen. *Pearl Harbor Is Burning*. New York: Puffin, 1993.

Mochizuki, Ken. *Baseball Saved Us*. New York: Lee & Low Books, 1993.

Something Strong Within. Japanese American National Museum, 1994. Videotape.

Uchida, Yoshiko. *Journey to Topaz*. Berkeley, Calif.: Creative Arts, 1983.

Yep, Laurence. *Hiroshima*. New York: Scholastic, 1995.

Suggested Writing Prompts for Response Journals for
Journey to Topaz

- What went through the family's members' minds when they heard the report of the bombing of Pearl Harbor?
- When the FBI man left the house after his phone call, why did he have trouble expressing something friendly and reassuring to Mrs. Sakane?
- Why were cameras, radios, binoculars, and guns taken from the Japanese Americans?
- What would you have to do if you had to move from your house in ten days? Where would the big stuff go?
- Why did the Japanese Americans get taken to camps while the Americans of German and Italian descent were left alone?
- Why would Yuki's mother stop and write poetry during busy times such as packing, organizing, and moving?
- Describe Tanforan Racetrack Internment camp. Describe the Sakane's "apartment" in the camp.
- Pretend that you and your family are among the group to be evacuated. How would you solve the problem of having to store, sell, or give away your belongings? What would be the feelings that you would have? Make a list of things you absolutely have to take to the internment camp.

Classroom Activities and Ideas for Literature Studies

1. Research the traditions of a cultural group through a study of music, art, food, and dance. Create a celebration of the culture through an interactive presentation of these cultural traditions.
2. Research the geographical history of a particular cultural group and its impact on their traditions, language, and belief systems.
3. Research what your classroom history books say about a particular cultural group and compare those findings with selections from historical fiction.
4. Research the historical events that have had major effects on cultural groups in this country and compare and contrast the retellings of those events in picture books and novels for young people. Some suggestions might be the slave revolts, the Civil War, the Underground Railroad, the building of the transcontinental railroad, Japanese interment camps, the civil rights movement, the 1970s Wounded Knee Stand, Native American boarding schools, and the plight of migrant workers.
5. Research and present historical background on immigration laws and their effect on particular cultural groups.

6. Invite outside speakers in to discuss the historical effects on the lives of those in their cultural group. Some speakers might relate experiences of the Holocaust, the Japanese internment during World War II, Native American treaty rights, or the civil rights movement of the 1960s.

7. Use movies to broaden understanding about historical struggles of particular cultural groups. Some film suggestions for use might be *Devil's Arithmetic*, *Amistad*, and *Where the Spirit Lives*.

8. Develop a list or database of multicultural historical fiction picture books and novels available in your school. Invite students to write critiques of the books they read and compile them so students can see what their peers think about the literature they are reading.

9. Encourage older students to mentor the younger students into reading historical fiction by sharing books through book talks to lower grades or through library book talks.

10. Ask students to create a list of historical fiction books that they believe their teachers should read. Encourage them to base their suggestions on clear criteria using the elements of story to develop a reason for inclusion.

11. Present any and all findings or projects in a student creative endeavors day when students may be honored for their work in multicultural historical fiction. Celebrate learning.

WORKS CITED

American Heritage Dictionary. 2nd ed. Boston, Mass.: Houghton Mifflin, 1982.

Berry, James. *Ajeemah and His Son*. New York: Willa Perlman, 1991.

Bruchac, Joseph. *Children of the Longhouse*. New York: Dial Books for Young Readers, 1996.

Burks, Brian. *Runs with Horses*. New York: Harcourt Brace, 1995

Cameron, Ann. *The Kidnapped Prince: The Life of Olaudah Equiano*. New York: Random House, 2000.

Choi, Sook-Nyul. *Echoes of the White Giraffe*. Boston: Houghton Mifflin, 1993.

———. *Year of the Impossible Goodbyes*. Boston: Houghton Mifflin, 1991.

Culleton, Beatrice. *In Search of April Raintree*. Winnipeg: Peguis, 1995.

Curtis, Christopher Paul. *Bud, Not Buddy*. New York: Delacorte, 1999.

———. *The Watsons Go to Birmingham—1963*. New York: Delacorte, 1995.

Davis, Ossie. *Just Like Martin*. New York: Simon & Schuster, 1992.

Dorris, Michael. *Guests*. New York: Hyperion Books for Children, 1994.

———. *Morning Girl*. New York: Hyperion Paperbacks for Children, 1992, 1999.

———. *Sees Behind Trees*. New York: Hyperion Books for Children, 1996.

English, Karen. *Francie*. New York: Farrar, Straus and Giroux, 1999.

Erdrich, Louise. *The Birchbark House*. New York: Hyperion Books for Children, 1999.

Forrester, Sandra. *Sound of Jubilee*. New York: Puffin, 1995.

Garland, Sherry. *Indio*. New York: Harcourt Brace, 1995.

———. *Song of the Buffalo Boy*. San Diego: Harcourt Brace Jovanovich, 1992.

Goldin, Barbara. *Red Means Good Fortune: A Story of San Francisco's Chinatown*. New York: Viking, 1994.

Hansen, Joyce. *The Captive*. New York: Scholastic, 1994.

Ho, Minfong. *The Clay Marble*. New York: Farrar, Strauss and Giroux, 1991.

Hopkinson, Deborah. *Sweet Clara and the Freedom Quilt*. New York: Knopf, 1993.

Houston, Gloria. *Bright Freedom's Song: A Story of the Underground Railroad*. New York: Harcourt Brace, 1998.

Houston, Jeanne Wakatsuki. *Farewell to Manzanar*. San Francisco: Bantam, 1974.

Hudson, Jan. *Sweetgrass*. New York: Scholastic, 1984.

Lasky, Kathryn. *True North*. New York: Scholastic, 1996.

Lyons, Mary E. *Letters from a Slave Girl: The Story of Harriet Jacobs*. New York: Scribners, 1992.

McKissack, Patricia, and Fredrick McKissack. *Christmas in the Big House, Christmas in the Quarters*. Illustrated by John Thompson. New York: Scholastic, 1994.

Mochizuki, Ken. *Baseball Saved Us*. Illustrated by Dom Lee. New York: Lee & Low Books, 1993.

———. *Heroes*. Illustrated by Dom Lee. New York: Lee & Low Books, 1995.

Mohr, Nicholasa. *Nilda*. New York: Harper & Row, 1973.

O'Dell, Scott. *Carlota*. Boston: Houghton Mifflin, 1981.

Patterson, Katherine. *Jip: His Story*. New York: Lodestar Books, 1996.

Paulsen, Gary. *Nightjohn*. New York: Delacorte Press, 1993.

———. *Sarny*. New York: Delacorte Press, 1997.

Pinkney, Andrea Davis. *Silent Thunder: A Civil War Story*. New York: Hyperion, 1999.

Polacco, Patricia. *Pink and Say*. New York: Philomel Books, 1994.

Ringgold, Faith. *If a Bus Could Talk: The Story of Rosa Parks*. Illustrated by Faith Ringgold. New York: Simon & Schuster, 1999.

Salisbury, Graham. *Under the Blood Red Sun*. New York: Delacorte Press, 1994.

Santiago, Esmeralda. *When I Was Puerto Rican*. New York: Vintage Books, 1993.

Slipperjack, Ruby. *Honour the Sun*. Winnipeg: Pemmican, 1987.

Sterling, Shirley. *My Name Is Seepeetza*. Vancouver: Groundwood Press, 1992.

Stolz, Mary. *Cezanne Pinto: A Memoir*. New York: Knopf: Distributed by Random House, 1994.

Taylor, Mildred. *Let the Circle Be Unbroken*. New York: Dial Press, 1981.

———. *The Mississippi Bridge*. New York: Dial Books for Young Readers, 1990.

———. *The Road to Memphis*. New York: Puffin Books, 1990.

———. *Roll of Thunder, Hear My Cry*. New York: Dial Press, 1976.

———. *Song of the Trees*. New York: Bantam Skylark, 1975

———. *The Well: David's Story*. New York: Dial Books for Young Readers, 1995.

Uchida, Yoshiko. *Journey Home*. New York: McElderry, 1978.

———. *Journey to Topaz: A Story of the Japanese American Evacuation*. Berkeley, Calif.: Creative Arts, 1985.

Wallis, Velma. *Bird Girl*. New York: HarperCollins, 1996.

Whelan, Gloria. *Goodbye, Vietnam.* New York: Knopf Books for Young Readers, 1992.

Winter, Janette. *Follow the Drinking Gourd.* New York: Knopf, 1988.

Yep, Laurence. *Dragon's Gate.* New York: HarperCollins, 1993.

———. *Dragonwings.* New York: Harper, 1975.

———. *The Star Fisher.* New York: Morrow Junior Books, 1991.

Chapter Six

Nonfiction

Biography, Informational
Texts, and Autobiography

Curiosity: 1 a desire to learn; 2 inquisitiveness; 3 anything curious or rare

—Adapted from *Webster's Dictionary*

As any young parent or teacher quickly discovers, children are enormously curious. They are constantly seeking an understanding of their world, and they have a boundless capacity to learn. The genres of nonfiction such as biography, informational texts, and autobiography flourish as a result of their inquisitive minds, as texts in these categories offer answers to young readers' questions in a multiplicity of ways.

Probably one of the most difficult things for authors of nonfiction to do is to determine how to relate the factual information about a given subject within the parameters of being developmentally appropriate for young people. The balance between enough and too much is essential if students are to be satisfied with the information they receive and yet still be interested in learning more at a later date. Students' interest must be piqued, not squelched. Children use nonfiction texts in much the same way that adults might use an encyclopedia or resource manual: they want information. Thus, as teachers, we must be able to review and evaluate nonfiction texts to determine their appropriateness for the children we teach. In making those determinations, we help our students discover another path—the path of the nonfiction genre—in their own cultural journey through literature.

The classification of nonfiction literature is a broad grouping of texts that includes *biography, autobiography,* and *informational narratives.* For our purposes, the genres are grouped together in this chapter to provide you with an opportunity to review the variety of available sources that provide us with opportunities to understand the historical and contemporary facts about people and cultures.

Biography tells the story of the life of a person and his or her achievements, while autobiography is the story of the author's life. Informational texts are intended to inform the reader about people, places, cultures, and events on the basis of specific data or observations. In defining each of the genres, we find that the thread that binds all of them together is the nonfiction quality. Although texts in this group can vary greatly in their literary quality and readability, this chapter seeks to provide particularly strong selections for review.

When evaluating biography, autobiography, and informational narratives, we must remember that all of the elements of plot, setting, characterization, theme, and style, mood, and tone apply to these genres. To entice young readers, the information or story must be engaging and worthwhile to them. In addition, it must be based on factual data about the life and times of people and events.

CRITERIA USED IN THE EVALUATION OF
MULTICULTURAL NONFICTION LITERATURE

Biography

In evaluating biographies, we must determine if they *are rooted in facts, relate the story of a real person, not an idealized portrayal of one*, and *accurately depict the period and geographical region.* In addition to these general characteristics, high-quality selections of biography that are multicultural must contain several specific features. First of all, as with all biographical selection, *accuracy and authenticity* are essential. One way to check for accuracy and authenticity is to determine whether the author adhered to the facts without adding nonexistent dialogue or perceptions that were not based on evidence. Other ways to check for accuracy are to check names, dates, or events that may be cited in the references or author's comments.

Although a biography often focuses only on the merits of an individual, the skilled author still weaves the events of the individual's life into a sound plot structure (or organization). In evaluating the plot structure for accuracy and authenticity, we must then determine if the story's plot is based on actual events and then if the author retells the events in ways that engage the reader.

The setting of a biography often alerts the reader to the social climate of the times and region. Thus, the description of the setting must be consistent with the factual information about the period and place of the events. In reviewing a biography, we need to question, therefore, whether the social milieu (or environment) is portrayed fairly and without any overt bias.

The individual about whom the biography is written is most often a person of some distinction. In evaluating the author's portrayal of that individual, we should ask if the character seems fully developed on the basis of reliable data. We should also question whether stereotypes have been avoided. As readers, we need to find the character believable by seeing someone who displays human strengths and weaknesses and is not idealized or a paragon. Finally, we need to determine if the secondary characters are also believable and based on real people.

The theme of any story often is universal in nature and biographies are no exception. In conjunction with that, the theme in a biography must represent the character's life accurately, as well as be noteworthy and memorable for the reader.

The style, tone, and mood of a biography refer to the language and choice of diction that the author uses to tell the story. Within this category, the author must use language that portrays the characters, events, and setting accurately. In addition, when writing for children, an author must represent the issue or topic in language that is age appropriate and avoids an oversimplification of the problems.

Many biographies are now presented in a picture book format in which the illustrations are either reproductions of original photographs or beautifully detailed works of art. In evaluating the illustrated biographies, we must question whether the illustrations complement and enrich the text and if the illustrations accurately portray the setting without stereotyped images or details.

By applying the criteria consistently, we are able to provide the very best representations of the genre to our students. Since young people rely on biographies, autobiographies, informational texts, and other books of nonfiction to inform them about important people, places, and events, we must provide texts that accurately and authentically represent cultural groups.

Accuracy and Authenticity

- Are facts adhered to? (Are dialogue and character's thoughts supported by data?)
- Are the names, dates, and events used in the text supported by documented resources?
- Is there reference to the sources or documentation used by the author?

Plot

- Is the story plot based on actual events?
- Does the author retell the events in ways that engage the reader?

Setting

- Is the description setting consistent with the factual information of the time and place of the events?
- Is the social milieu portrayed fairly?

Characterization

- Is the character fully developed on the basis of reliable data?
- Are stereotypes avoided?
- Is the character believable in his or her strengths and weaknesses and not idealized?
- Are the secondary characters believable and based on real people?

Theme

- Is the theme universal in nature?
- Does the theme represent the character's life accurately?
- Is the theme noteworthy and memorable to the reader?

Style, Tone, Mood

- Does the language portray the characters, events, and setting accurately?
- Are the issues or topics explained in language that is age appropriate?
- Does the author avoid oversimplification?

Illustrations

- Do the illustrations complement and enrich the text?
- Do the illustrations accurately portray the setting?
- Does the illustrator avoid use of stereotyped images and details?

Autobiographies and Memoirs

Although generally the criteria just discussed can be applied also to *autobiography*, certain elements of the criteria specifically relate to the genre. Autobiography is the author telling the story of his or her life. Sometimes the author will choose a particular period or series of events to relate rather than his or her whole life. When he or she does this, the work is sometimes signified by a special term, *memoir*, to distinguish it from autobiography that is wider in scope. Esmeralda Santiago, for instance, has written two memoirs that reflect significantly different periods in her life. Although both books are appropriate for older readers, her first memoir, *When I Was Puerto Rican*, shares her early years as a child in Puerto Rico and her family's move to New York City. It ends with her audition to New York City's High School for Performing Arts. Her second memoir, *Almost a Woman*, begins with her arrival in New York City. It quickly moves into her teenage years and experiences at the Academy for Performing Arts and the years following her graduation—including her first love affair—and concludes with her decision to move to Florida at the age of twenty-one. Santiago uses these different periods to introduce readers to the nuances of life experiences for a young Puerto Rican—first as a child and later as a young woman. The reflective quality of memoir is emotionally engaging in ways that some autobiographies are not.

In contrast to the memoir genre, autobiographies for young people are often more inclusive of the author's life. Not unusual are texts that present the life and craft of popular authors of literature for children and young adults. Jean Fritz, Beverly Cleary, Ronald Dahl, Richard Peck, and many others tell the stories of their childhood and how they came to be writers. Like memoirs and biographies, autobiographies must be engaging for the reader and the elements of story must exist. Unlike biographies, however, autobiographies seldom give readers documentation or resources to validate the accuracy of the events. Authors will often include notes for the readers, providing background or what happened later, but since the story is one of personal experiences, the reader relies on the author to tell us the facts of his or her life. There is no need for further supporting documentation. However, the criteria for evaluating the elements of story—plot, setting, characterization, theme, style, tone, and mood—are all valid, and we apply them to autobiography and memoir genres to determine appropriateness, readability, and issues of quality.

Informational Texts

Informational texts provide readers with facts within a non-textbook approach. While facts and data can be obtained through encyclopedias and other resource materials, informational texts package those facts in ways that engage and satisfy readers, linguistically and often visually. Walter Dean Myers, Patricia and Fredrick McKissack, Russell Freedman, David McCauley and many others have introduced complex subject matter and issues to students in ways that are developmentally appropriate and extremely engaging for young readers. An interesting phenomenon seen frequently in this genre is the collaborative effort of a children books author and an expert in the particular field being presented. Whether simply interested in the topic or whether seeking information for a research project, children have the ability to become engaged with a plethora of topics through quality informational texts.

To evaluate these texts, we must examine them in terms of organization, style, and accuracy. First of all, informational texts should be organized in terms of structure and format. In other words, the author should provide such things as indexes, glossaries, and graphics that will help the reader understand all facets of the intended content. The layout and design of the book should support the content in a visually appealing way for the reader, and the information should be easily decipherable. The style of the text refers to the language used to explain the content. The author should use language or terms that are accurate without overwhelming the readability of the text. In other words, the explanations should include interesting details yet not be beyond the capabilities of the intended audience. Finally, informational texts must present accurate and complete facts about the topic. High-quality informational texts will provide the reader with multiple views and documentation to support the information given. Generalizations will be limited, while fact and theory will be identified and those given will be qualified through appropriate sources.

While these criteria might be applied to any textbook, most quality informational texts attend to these criteria with the intent to engage readers' curiosity and to foster the love of learning.

Organization

- Informational texts should be well organized in terms of structure and format.
- Indexes, glossaries, and graphics that help the reader to understand all facets of the intended content should be provided.
- The layout and design of the book should support the content and be visually appealing to the reader.
- The information should be easily decipherable.

Style

- The author should use language or terms that are accurate without overwhelming the readability of the text.
- The explanations should include interesting details yet not be beyond the capabilities of the intended audience.

Accuracy

- Informational texts must present accurate and complete facts about the topic.

- Quality informational texts will provide the reader with multiple views and documentation to support the information given.
- Generalizations will be limited, while fact and theory will be identified and those given will be qualified through appropriate sources.
- A list of further resources and documentation will be listed to provide readers with additional information on the topic.

SELECTIONS OF BIOGRAPHY, AUTOBIOGRAPHY, MEMOIR, AND INFORMATIONAL TEXTS

African American

The publishing companies of the 1990s have provided readers with many new biographies of African Americans. Important people of the past come alive for young readers through the retelling of their experiences by authors and illustrators. Often, we find multiple biographies of the same person presented by different authors. People such as Rosa Parks, Martin Luther King Jr., and Malcolm X have been the focus of many biographical representations. In recent years, other individuals have had their stories told by multiple representations as well.

Biographies

Duke Ellington, for instance, is the focus of two different biographies during recent years. In 1991, James Collier authored a biography for older readers titled *Duke Ellington*. In this biography of 140 pages, Collier traces the life of Edward Kennedy Ellington (Duke) with a special focus on his musical career. Seven years later, in 1998, Hyperion Press published a picture book version of Ellington's life story as a musician. Under the same title, *Duke Ellington*, Andrea Davis Pinkney retells the jazz musician's accomplishments for younger readers in just 32 pages. The illustrations of this book are beautiful representations of the period rendered on scratchboard with gouache and oil by Brian Pinkney. The creative depictions are highly detailed and won a Caldecott Honor for 1999. Both books provide young readers with the opportunity to learn about this great jazz musician whose work changed the face of music in the early years of the twentieth century.

Another prominent African American figure who received multiple biographical representations during the 1990s was Zora Neale Hurston. As with Duke Ellington, Zora Hurston's biography was also presented in both novel and picture book formats. Mary Lyons's *Sorrow's Kitchen: The Life and*

Folklore of Zora Neale Hurston presents older readers with a colorful look into the life of this Harlem Renaissance writer. Combining the facts and folklore of her life as a writer, Lyons supports the retelling of this important writer's life with reproductions of photographs taken throughout Hurston's life.

A. P. Porter's depiction of Zora Neale Hurston is found in *Jump at de Sun: The Story of Zora Neale Hurston.* This ninety-eight-page biography provides older readers with an interesting look at the early life and work of Hurston. Porter uses the phrase "jump at de sun" to emphasize the influence of Hurston's mother on her ability to become an anthropologist, a folklorist, and a writer. A favorite phrase used by Hurston's mother to her young child, it epitomized the confidence and emotional support Zora received during her early childhood.

A presentation of Zora Neale Hurston was written for younger readers by William Miller in his book titled *Zora Hurston and the Chinaberry Tree.* In this beautifully illustrated book, readers are introduced to Hurston as a child whose independence allows her to gather the stories of her community. This coupled with the encouragement of her dying mother gives readers another opportunity to gain insight into the early makings of this remarkable writer.

Sports figures are often interesting biographical subjects for young readers. One important and frequently researched figure is Jesse Owens. In a picture book format for young readers, author David Adler and illustrator Robert Casilla recreate the life of Jesse Owens in *A Picture Book of Jesse Owens.* Walter Dean Myers details the life of another sports hero in his book *The Greatest: Muhammad Ali.* Myers eloquently tells of the struggles of segregation faced by the young Cassius Clay and his transformation into Muhammad Ali.

Biographies of historical figures provide readers with a sense of the people who contributed to society in significant ways. Patricia and Fredrick McKissack have provided older readers with a portrait of the life and times of one such figure in *Sojourner Truth: Ain't I a Woman?* This novel details the life of this important woman who, although born a slave, became an abolitionist and an advocate for women's rights. The McKissacks have retold the story on the basis of historical documents that is both informative and engaging for readers.

Walter Dean Myers has chronicled the life stories of important historical figures as well. In two separate texts, Myers tells the story of Malcolm X. In his first biography geared for young people, Myers tells of the challenging life of Malcolm X in a chapter book. Depicting poignant and harsh realities of the times and life, *Malcolm X: By Any Means Necessary* received a Coretta Scott King honor award in 1994. In a more recent illustrated biography, *Malcolm X: A Fire Burning Brightly*, Myers details the life story again of one of the most interesting figures of the civil rights era. Within this text, Myers not only depicts the adversity that was a prominent element in the life of Malcolm X, but he also tells of his ability to change—moving from hatred to tolerance.

Other historical biographies are broader than a single individual and focus on the events of a group of important people of the culture. Clinton Cox's *Undying Glory* gives readers a perspective on the all-black 54th Massachusetts Regiment who fought in the Civil War. This group of soldiers' experiences of discrimination, lower wages, and incredible odds are detailed through photographs and primary sources.

Another type of biographical writing appeared during the decade of the 1990s in the form of collections. These novel-length collections provide readers with many different biographical sketches of individuals focused on a particular topic. In *And Not Afraid to Dare* by Tonya Bolden, readers are exposed to the stories of ten African American women including Ellen Craft, Charlotte Forten Grimke, Mary Fields, Ida B. Wells, Mary McLeod Bethune, Clara Hale, Leontyne Price, Toni Morrison, Mae C. Jemison, and Jackie Joyner-Kersee. Each story exemplifies the personal qualities of these women, qualities that provided them the strength to overcome struggles of racism, prejudice, and social restrictions.

In Nikki Giovanni's edited collection titled *Grand Fathers*, the author provides her readers with forty-seven biographical snapshots of grandfathers through prose, poetry, and song. For most of these brief character sketches, we are given a glimpse of the grandfathers who touched the lives of the forty-seven featured authors. Though undocumented in the traditional sense of a biography, the realities of the authors' experiences and memories of their grandfathers or grandfather figures ring true to the reader.

Another author who has provided young readers with several biographical collections is James Haskins. His texts, *Against All Opposition: Black Explorers in America*, *One More River to Cross: The Stories of Twelve Black Americans*, and *Outward Dreams: Black Inventors and Their Inventions*, provide readers with many brief biographies of African Americans who have made significant contributions to the success of this country.

Autobiographies and Memoirs

Autobiographies and memoirs help us understand the life experiences of African Americans on a much more personal level than biographies. By reading the story in someone's own words, we can often develop a level of empathy that is incredibly strong for us as readers. One such memoir is found in Melba Beals' *Warriors Don't Cry: A Searing Memoir of the Battle to Integrate Little Rock's Central High*. Written nearly forty years after her experience as one of the nine high school students who, with a court order and protection of the National Guard, was among the first students to integrate Central High School, Beals tells the powerful story with a sense of clarity. This first-person account leaves us, as readers, stunned by the courage and determination these teenagers had in the face of so much hostility. The power and climate of the period are richly detailed through the eyes of one who lived it.

Nonfiction or Informational Texts

Nonfiction or informational texts as they are sometimes called refer to writing that is designed to inform. As the discussion about this genre earlier in this chapter indicated, there are many authors who provide young readers with an excellent array of texts that inform and educate them about a variety of topics and issues. Two people who have been major contributors to this genre are Patricia and Fredrick McKissack. In their 1999 publication, *Black Hands, White Sails*, the McKissacks tell the little-known history of the role African Americans played in the whaling industry and of its significance to the abolitionist movement and the Underground Railroad. This East Coast industry provided work for free black men and runaway slaves despite the lower wages and high risk that the sea posed. The McKissacks provide details of whaling ship voyages and introduce readers to the danger and the drama of the work. Thoroughly supported by archival drawings and photos of the period, *Black Hands, White Sails* is an informative and enlightening story about the contributions of African Americans to the whaling industry during a time fraught with the turmoil of the pre-Civil War.

Another important informational text provided by the McKissacks is *Rebels Against Slavery: American Slave Revolts*. This collection of stories about the slave revolts from the colonial times to the emancipation proclamation provides readers with a sense of the dire circumstances faced by slaves. Without either a sense of sentimentality or a glorification of the violence that occurred, the McKissacks painstakingly tell of the revolts that were waged. Although many readers may know of the revolts led by Nat Turner in 1831 or Cinque of the Amistad in 1839, far fewer will know of the Maroons who were the slaves that revolted by escaping and setting up hidden communities in the South. The McKissacks have based their retellings of these events on detailed documented research—all of which makes this text a valuable resource to students and teachers.

Another little-known historical contribution of African Americans is presented by Cox in *Come All You Brave Soldiers: Blacks in the Revolutionary War*. This informational text captivates the readers by bringing them into the period of the Revolutionary War through the descriptive retelling of the events. Through the research of primary and secondary sources, Cox provides young readers with a well-documented narrative that clearly shows the strong role that African Americans played in gaining freedom for this country. Cox begins his narrative with a quote from Rev. William Howard Day, an abolitionist and educator, who addressed the convention of black veterans of the War of 1812 in Cleveland, Ohio, in 1852, about the lack of recorded history of black Revolutionary War soldiers. As Cox reflects upon this quote, he notes that it has been nearly 150 years since Rev. Day's address and yet, "the role of black soldiers in the American Revolution is still largely buried in the graveyard of forgotten history" (1999, v). Through his diligence, Cox has given readers an opportunity to unearth the unacknowledged role of African Americans and to understand to a greater degree its importance to us all.

Two other texts that help students explore the historical struggles of African Americans are *Now Is Your Time!* by Walter Dean Myers and *Mississippi Challenge* by Mildred Walter. Both texts provide information about the role of African Americans in the history of the United States. In *Now Is Your Time!*, Myers provides young readers with an easily accessible history of African Americans. With factual information laid out in a chronological order, Myers presents historical content in such a clear way that students are able to understand key events within a narrative format. From the early days of slavery to the civil rights movement, Myers explains the strife endured by generations of African Americans to young readers in a way that helps all of us understand better the long struggle for freedom.

Walter's *Mississippi Challenge* focuses more directly on the period of the civil rights movement and in particular on the events in Mississippi. The incredible level of violence and hatred displayed in Mississippi is difficult to understand, but Walter narrates the story of this period with clarity of purpose. Her descriptions and explanations of the movement and the people are poignant reminders of our past. This is an excellent text for older readers and I would not hesitate in using it with students in grades six and up.

Asian American

Biographies

The richness of biographies offers young people an opportunity to read about the strange and the unusual. Such is the case with Allen Say's biography of Billy Wong titled *El Chino*. In this beautifully illustrated picture book, Say gives young readers the story of a young Chinese American man who takes his father's words to heart when he says, "In America, you can be anything you want to be." Although trained as an engineer, Billy Wong had always wanted to be a professional athlete. His fascination with bullfighting ultimately brings him to the ring, and against all odds he becomes one of Spain's famous matadors—El Chino. The richness of Say's watercolor illustrations provides readers with a visual appreciation for this man and his love of bullfighting.

Other biographies that offer young people insight into the lives of famous individuals are Mary Fox's *Bette Bao Lord: Novelist and Chinese Voice for Change*, Pamela Dell's *I.M. Pei: Designer of Dreams*, Jim Hargrove's *Dr. An Wang: Computer Pioneer*, Mary Malone's *Maya Lin: Architect and Artist*, and Gail Riley's *Wah Ming Chang: Artist and Master of Special Effects*. As Fox documents the life of author Bette Bao Lord, readers are able to see the details of her early life in China and the United States and their influence on her novel for children *In the Year of the Boar and Jackie Robinson*.

Societal contributions through technology, art, and architecture are revealed through the biographies of Dr. An Wang, Wah Ming Chang, and Maya Lin. From the computer industrialist whose $600 investment grew into a multibillion-dollar enterprise, to the artist whose work in special effects changed the face of the movie industry, and to the twenty-one-year-old artist-architect who designed the Vietnam Wall in Washington, D.C., young readers are informed and entertained by these well-documented stories. With each new biographical addition, readers have the opportunity to gain knowledge and respect for individuals who represent heritages different from the dominant culture.

Autobiographies and Memoirs

In recent years, literary attention has been given to the shameful treatment of Japanese American citizens during World War II. A number of excellent autobiographies, memoirs, and biographies have been written and provide young readers with real-life stories about the internment camps. One author, Yoshiko Uchida, made significant literary and social contributions to this body of literature by writing about her own internment experiences first in the Tanforan Race Track Center and later in Topaz, Utah. Through her memoir, *The Invisible Thread*, young readers are able to learn what it was like to be Nisei—second generation Japanese—prior to and during World War II (Uchida 1991). As Uchida and others tell their stories, students become literary witnesses to government action against U.S. citizens of Japanese heritage who were rounded up and forced to leave their homes and businesses to live in horse stalls before being shipped off to internment camps in the desert.

Uchida and her family were relocated to Topaz, Utah—one of ten internment camps for Japanese Americans. Her detailed description of family life before, during, and immediately after the internment camp experiences of World War II can help students understand the physical and emotional hardships endured because of racial prejudice and war hysteria.

Jeanne Wakatsuki Houston is another author who has written about her experiences of internment. While Uchida was a young adult just finishing her BA degree at the University of California when Pearl Harbor was bombed, Houston was a seven-year-old child. In her autobiography, *Farewell to Manzanar*, Houston shares with her readers the difficulties she had as a Nisei child who spoke English and had lived in the predominately affluent Caucasian neighborhood of Ocean Park, Calif. The youngest of ten children, she was curious about the arrest of her father and the removal of their family to Manzanar. She sometimes looked upon the experience as an adventure—aware and confused by the uprooting, at times fearful, but most often secure because she was surrounded by older siblings and their spouses. Her story seems at times surrealistic with its prison camp background of armed guards, barbed wire confinements, and tar paper barracks and the day-to-day life of the camp filled with dances, baton twirling lessons, cheerleaders, Boy Scouts, and dance bands. What readers discover is that the Japanese Americans who were torn from their homes, jobs, and families were spirited survivors full of dignity and perseverance.

There are also excellent autobiographies or memoirs that help readers understand better the writers who create their literature. Laurence Yep, a prolific writer of fiction—both contemporary and historical—tells young readers about his life as a child who is "too American to fit into Chinatown . . . too Chinese to fit anywhere else . . ." His story resonates the feelings that many children have—particularly when they feel like outsiders. *The Lost Garden* is an articulate and insightful story of how Yep came to understand and accept himself as a writer and as a person.

Another autobiography/memoir written for older readers is *Chinese Cinderella* by Adeline Mah. This story details the events—physical and emotional—of Mah's life from early childhood through her late teen years. Although set in China, Mah, who now resides in California, tells a story all too familiar to children who are neglected by parents and stepparents. Her determination is phenomenal and readers will be amazed at the author's postscript that tells the rest of her story after leaving China. The author has written two versions of her autobiography: *Chinese Cinderella* is written for younger readers, while *Falling Leaves* is intended for an adult audience.

Informational Texts

Informational texts that explore and present the Asian American experiences are valuable resources for the classroom. From the celebrations of the Chinese New Year to photo essays of immigration experiences to the United States, we can learn a great deal from these stories of real life experiences.

An interesting addition to understanding the emigration stories of people from China, Korea, and Vietnam is the Footsteps to America series books authored by Alexandra Bandon in 1994. This multivolume set presents the historical and political factors behind the emigration of people from China, Korea, and Vietnam to the United States. Photographs and personal narratives of recent immigrants and their experiences provide young readers with a substantive understanding of why these people chose to move to the United States.

Another series that has focused its efforts in presenting cultural information is the American Family Album series. Within this series generally, and this volume in particular, Dorothy and Thomas Hoobler use photographs to support the narrative in *The Chinese American Family Album*. Issues such as legal discrimination and cultural persecution are dealt with in a forthright way that makes this text an excellent resource for students who seek to learn more about the levels of racism and prejudice endured by Chinese Americans.

War is often a common thread that runs through many of the informational texts written for young people. Supported by photographs, Nancy Graff details the life of a Cambodian family who struggle to start over in the United States after fleeing their homeland during a civil war. In *Where the River Runs: A Portrait of a Refugee Family*, young readers become aware of the difficulties in starting a new life in a place where the language, culture, and religion are all different. To read the story of this family struggling to hold onto the ways of their homeland is very important if we are to begin to develop a level of empathy with immigrants to this country.

Two Lands, One Heart: An American Boy's Journey to His Mother's Vietnam by Jeremy Schmidt and illustrated by Ted Wood is another photographic narrative that details the experiences of a seven-year-old American boy who travels with his mother to her homeland of Vietnam. Taken to the United States during the fall of Saigon and after being separated from her family as a young child, TJ's mother finds her family in Vietnam and takes her son to meet his overseas relatives. Rather that focusing on the traumas of the relocation experience, the narrative revels in the joy of rediscovery of family and culture.

A text that explains the rituals and beliefs associated with the celebration of the Chinese New Year is *Lion Dancer: Ernie Wan's Chinese New Year* by

Kate Waters and Madeline Slovenz-Low. Through the narration given by Ernie Wan, who lives in New York City's Chinatown, readers are invited to share the Chinese New Year Celebration with Ernie and his family. The highlight of the celebration in the text is Ernie's performance in the New Year's parade of the lion dance.

Latino and Hispanic Americans

While there has been an increase in the number of Spanish-language books over the past few years, many of those texts often do not significantly reflect the Latino culture. What is important, therefore, is to provide a wide selection of texts that accurately and authentically portray the nuances of the Latino people and culture. One way to broaden that selection is again with the inclusion of biographies and autobiographies/memoirs of, for example, authors, political figures, athletes, and entertainment personalities.

Biographies

Helping young people understand the importance of social responsibility is sometimes a benefit derived from biographies that highlight important political figures. Three such examples can be found in Carmen Bredeson's *Henry Cisneros: Building a Better America*, Mary Wade's *Guadalupe Quintanilla: Leader of the Hispanic Community*, and Nicholasa Mohr's *All for the Better: A Story of El Barrio*, which is illustrated by Rudy Gutierrez. All three of these biographies offer young readers the life stories of individuals who struggled to honor their Latino traditions in the face of discriminatory attitudes and practices.

In Bredeson's *Henry Cisneros*, the life of the former mayor of San Antonio and former secretary of Housing and Urban Development is documented. Full of family pictures and other photographs, Bredeson details Cisneros's work as a public servant and as a man dedicated to improving the lives of his constituents.

Wade tells of the frustrations and challenges faced by Mexican immigrant Guadalupe Quintanilla in her biography titled *Guadalupe Quintanilla*. Wade provides an account of the struggles encountered by Quintanilla as a thirteen-year-old placed in a first-grade classroom because of her lack of English language skills and her eventual self-schooling to educate herself to become a leader for immigrants.

In Mohr's *All for the Better*, we find another story of emigration, this time from Puerto Rico. This is the story of Evelina Lopez Antonetty, a Bronx community activist, who worked to improve educational opportunities for children. Done in a picture book format, Rudy Gutierrez does a wonderful job expressing the cultural nuances of the life in the neighborhoods of New York City during the 1930s.

Influential sports figures also have found their way into picture books and novels for young readers. Baseball great Roberto Clemente is remembered for his love of the sport and his dedication to the people of Puerto Rico and Central America. In the picture book *Roberto Clemente: Young Baseball Hero* written by Louis Sabin and illustrated by Marie DeJohn, we see the details of Clemente's childhood and family values in Puerto Rico prior to his baseball career. Young readers are introduced to the culture and its influences on Clemente.

Another biography focused on Roberto Clemente is *Pride of Puerto Rico: The Life of Roberto Clemente* written by Paul Walker. In this novel for upper elementary students, readers are provided with the harsh realities of racial and cultural insults incurred by this famous baseball player. Readers also learn of the support provided by family and friends that helped Clemente rise above the discriminatory behaviors of others and of his dedication to reach out to those less fortunate. His dedication and commitment ultimately cost him his life as he died on a mission to help the Nicaraguan people after the devastating earthquake of 1972.

Autobiographies and Memoirs

As noted earlier, one author who has written two memoirs for young adult readers is Esmeralda Santiago. Within both of her memoirs, *When I was Puerto Rican* and *Almost a Woman*, Santiago shares with her readers the joys and frustrations of being one of eleven children, where poverty and being different permeate all aspects of her life. From her first novel, *When I was Puerto Rican*, we see a family that is incomplete and struggles with poverty in Puerto Rico. A bicycle accident severely injures the foot of a younger brother, Raymond, and its lack of healing prompts Esmeralda's mother to move her children first to the barrio of El Mangle and then on to New York to seek medical care. Once in New York with her mother's relatives, Esmeralda, or Negi as her family calls her, is focused on surviving the new experiences of tenement life and ghetto poverty. This first memoir ends with Negi's acceptance to the Performing Arts High School.

Santiago's second memoir, *Almost a Woman*, begins in 1961 with her arrival in New York with her mother and two of her siblings. At the age of thirteen, Negi faces the strangeness of a new city and of starting over. Although surrounded by many relatives, Negi often feels alone and different in this strange city where she must be *Hispanic*, not Puerto Rican. Young adult readers of this novel will follow Negi through her acceptance to the Performing Arts High School, her years there, and the first few years following graduation when, as a young actress, she falls in love for the first time. Readers may be surprised by the frankness and honesty of this young woman's experiences and will certainly come to understand the difficulty of her decisions. The family bond that pulls at Negi, while she yearns for independence and a sense of normalcy, will appeal to young adults who often empathize with Negi's struggles.

Informational Texts

Informational texts provide opportunities for learning about cultural experiences at both the factual and the personal levels. In Kathleen Krull's *The Other Side: How Kids Live in a California Latino Neighborhood*, we see how children learn to negotiate the language, social, and cultural barriers posed to recent immigrants from Mexico to California. Through color photographs, we are provided a window into the bilingual and bicultural lives of three children and their families.

The understanding of a culture is often enriched through learning about the celebrations of the people. In George Ancona's *Pablo Remembers: The Fiesta of the Day of the Dead*, we are invited into the lives of Pablo and his family as they prepare for the "Dia de los Muertos" (Day of the Dead) celebration. Through the preparation of food and assorted offerings brought to the home, we see the cultural significance placed on honoring the lives of the family members who have died.

In another of his photo narratives, *Fiesta, U.S.A.*, Ancona further enriches our understanding of the Latino cultural celebrations. In a vivid display of the four celebrations of Dia de los Muertos, Las Posados, Los Matachines, and La Fiesta de los Reyes Magos, Ancona's photography provides young readers with an authentic representation of the Latino community through text and colorful illustrations.

Mary Lankford also uses a photo essay approach to inform young readers about a traditional Latino birthday celebration in *Quinceanera: A Latina's Journey to Womanhood*. As we quickly learn, a young woman's fifteenth birthday carries a special significance in many Latino families and communities at the social and religious levels.

In a narrative about the history of the United Farm Workers, Dana De Ruiz and Richard Larios provide readers with a clearly written documentation of the events that fostered the working contracts in the agricultural areas of California in the late 1960s. In *La Causa: The Migrant Farmworkers' Story*, we see again illustrations by Rudy Gutierrez that help readers gain a sense of the

life and work that migrant workers experienced during the decades of the
1940s, 1950s, and 1960s.

Another narrative that presents the historical perspective of Mexican
Americans is *The Mexican-American Experience* by Elizabeth Martinez.
Supported by illustrations and photographs, the text provides younger readers
with not only a historical background of the Mexican American experiences
but also more recent experiences of immigrants to the United States from
Mexico.

As more informational texts are published, young readers are given the
opportunity to see how cultural identities are linked to traditional celebrations
and events.

Native American

Biographies

Through biographies, we are able to see more clearly into the world of prominent Native Americans. In *A Boy Becomes a Man at Wounded Knee*, Ted
Wood with Wanbli Numba Afraid of Hawk tells the story of the one hundredth anniversary of the massacre of 350 Lakota Indians at Wounded Knee,
S.Dak. Photographs detail the trip on horseback through the South Dakota
Badlands in December taken by Wanbli Numba as he seeks to honor his
ancestors in the Big Foot Memorial Ride.

In another biography, *The Life and Death of Crazy Horse* by Russell
Freedman with drawings by Amos Bad Heart Bull, the story of the life and
death of Crazy Horse, the great warrior, is told. On the basis of interviews
conducted by Eleanor Hinman and Mari Sandoz with his surviving relatives
and fellow warriors on Pine Ridge Reservation in 1930, Freedman constructs
an interesting and informative narrative of Crazy Horse. Supplemented by the
drawings of Amos Bad Heart Bull, cousin to Crazy Horse, the biography creates a clear sense of the struggles faced by Native Americans at the close of
the nineteenth century.

Other biographies such as *Chief Joseph: Nez Percé Warrior, Crazy Horse:
Sioux Warrior, Quanah Parker: Comanche Warrior, Sitting Bull: Sioux Warrior,* and *Osceola: Seminole Warrior* were all written by William Sanford as
part of the Native American Leaders of the Wild West series. These texts
include archival photographs, maps, and drawings to support the depictions
of these men and the struggles they faced in their attempts to defend their
territories.

Autobiographies and Memoirs

Literature that informs us about the Native American experiences is a valuable resource for the young people we teach. As cultural experiences are celebrated through powwows across the country, young people are being given the opportunity to see the beauty of dance and drumming. The concern, however, is that students need more than an occasional visit to a powwow if they are to understand the indignities that Native Americans have endured, and to appreciate their contribution to this country. From the earliest days of the Europeans on this soil, Native Americans have faced disenfranchisement. There are several picture books and novels that now provide information about this struggle—one that threatened families and traditional life of Native Americans. Memoirs are finding their way into literature for young people. *My Name Is Seepeetza* by Shirley Sterling relates the story of one girl's experiences in a Native American boarding school. The level of insensitivity to culture and traditions is evidenced by the teachers and administrators of the school. While there is an assumption that all children will attend the school, there is also a sense of sadness at the community and family loss when the children are uprooted from their homes for months at a time. The journal that Seepeetza keeps documents the year's events and the loneliness she experiences with a frank and candid approach for young readers.

Informational Texts

Informational texts provide valuable resources in understanding the history of racism and prejudice experienced by Native Americans. In *Wounded Knee* by Dee Brown and adapted for younger readers by Amy Ehrlich, the historical significance of the events that led up to the massacre of Native Americans at Wounded Knee are reissued in a format that is more appropriate for use with younger readers in upper elementary schools. Ehrlich is careful to retain the key passages and events that allow young people to experience the power of Brown's original work without overwhelming them with its 450-plus-page length.

Some other informational texts that are important resources for younger readers vary from the historical perspectives of *Trail of Tears: The Cherokee Journey* by Marlene Brill and The First Americans series by Virginia Driving Hawk Sneve, to contemporary cultural experiences such as *Shannon: An Ojibway Dancer* by Sandra King or *Kinaalda: A Navajo Girl Grows Up* by Monty Roessel.

Learning about a culture through well-documented narratives of historical events and traditions provides young readers with some background for understanding the discrimination and displacement endured by Native Americans. One particularly powerful narrative is Brill's *The Trail of Tears* in which the author supports her textual information with maps, photographs, and illustrated drawings that help students understand the incredible injustice thrust upon the Cherokee nation by the Indian Removal Bill of 1830. In one removal example, the Cherokee were forced to leave their homelands in the Appalachian Mountains and move to Oklahoma; this removal has been highly documented for its inhumane treatment of a group of people.

Sneve has authored several volumes that describe the traditional ways of individual Native American groups of people. Providing her readers with geographical and historical data in *The Hopis*, *The Iroquois*, *The Navajos*, *The Nez Percé*, and *The Sioux*, Sneve shares carefully researched cultural information that details their past two centuries. Beginning with the group's creation story and illustrated with watercolor paintings by Ronald Himler, this picture book series is a valuable classroom resource.

Contemporary information about Native American culture is essential for a balanced cultural understanding for students. To hear or read only about historical experiences of Native Americans poses the potential threat of diminishing the role of Native Americans today. Through *Shannon* (King) and *Kinaalda* (Roessel), young readers are able to see how traditional customs are integrated into the daily lives of young people today.

In the photo essay written by Sandra King and illustrated by Jesse Herrera, we are able to see modern and traditional Ojibwa practices. The focus of the text is on a thirteen-year-old girl from Minnesota whose daily life epitomizes the combination of these traditional and modern ways. Young readers will see a young woman whose life is full of the activities of school, family, and friends. The culmination of Shannon's story with us is her dance performance honoring her heritage at a powwow.

Another fascinating photo essay is given by Navajo writer and photographer Monty Roessel. In *Kinaalda*, readers are invited into the coming of age ceremony for a Navajo girl. By adapting this ancient ceremony to the present-day lifestyle and circumstances, this New Mexico girl and her family are able to recapture an important ceremony that was nearly lost owing to the disruptive influences outside of the Navajo culture.

CONCLUSIONS

With new publications appearing yearly, students and teachers are given the opportunity to develop greater breadth and a deeper level of understanding for cultures that are not their own. Nonfiction texts provide information about real people and experiences that offer all of us a fuller sense of who we were and who we are as a country. One of the key elements of nonfictional literature is its authenticity. To really get to know about a person, to experience an event, or to visualize a certain period is what authors of good nonfiction literature should strive for. Teachers can supplement readings with videos, guest speakers, monologues, and dramatic interpretations. Once students are aware of this information, understand its meaning, and accept those realities, then they can move on and interpret its true effect on them.

Students should be given opportunities to learn about people who contributed to our country from every walk of life. This includes African Americans, Asian Americans, European Americans, Latino Americans, and Native Americans. And within these specific groups, students should reach beyond the traditional role model that everyone has condoned as being politically acceptable. Not only should they know about Martin Luther King Jr. and all of his contributions toward the civil rights movement, but also they should be taught about Mae Jemison and C. J. Walker. Students should know about the accomplishments of people such as Billy Wong, Dr. An Wang, and a host of other heroes and heroines of color. If there are so many of these heroes and heroines from all racial groups for our young readers to learn about, why then do we stifle their intellectual growth?

UNIT PLAN: CIVIL RIGHTS MOVEMENT
By Susan Horgan

Susan Horgan has taught at the elementary level for thirty-five years and is presently serving as a literacy consultant for the Mt. Pleasant, Mich., school district. Horgan spent thirty-three years teaching upper-elementary self-contained classrooms at Mary McGuire Elementary School in Mount Pleasant. This school has had a history of serving the Native American children of the community who are members of the Saginaw Chippewa Reservation in Mt. Pleasant. Horgan graduated from Central Michigan University in Mount Pleasant with a degree in English. Her professional focuses are in cooperative learning, curriculum development, educational policy, multicultural education, and literacy.

Horgan worked collaboratively with, Nancy Cantrell, her grade mate at the sixth-grade level for 16 years, using multicultural literature to raise the students' awareness of the damage that racism and prejudices inflict on daily lives. The use of multicultural literature was the vehicle for both to teach the outcomes required by the district and to examine ideas, histories, and situations that are engaging to the students. Horgan finds it very rewarding and satisfying to watch children gain awareness and develop new attitudes.

By the end of each year, a poster titled *Prejudice in Our Daily Lives* was filled with articles, recounts, pictures, and fliers that demonstrated how students in both classes looked at the world through a different lens. According to Horgan and Cantrell, this was due to the fact that they, as teachers, had looked at the curriculum through a different lens when planning and choosing materials for the students.

Rationale

This unit is taught to help students establish their own point of view as they continue to explore the topic of racism and prejudice among different groups of people. Some outcomes for sixth-grade language arts and social studies are also met throughout this study.

Goals and Objectives

- To understand the treatment of African Americans after the Civil War.
- To understand why African Americans allowed themselves to be controlled by whites after the Civil War.
- To see the need for civil rights.
- To understand that the success of the civil rights movement depended on the groundwork laid by Thurgood Marshall in the courts.
- To understand the roles Martin Luther King Jr., Rosa Parks, and Malcolm X played in the civil rights movement.
- To use their understanding of the civil rights movement to understand the issues of apartheid.
- To understand the power of fear.
- To use oral, written, and visual texts to research community, national, and global issues and to explore how to make a difference.
- To use conclusions based on understanding of differing views presented in text to support a position.
- To compare the basic concepts of Christianity and Islam.

Materials Needed

- Response journals
- Art material
- Large cutout silhouettes of a human figure

Assessments and Evaluations

The student writes an essay using his or her conclusions about the role various people played in the civil rights movement.

Extensions

Students read additional books on the topic. Students watch for local speakers, exhibits, and appropriate television shows.

Resources

Arthur, Joe. *The Story of Thurgood Marshall: Justice for All.* New York: Bantam Doubleday Dell, 1995.

Davidson, Margaret. *I Have a Dream: The Story of Martin Luther King.* New York: Scholastic, 1986.

The Ernest Green Story. The Disney Educational, 1993. Videotape.

Golenbock, Peter. *Teammates.* New York: The Trumpet Club, 1990.

Milton, Joyce. *Marching to Freedom: The Story of Martin Luther King, Jr.* New York: Bantam Doubleday Dell, 1987.

Myers, Walter Dean. *Malcolm X: By Any Means Necessary.* New York: Scholastic, 1993.

———. *Now Is Your Time! The African-American Struggle for Freedom.* New York: HarperCollins, 1991.

Parks, Rosa (with Jim Haskins). *Rosa Parks: My Story.* New York: Dial Books, 1992.

Taylor, Mildred D. *The Friendship.* New York: Puffin, 1987.

———. *Mississippi Bridge.* New York: Bantam, 1990.

———. *Song of the Trees.* New York: Bantam, 1975.

———. *The Well.* New York: Puffin, 1995.

Suggested Writing Prompts

The Friendship

- Do you think Mr. John Wallace was right to shoot Mr. Tom Bee? What made it right or wrong?
- Do you wonder if incidents like this happened often in the South in the early 1900s? Why or why not?

- Could this incident happen today? Could it happen in your community? Why did you make these decisions?
- When you read the word "nigger" in *The Friendship*, what connections did you make to your life? What feelings did you have?
- How did you feel when I read the part about the shooting?

Mississippi Bridge

- Why couldn't Rudine try on "the summer sky blue hat" but Miss Hattie could?
- Why was Josias given a hassle about going on the bus?
- Tell everything you have figured out about the boy who is telling the story.
- Why did Mildred Taylor choose this character to tell the story in *Mississippi Bridge*?

Song of the Trees

- Write down everything you learned about Little Man.
- Why couldn't Mr. Anderson look Tom, Big Ma, or Papa straight in the eyes?
- Compare the Logan family to other families during the Depression. How does what they had compare with what your family has?
- What did Mr. Anderson mean when he said, "'You won't always have that black box, David,' he warned. 'You know that, don't you?'"

The Ernest Green Story *(video)*

- Elizabeth had to go to the school alone. Could you have done what she did? Why or why not?
- What did the crowd mean when they shouted at her, "Go back to Africa!"?
- Would you have helped Elizabeth as the white woman on the bus did? Why did she help?
- If you were one of the black students, what would you need to do to go back to the school on the second day?

Teammates

- What was the challenge for Jackie Robinson?
- What was the challenge for Pee Wee Reese?

- What was so amazing about having Jackie Robinson play on the Dodgers' team?

WORKS CITED

Adler, David. *A Picture Book of George Washington Carver.* Illustrated by Dan Brown. New York: Holiday House, 1999.

———. *A Picture Book of Jesse Owens.* Illustrated by Robert Casilla. New York: Holiday House, 1992.

Ancona, George. *Fiesta, U.S.A.* New York: Lodestar Books, 1995.

———. *Pablo Remembers: The Fiesta of the Day of the Dead.* New York: Lothrop, Lee, & Shepard Books, 1993.

Bandon, Alexandra. *Chinese Americans.* New York: New Discovery Books, 1994.

———. *Korean Americans.* New York: New Discovery Books, 1994.

———. *Vietnamese Americans.* New York: New Discovery Books, 1994.

Beals, Melba P. *Warriors Don't Cry: A Searing Memoir of the Battle to Integrate Little Rock's Central High.* New York: Archway, 1995.

Bolden, Tonya. *And Not Afraid to Dare.* New York: Scholastic, 1998.

Borden, Louise, and Mary Kay Kroeger. *Fly High! The Story of Bessie Coleman.* Illustrated by Teresa Flavin. New York: McElderry Books, 2001.

Bradshaw, Douglas. *Shaquille O'Neal: Man of Steel.* New York: Grosset & Dunlap, 2001.

Bredeson, Carmen. *Henry Cisneros: Building a Better America.* Berkeley Heights, N.J.: Enslow, 1995.

Bridges, Ruby. *Through My Eyes.* New York: Scholastic, 1999.

Brill, Marlene T. *The Trail of Tears: The Cherokee Journey.* Brookfield, Conn.: Millbrook Press, 1995.

Brown, Dee. *Wounded Knee.* (Adapted from *Bury My Heart at Wounded Knee.*). New York: Henry Holt, 1993.

Collier, James L. *Duke Ellington.* New York: Macmillan, 1987.

Cox, Clinton. *Come All You Brave Soldiers: Blacks in the Revolutionary War.* New York: Scholastic Press, 1999.

———. *Undying Glory: The Story of the Massachusetts 54th Regiment.* New York: Scholastic, 1991.

Dell, Pamela. *I.M. Pei: Designer of Dreams.* Chicago: Children's Press, 1993.

De Ruiz, Dana, and Richard Larios. *La Causa: The Migrant Farmworkers' Story.* Illustrated by Rudy Gutierrez. Austin, Tex.: Raintree Steck-Vaughn, 1993.

Ehrlich, Amy. *Wounded Knee: An Indian History of the American West.* New York: Holt, Rinehart and Winston, 1974.

English, Karen. *Francie.* New York: Farrar, Straus and Giroux, 1999.

Fox, Mary V. *Bette Bao Lord: Novelist and Chinese Voice for Change.* Chicago: Children's Press, 1993.

Freedman, Russell. *The Life and Death of Crazy Horse.* Illustrated by Amos Bad Heart Bull. New York: Holiday House, 1996.

Giovanni, Nikki. *Grand Fathers.* New York: Henry Holt, 1999.

Graff, Nancy P. *Where the River Runs: A Portrait of a Refugee Family.* Boston: Little, Brown, 1993.

Hargrove, Jim. *Dr. An Wang: Computer Pioneer (People of Distinction).* Chicago: Children's Press, 1993.

Haskins, James. *Against All Opposition: Black Explorers in America.* New York: Haskins, 1992.

———. *One More River to Cross: The Stories of Twelve Black Americans.* New York: Scholastic, 1992.

———. *Outward Dreams: Black Inventors and Their Inventions.* New York: Walker, 1991.

Hoobler, Dorothy, and Thomas Hoobler. *The Chinese American Family Album.* London: Oxford University Press, 1994.

Houston, Jeanne W. *Farewell to Manzanar.* Boston: Houghton Mifflin, 1973.

King, Sandra. *Shannon: An Ojibway Dancer.* New York: Lerner, 1993.

Krull, Kathleen. *The Other Side: How Kids Live in a California Latino Neighborhood.* New York: Lodestar Books, 1994.

Kudlinski, Kathleen. *Rosa Parks: Young Rebel.* Illustrated by Meryl Henderson. New York: Aladdin, 2001.

Lankford, Mary D. *Quinceanera: A Latina's Journey to Womanhood.* Brookfield, Conn.: Millbrook Press, 1994.

Lasky, Kathryn. *True North.* New York: Scholastic, 1996.

———. *Vision of Beauty: The Story of Sarah Breedlove Walker.* Illustrated by Nneka Bennett. New York: Candlewick, 2000.

Lord, Bette Bao. *In the Year of the Boar and Jackie Robinson.* New York: HarperCollins, 1984.

Lyons, Mary E. *Sorrow's Kitchen: The Life and Folklore of Zora Neale Hurston.* New York: Charles Scribner's Sons, 1990.

Mah, Adeline Y. *Chinese Cinderella.* New York: Delacorte Press, 1999.

———. *Falling Leaves: The Memoir of an Unwanted Chinese Daughter.* New York: Wiley, 1998.

Malone, Mary. *Maya Lin: Architect and Artist.* Berkeley Heights, N.J.: Enslow, 1995.

Martinez, Elizabeth Coonrod. *The Mexican-American Experience.* Brookfield, Conn.: Millbrook Press, 1995.

McKissack, Fredrick. *Black Hoops: The History of African Americans in Basketball.* New York: Scholastic, 1999.

McKissack, Patricia, and Fredrick McKissack. *Black Hands, White Sails: The Story of African American Whalers.* New York: Scholastic Press, 1999.

———. *Rebels Against Slavery: American Slave Revolts.* New York: Scholastic, 1996.

———. *Sojourner Truth: Ain't I a Woman?* New York: Scholastic, 1992.

Miller, William. *Zora Hurston and the Chinaberry Tree.* New York: Lee & Low Books, 1994.

Mohr, Nicholasa. *All for the Better: A Story of El Barrio.* Illustrated by Rudy Gutierrez. Austin, Tex.: Raintree Steck-Vaughn, 1993.

Monceaux, Morgan, and Ruth Katcher. *My Heroes, My People: African Americans and Native Americans in the West.* Illustrated by Morgan Monceaux. New York: Frances Foster Books, 1999.

Myers, Walter Dean. *The Greatest—Muhammad Ali.* New York: Scholastic, 2001.

———. *Malcolm X: By Any Means Necessary.* New York: Scholastic Trade,1993.

———. *Malcolm X: A Fire Burning Brightly.* Illustrated by Leonard Jenkins. New York: HarperCollins, 2000.

———. *Now Is Your Time!* New York: HarperCollins, 1991.

Parks, Rosa (with Jim Haskins). *Rosa Parks: My Story.* New York: Dial Books, 1992.

Pinkney, Andrea. Davis. *Duke Ellington.* Illustrated by Brian Pinkney. New York: Hyperion, 1998.

Porter, A. P. *Jump at de Sun: The Story of Zora Neale Hurston.* Minneapolis, Minn.: Carolrhoda Books, 1992.

Rappaport, Doreen. *Freedom River.* Illustrated by Bryan Collier. New York: Hyperion, 2000.

Riley, Gail B. *Wah Ming Chang: Artist and Master of Special Effects.* Berkeley Heights, N.J.: Enslow, 1995.

Roessel, Monty. *Kinaalda: A Navajo Girl Grows Up.* Minneapolis, Minn.: Lerner, 1993.

Ruffin, Francis E. *Martin Luther King, Jr. and the March on Washington.* Illustrated by Stephen Marchesi. New York: Grosset & Dunlap, 2001.

Sabin, Louis. *Roberto Clemente: Young Baseball Hero.* Illustrated by Marie DeJohn. New York: Troll Associates, 1992.

Sanford, William R. *Chief Joseph: Nez Percé Warrior.* Berkeley Heights, N.J.: Enslow, 1994.

———. *Crazy Horse: Sioux Warrior.* Berkeley Heights, N.J.: Enslow, 1994.

———. *Osceola: Seminole Warrior.* Berkeley Heights, N.J.: Enslow, 1994.

———. *Quannah Parker: Comanche Warrior.* Berkeley Heights, N.J.: Enslow, 1994.

———. *Sitting Bull: Sioux Warrior.* Berkeley Heights, N.J.: Enslow, 1994.

Santiago, Esmeralda. *Almost a Woman.* New York: Vintage Books, 1998.

———. *When I Was Puerto Rican.* New York: Vintage, 1993.

Say, Allen. *El Chino.* Boston: Houghton Mifflin, 1990.

Schmidt, Jeremy. *Two Lands, One Heart: An American Boy's Journey to His Mother's Vietnam.* Illustrated by Ted Wood. New York: Walker Books for Young Readers, 1995.

Sneve, Virginia Driving Hawk. *The Hopis.* Illustrated by Ronald Himler. New York: Holiday House, 1995.

———. *The Iroquois.* Illustrated by Ronald Himler. New York: Holiday House, 1995.

———. *The Navajos.* Illustrated by Ronald Himler. New York: Holiday House, 1993.

———. *The Nez Percé.* Illustrated by Ronald Himler. New York: Holiday House, 1994.

———. *The Sioux.* Illustrated by Ronald Himler. New York: Holiday House, 1994.

Sterling, Shirley. *My Name Is Seepeetza.* Vancouver: Groundwood Press, 1992.

Taylor, Mildred D. *The Friendship.* New York: Puffin, 1987.

———. *Mississippi Bridge.* New York: Bantam, 1990.

———. *Song of the Trees.* New York: Bantam, 1975.

———. *The Well.* New York: Puffin, 1995.

Uchida, Yoshiko. *The Invisible Thread: An Autobiography.* Englewood Cliffs, N.J.: Messner, 1991.

Wade, Mary D. *Guadalupe Quintanilla: Leader of the Hispanic Community.* Springfield, N.J.: Enslow, 1995.

Walker, Paul R. *Pride of Puerto Rico: The Life of Roberto Clemente.* San Diego: Harcourt Brace Jovanovich, 1988.

Walter, Mildred P. *Mississippi Challenge.* New York: Aladdin, 1992.

Waters, Kate, and Madeline Slovenz-Low. *Lion Dancer: Ernie Wan's Chinese New Year.* New York: Scholastic, 1990.

Weidt, Maryann N. *Voice of Freedom: A Story about Frederick Douglass.* Illustrated by Jeni Reeves. New York: Carolrhoda Books, 2001.

Wood, Ted and Wanbli Numba Afraid of Hawk. *A Boy Becomes a Man at Wounded Knee.* New York: Walker, 1992.

Yep, Laurence. *The Lost Garden.* Englewood Cliffs, N.J.: Messner, 1991.

Chapter Seven

Realistic Fiction

Elements of realistic fiction were best defined by Lloyd Alexander over two decades ago when he said, "The raw materials of story are the raw materials of all human culture. Story deals with the same questions as theology, philosophy, psychology. It is concerned with polarities: love and hate, birth and death, joy and sorrow, loss and recovery." In applying these concepts to realistic fiction generally, and to multicultural contemporary fiction specifically, we note that the problems seen as societal problems are also deemed as some of the most poignant issues found in contemporary realistic fiction. Drugs, alcoholism, sexuality, illness, death, and abuse are issues faced across all ethnic and socioeconomic cultures, and well-written stories about these issues may help us see how others face these difficult and often painful life situations. While providing answers to difficult life situations is not the purpose of realistic fiction, it does sometimes present the reader with plausible scenarios on which to reflect. Often, young readers will tell us that they have felt the same feelings of fear, frustration, sadness, or elation that the characters express in the stories they read and that they felt less alone knowing that there were others out there just like them. The importance of realistic fiction for young readers lies in the ability for young people to read about events, situations, and characters that either mirror their own experiences or open a window into another's experiences through which they can experience and learn vicariously. These opportunities become vitally important with multicultural realistic fiction since students of color need to see themselves and their experiences validated in good literature. At the same time, all students need to learn about others who have different cultural and ethnic backgrounds that frame and sometimes influence their daily experiences.

Realistic fiction, or the contemporary problem novel as it is sometimes classified, is often filled with challenges faced by young people finding their way into adulthood. How the young protagonist deals with the problem or

149

problems presented before him or her is key in determining whether the resulting outcomes or resolutions seem viable to the reader. In other words, the content and context must seem real and plausible to the reader if the problems and resolutions presented are to be believable. While this is an important element with any form of realistic fiction, it is essential when evaluating multicultural literature. Authentic details and responses become grounded if they are true to the cultural context and the people they represent.

CRITERIA FOR EVALUATING MULTICULTURAL REALISTIC FICTION

Plot structure that is believable is essential in realistic fiction. When a young person reads a novel, the conflict or problems faced by the protagonist must seem real and viable. The reader must recognize the dilemma as one that could be faced by himself or herself or by his or her peers. In multicultural literature, believability must cross cultural boundaries—if the mirror or window analogy is to ring true.

Characterization is another important element in realistic fiction. First of all, the characters we meet in realistic fiction must epitomize human beings we know. In other words, they must exhibit all the strengths and weaknesses that we find in any real person. Human beings, whether young or old, do not possess supernatural powers or superhuman strength, but they do face and undertake some incredible life challenges. Characters in contemporary realistic fiction often are faced with life-altering challenges and experiences; how they respond and resolve these challenges defines the strength of a quality piece of literature. If young people can vicariously experience those journeys with multidimensional, fully developed characters, then they are provided with the window or mirror. Shallow, undeveloped, or unbelievable characters leave readers dissatisfied and minimize the nature of the conflict in the book and its ultimate resolution. This becomes even more important when the literature reflects a particular cultural component, if we are to alleviate the potential of negative stereotypes.

Setting in realistic fiction carries the requirement of a time and place that does or could exist. Whether fully described or left generally vague in nature, the setting in multicultural realistic fiction should authentically reflect the culture and region without stereotyped influences or imagery but with supporting events and characters.

Themes in contemporary realistic fiction always reflect important issues in the lives of young people. Whether playful, poignant, or painful, any issue found in society also finds its way into contemporary realistic fiction. These issues also are found as part of multicultural realistic fiction, and the importance of telling the story without establishing or reinforcing negative stereotypes becomes paramount to the author.

Style, tone, and mood are reflected in the language used to tell the story. Dialogue should accurately reflect the cultural regions and people it represents, and attention to dialect, language differences, or foreign phrases should be woven in without becoming burdensome for the young reader.

That said, we have identified some characteristics that one should look for when evaluating contemporary multicultural realistic fiction.

- The experiences, conflicts, and ultimate resolutions must be consistent and believable with respect to the people and culture represented.
- The setting must support the events of the story and ring true to the reader by depicting authentic and realistic places.
- Primary and secondary characters must reflect and express appropriate and authentic contemporary values and beliefs, including socioeconomic differences.
- Explicit and implicit themes of the story must be contemporary in nature and not dated.
- The language used to reflect the dialogue and inner thoughts of the characters must authentically represent them. Dialect and diction should be appropriate to their cultural setting and age group.
- If illustrations are used, they should complement the text and represent the characters and setting in realistic and believable ways.
- The language, illustrations, theme, or characters should accurately portray contemporary ethnic or cultural representations without stereotypes.

SELECTIONS OF MULTICULTURAL REALISTIC FICTION

The intent of this section is to provide you with several selections of contemporary realistic fiction once again divided into particular cultural groups. By sharing the stories of cultural groups in contemporary settings, we may be able to understand better the challenges that young people continue to face today. Although it is our intent to present quality selections of realistic fiction, we do not mean to suggest that those discussed are free of criticism. We do believe, however, that this is our opportunity to share some of our favorite examples of realistic fiction and that those chosen provide accurate and sometimes new information for young readers without the stereotypes that have often misrepresented groups of people. Although expressed earlier, it is important to restate that we do not suggest that the selections provided are the only representations or even the best representations available as it is impossible to know every published text or source. We have chosen texts that we have used and discussed with our students and ones which have provided excellent discussions about societal issues for young people—discussions that have promoted an open examination of the continued forces of racism, prejudice, and ignorance. While some of these selections tell of extreme hardship and pain, others tell of the hopes and dreams of youth. These story snapshots are meant to whet your reading appetite and provide a window or mirror into the lives of some of the most exciting characters we have ever met.

African American Contemporary Fiction

To begin this section is to first acknowledge the wealth of contemporary realistic fiction available to young people and to applaud the outstanding authors who have created that richness. Authors such as Ann Cameron, Lucile Clifton, Floyd Cooper, Christopher Paul Curtis, Leo and Diane Dillon, Ossie Davis, Valerie Flournoy, Eloise Greenfield, Virginia Hamilton, Sharon Bell Mathis, Fredrick and Patricia McKissack, Angela Shelf Medearis, Walter Dean Myers, the Pinkneys: Gloria, Jerry, Brian, and Andrea Davis, Mildred Pitts Walter, and Jacqueline Woodson have wowed us with their prolific writings for young people. While their works span all genres, they and the many other authors not mentioned above have created a body of work that provides young people with cultural representations second to none—reflecting poetical and contemporary images to the youth of the culture while providing a window into the past and for all those outside the culture. In attempting to choose a few books to review for this section, we immediately recognized the daunting challenge before us and compromised by choosing just a few titles to discuss, and we have provided a lengthy bibliography of contemporary realistic fiction titles. Although there are some wonderful selections of realistic fiction that are not significantly dated in their content, publication date, or thematic qualities, such as *Baby Grand, the Moon in July, and Me* by Joyce Annette Barnes, *Circle of Gold* and *Forever Friends* by Candy Dawson Boyd, or *The Hundred Penny Box* by Sharon Bell Mathis, we chose to share some selections of realistic fiction that were written during the last decade and that address a number of key issues that some young adolescents face. Thematically, the discussions are divided between those related to family and those related to friends.

Families

Families are not all the same, and few tell family stories better than Jacqueline Woodson. In the book *From the Notebooks of Melanin Sun*, we meet thirteen-year-old Melanin Sun who has what he considers to be a great life. Living with his single mom, Melanin feels lucky because he has such a close relationship with her and can tell her anything, and even his friends think she's beautiful. However, his whole world changes one day when his mother tells him that she is in love with a white woman. Angry and frustrated, Melanin faces his greatest challenge—to adjust his own sense of values and perceptions before he loses everything that matters to him.

Another poignant story about family from Jacqueline Woodson is found in *Miracle's Boys*. Orphaned after the death of their mother, three brothers living in New York City struggle to overcome and survive the grief, poverty, and violence that threaten the very core of their existence. Hanging on to the dying promise of their mother's love, they face the emotional tragedies of their lives and eventually find strength through their love for one another. Once again, Woodson challenges her readers with a story of hardship laced with hope.

In yet another approach to the theme of family, Woodson brings us *Hush*, the incredible story of a family that is stripped of its identity and its once idyllic life when they are forced to become part of the witness protection program. Each family member struggles to hang on, but the supportive, healthy unit once known to Evie Thomas, formerly known as Toswiah Green, disintegrates before her very eyes and she is caught in a nightmare of family turmoil and depression. Once again, Woodson gives her readers a window into tragedy precariously balanced with a ray of hope.

A final tale of family from Jacqueline Woodson is found in *Locomotion*. In this story of family, we learn about Lonnie Collins Motion, nicknamed Locomotion, who is a New York City fifth grader who writes poetry as part of a class assignment. Through a series of poems, Woodson reveals the tragic fire that killed Lonnie's parents and orphaned him and his younger sister, Lili, four years earlier. Now living apart from his sister in separate foster homes, Lonnie tries to come to grips with his sadness, his loneliness, and his determination to someday put a sense of family back together with his sister. While the tragedy that orphaned Lonnie and Lili is a poignant part of the story, so, too, is finding one's place with a different family and different support, as he found with his foster mother and with his teacher.

Another author who has written about family is Walter Dean Myers. His 1989 Newbery Honor Award book *Scorpions* tells the story of Jamal—a twelve-year-old boy in Harlem who is expected to fill the shoes of his older brother who has been sent to prison. Balancing the role of student, son, and brother against the pressures of the Scorpions—his brother's gang—is hard enough, but when he comes into the possession of a gun, he is forced to make the hard choice between peer pressure and family. The meaning of family is a challenging one in the 1993 Newbery Honor book by Myers titled *Some-*

where in Darkness. In this tale, the reader meets Jimmy, another teen from Harlem. Crab, Jimmy's father, is an escaped convict who shows up and takes him off on a cross-country trip to Chicago. While father and son know very little of each other, they begin to learn some difficult and painful lessons about the meaning of family and the role of trust in relationships.

Two family stories that deal with issues of adoption and friendship are found in Myers's *Me, Mop, and the Moondance Kid* and *Mop, Moondance, and the Nagasaki Knights*. In the first story, we are introduced to TJ, his younger brother Moondance, and their friend Mop, a girl they knew from their orphanage. When TJ and Moondance are adopted, the three continue to work hard at playing baseball and at finding a home for Mop. In the sequel, *Mop, Moondance, and the Nagasaki Knights*, we follow the three as they face tough baseball tournament action from visiting teams from Japan, Mexico, and France.

Family stories also are a great way for students to sort through a sense of place and feelings of self-esteem. Candy Dawson Boyd gives us Joey Davis in *Chevrolet Saturdays*, a story about a young boy's year of adjustment to his mother's remarriage, to his stepfather's attempt to form a father-and-son bond with him, and to a teacher who is trying to move him into a special education program, despite his success in science. In Boyd's two novels, *Fall Secrets* and *A Different Beat*, we meet Jessie who is eager to enter a performing arts middle school. While she is a talented young actress, she soon begins to struggle with the rigors of academics, relationships, and self-esteem. Her concerns about the darkness of her skin color threaten to undermine her dreams of becoming an actress. In the sequel, *A Different Beat*, Jessie's self-esteem begins to improve as she strives to prove to her father and to herself that she can succeed as a student, as an actress, and as a daughter.

In the 1994 Coretta Scott King Award book *Toning the Sweep* by Angela Johnson, we meet Emmie who is visiting her grandmother who is dying of cancer. While Emmie is there to visit and care for her grandmother, the young teen is showered with stories of relatives and family history and discovers its importance in her own life.

Finally, throughout her life, Virginia Hamilton captivated us with wonderful stories of families, of mysteries, of tales and of the importance of our heritage. In *Plain City*, we meet twelve-year-old Buhlaire, a "mixed" child who struggles to discover her family history and a sense of belonging. In *Cousins*, we are invited into the dynamics of a family as they struggle with the accidental death of a cousin and the deep depression of Cammy who witnessed it. Hamilton's *Second Cousins* reunites readers with Cammy and her family a year after the death of Patty Ann. New family dynamics and tensions arise with the introduction of distant relatives and the irritating cousin, Jahnina, at the Coleman family reunion.

Whether it be finding one's place in a big family, or finding one's place in a new or different family, the dynamics of family relationships are ones that most of us understand. The challenges young people face extend outside the boundaries of families, however, and it is often the relationships they have within friendships or peer groups that provide the most daunting aspects of growing up. The following authors have found ways of telling the tales that these outside challenges present to young people

Friendship, Peer Pressure, School, and Rites of Passage

Alice Mead introduces young readers to a nine-year-old protagonist in her 1995 novel *Junebug*. Living in a rough neighborhood, Junebug is afraid of turning ten—the age at which drugs, guns, and crime seems to come into the lives of boys like him. Even his best friend ran away to avoid a confrontation with a local drug lord. Readers learn quickly of Junebug's dream of becoming a sailor and his hopes that are captured in notes he stuffs in bottles and tosses into the sea. In a story of hope, Mead lays out the challenges and the dreams of a child who wishes to get out of an inner-city setting.

Andrea Davis Pinkney gives readers a look into what it means to be an outsider in *Hold Fast to Dreams*. When Dee's father is given a promotion, he moves the family to an all-white suburban community. Dee and her sister struggle in their new school, and her younger sister tries to fit in by "acting white" and joining the lacrosse team. Dee refuses to change and continues to pursue her love of photography and eventually makes a friend. The story revolves around the struggles of moving that the entire family faces, and Pinkney addresses the challenges others might face in similar relocation situations.

Jacqueline Woodson captured the interest of young readers with her stories about Maizon and her friend Margaret. In her first book, *The Last Summer with Maizon*, we see how major changes in the lives of two young friends can threaten the bonds of friendship. In the sequel *Maizon at Blue Hill*, readers follow Maizon into a private boarding school where she is forced to deal with issues of race and class. Both books offer readers an opportunity to watch two wonderfully dynamic characters wrestle with growing up, growing apart, and discovering the importance of friendship, family, and self-determination.

In some of her other books, Woodson tackles issues related with interracial friendships. In *I Hadn't Meant to Tell You This*, Woodson tells the heartbreaking story of Marie and Lena. Marie is middle class and black; Lena is poor and white. While Marie is struggling with the absence of her mother, she discovers the secret Lena is hiding—an abusive father. Together, they find support for each other in their friendship until one day, Lena runs away from the abuse with her younger sister, Dion. The sequel *Lena* tells the rest of the story through the dynamic voice of Lena, where disguised as boys, they hitchhike from Ohio to Kentucky in search of some relative who might help them.

Other Woodson novels that deal with friendship and painful issues are *The Dear One*, *If You Come Softly*, and *Behind You*. From the story of teen pregnancy and friendship in *The Dear One* to the story of love, loss, and recovery in *If You Come Softly* and its sequel, *Behind You*, Jacqueline Woodson weaves stories of life, loss, and hope for young readers with quiet eloquence.

Walter Dean Myers continues to tackle the tough issues faced by young teenage males in his novels *SLAM!* and *Monster*. In *SLAM!* we are introduced to seventeen-year-old Greg, nicknamed Slam because of his ability to slam on the basketball court. He is one of a few blacks who attend the Latimer Arts Magnet School in the Bronx. Although he is a junior, this is his first year at Latimer and he has problems keeping his grades up, and some teammates and even his coach resent his style and attitude on the court. Along with these struggles at school, Slam also faces problems of an alcoholic father, a good friend who is dealing drugs, and his own issues related to growing up. Myers uses basketball to weave parallels on and off the court to understand the challenges Slam faces and the decisions he must make for himself if he is to realize his dreams.

In *Monster*, Myers again brings his reader into the world of teen challenges. Steve is a young man who finds himself on trial as an accomplice in a murder. The story is told in the format of a film script in which Steve describes his time in jail and the trial itself. Throughout the story, the reader struggles with Steve to understand his role in the robbery-murder and how others will ultimately rule on his guilt or innocence. Filled with Steve's inner reflection, *Monster* illustrates the stark realities of the justice system and a young man's attempt to find himself in the process.

Finally, Myers deals once again with a young man's attempt to break away from the influences of the inner city in *The Beast*. When Anthony "Spoon" Witherspoon leaves Harlem to attend a prep school for his senior year, he thinks he is making the right decision for his future and for that of Gabi—his poet girlfriend, whom he plans to marry someday. Spoon finds that he is able to deal with the racial and class issues presented to him at this new school, but he becomes concerned when his letters from Gabi become fewer and fewer. The bulk of the story, however, occurs during the holiday break, when Spoon goes home to find that things have fallen apart. His biggest fear is realized when he finds a needle in Gabi's room and learns that she has started to use "the beast." The heartbreak and frustration are relayed once again through Myers's clear style in a voice that resonates with the voices of young people.

While the above discussions highlight only a few of the contemporary realistic fiction novels available, they do provide examples of how rich the genre is for African American literature. As you will soon discover, this subset provides far more offerings than the three cultures to follow. It is our hope, however, that the next decade will provide a substantial increase to those selections we now have for our classrooms.

Asian American

Contemporary realistic fiction books with Asian American protagonists vary in cultural backgrounds as has been discussed in earlier chapters. The Chinese American experience is not the same as the Japanese American or the Cambodian American. Acknowledging those differences in cultural heritage and experiences, we have divided this section by culture rather than by theme. We hope this provides a clearer delineation for cultural explorations. It is clear, of course, that themes can be pulled across cultures, and this always remains a way for teachers to discuss a variety of cultural experiences— through themes, rather than by culture.

Chinese American

Two authors whose work has focused on the experiences of Chinese American youth are Lensey Namioka and Lawrence Yep.

Lensey Namioka has provided young readers with a delightful series that focuses on the Yang family—recent Chinese immigrants who have settled in Seattle. Full of musical talent except for Yang the Youngest (Yingtao), the children of the family struggle with the challenge of becoming acclimated to life in the United States while continuing to embrace and honor the traditions of China. In *Yang the Youngest and His Terrible Ear*, we learn that Yingtao is born into a musical family. Despite the fact that he has no musical talent, his family continues to expect that his talent will emerge. Yingtao, however, wants to play baseball. Problems arise as this cultural shift threatens the family expectations.

In *Yang the Third and Her Impossible Family*, Yang is doing everything she can to be accepted at school. She is embarrassed by her family and even changes her name to Mary in an attempt to fit in. When a classmate offers her a kitten, she sees it as a way to be accepted, despite her parents' rule against pets. She soon discovers though that keeping a kitten hidden is more difficult than one might expect.

Namioka's third tale of the Yang family is found in *Yang the Second and Her Secret Admirers*. In this adventure, Yang the Youngest decides that his older sister needs to become more enamored with her new life in the United States. In an attempt to divert her attention from her former life in China, he decides to play matchmaker and gets more than he bargained for.

The final Yang family story involves Yang the Eldest and his desire to have a new violin. His family becomes worried when he seems to become obsessed about earning money and loses interest in his music. Yang the Youngest seems to be the only one capable of reaching him.

Throughout all of the Yang family tales, Namioka is able to weave the thread of the challenges faced by those who are trying to live in two cultures in ways that are understandable to young readers.

Another story of living between cultures is found in Namioka's *Half and Half*. Readers are introduced to Fiona Cheng whose father is Chinese and mother is Scottish. While she looks more like her father, she is interested in her Scottish heritage. A lively tension arises when both sets of grandparents come to town to celebrate a folk festival.

A final book worthy of discussing is *April and the Dragon Lady* by Namioka. While this text is written for older readers, it, too, deals with generation and culture clashes such as the one between 16-year-old April and her grandmother. The "dragon lady," as April refers to her grandmother, disapproves of April's Caucasian boyfriend and seems to disapprove of everything April hopes to do with her life; she even undermines April's attempts to go away to college. April's determination to follow her own path yet honor and respect her family creates a dilemma that Namioka is able to address with eloquence.

Laurence Yep has published several popular series for young people—two series that fall under the genre of contemporary realistic fiction. In the last three books of the Golden Mountain Chronicles series, Yep tells the stories of three different protagonists who live in San Francisco's Chinatown. In *Child of the Owl*, we are introduced to Casey—a young teen whose father's gambling problem gets the best of him and lands him in the hospital. Casey goes to live with her grandmother, PawPaw, in Chinatown, and realizes that she is a child caught between cultures. With the love and help of PawPaw, Casey begins to learn about her mother, her heritage, and her true Chinese name.

In *Sea Glass*, we meet Craig, a young boy who has just moved from San Francisco's Chinatown to Conception, Calif.—a place where he feels he won't ever fit in. His father pressures him to succeed in sports, and Craig feels like a failure until his Uncle Quail shows up.

The final book in this series, *Thief of Hearts*, is the sequel to *Child of the Owl*. In this book, readers are introduced to Stacy, the daughter of Casey. Stacy lives in the suburbs of San Francisco with her parents and great-grandmother and has never really cared about the stories of her mother's life in Chinatown. When Stacy is asked to show Hong Ch'un, a recent immigrant, around school, she suddenly becomes all too aware of bigoted comments. Later, when Hong Ch'un runs away because of an accusation of stealing, Stacy, her mother, and her great-grandmother travel to Chinatown in search of Hong Ch'un, and in the process, Stacy comes to understand her heritage as a Chinese American.

Another popular series by Laurence Yep is his Chinatown murder mysteries. In *The Case of the Goblin Pearls*, *The Case of the Firecrackers*, and *The Case of the Lion Dance* (1999), readers are entertained with the Chinatown sleuths of Lily and her great-aunt Tiger Lil as they solve each murder case. Full of action and surprises, Yep uses the backdrop of Chinatown to unravel the mysteries.

Yep's *Ribbons* is a story of a family who saves every bit of money they can to bring Robin's grandmother over from China. The financial strain is felt especially by Robin who is expected to give up her dance lessons as part of the savings. Angry, Robin struggles with her feelings as they spill over on her relationship with her grandmother. Cultural and generational misunderstandings abound, and it takes a shocking event to break through the barriers of emotional pain that separate Robin and her grandmother.

Japanese American

Ken Mochizuki has given readers a poignant story about feeling invisible in *Beacon Hill Boys*. Dan Inagaki is expected to be just like his brother—a model minority citizen. While his parents expect him to get high grades and a scholarship to college, Dan and his friends feel ignored and rejected by teachers and classmates. This sense of rejection angers Dan and his friends, and they struggle against a culture identity crisis.

Another story full of racism and ignorance is Jacqueline Turner Banks's *A Day for Vincent Chin and Me*. Based on the events surrounding the 1982 murder of Vincent Chin in Detroit, Mich., Banks weaves a story set in Kentucky. She uses the true events related to the death of Chin to create a climate for the story. In 1982, Chin was mistaken for being Japanese and was killed because of the auto industry's competition from Japan. Tommy, a Japanese American teenager fears his activist mother will take up Chin's cause—a real problem since Tommy and his friends just want to fit in. As life would have it, however, Tommy and his friends do find themselves involved in a cause of their own that helps them to value their own beliefs and heritage.

Cambodian American

Linda Crew tells the story of Sundara in her 1989 novel *Children of the River.* Sundara is a teenager when she and her aunt flee from the Khmer Rouge and resettle in the United States. This story relates the family tensions that arise when Sundara tries to fit into her high school. When she begins a new romance, balancing her new life with the traditional Cambodian customs demanded by her family, the story escalates into a major threat to Sundara's attempts to begin her new American life.

Korean American

If It Hadn't Been for Yoon by Marie Lee is a story about a seventh grader who has everything—popularity, a place on the cheerleading squad, and the interest of the cutest guy. But things change when her parents want her to be friends with the new kid from Korea and to learn more about her culture. Marie Lee handles the topic of being different in ways that appeal to young readers.

Vietnamese American

Onion Tears by Diana Kidd is the story of a young Vietnamese refuge child's adjustment to her new home and life in the United States. With the help of a teacher, Nam-Huong is able to write about the horrors she left behind in Vietnam. This poignant story of war's influences on the life of a child is full of sadness and hope.

Latino/Hispanic American

In recent years, selections of literature for Latino and Hispanic American young people have increased dramatically. While a number of publishing houses have begun to feature more literature written and illustrated by people of the culture, the bulk of the new releases in recent years have come from two publishing houses: Arte Publico in Texas and Children's Book Press in California. Both of these publishing houses feature a large number of new authors in the field while some other publishing houses feature such authors as Nicholasa Mohr and Gary Soto. For the sake of discussion, we have chosen to address contemporary realistic fiction in the two primary cultures presently well represented in the Hispanic literature for children and young adults: Puerto Rican American and Mexican American. While there are some selections that reflect the cultural heritages of Central America and Cuban Americans, they number far fewer at this point. We will, however, identify some authors who are addressing those particular cultural nuances in their writing such as Alma Flor Ada who authored *My Name Is Maria Isabel.*

Puerto Rican American

By far, the most prolific writer for children of this cultural area is Nicholasa Mohr. In *Felita*, readers are introduced to Felita as an eight-year-old in New York who is forced to leave her neighborhood when her family decides to move to a new neighborhood only to return when they find that they are faced with unrelenting prejudice. When they do return to their old neighborhood, Felita realizes that the experience has changed her and that she is now aware of the pain of discrimination.

In the sequel *Going Home*, Felita is now twelve and is preparing to travel to Puerto Rico to fulfill a vow she made to her grandmother before she died. When the family does finally arrive in Puerto Rico, it is not as they expected, and they soon realize that they feel caught between cultures.

In *Nueva York*, Mohr gives her readers a collection of stories that depict life in one of New York's Puerto Rican communities. Full of humor, readers are keenly aware of the poverty and duality of cultures that exist among its young people.

Another popular Puerto Rican author and scholar is Judith Ortiz Cofer. Her 1995 book *An Island Like You: Stories of the Barrio* is a young adult collection of stories that focus on the adolescent experiences of a barrio in New Jersey.

Mexican American

One of the most popular authors of stories featuring Mexican American youth is Gary Soto. With over two dozen books to his credit, teachers are able to share Soto's picture books, novels for young readers, collections of short stories, collections of poetry, and novels for young adults. Some favorites used in our classrooms include *Too Many Tamales, Baseball in April, Taking Sides,* and *Jesse.*

In *Too Many Tamales*, we meet Maria who is helping her mother make tamales and admiring her mother's diamond ring, which had been placed on the counter. When Maria's mother leaves to answer the phone, Maria decides to try it on and places it on her thumb, and then she returns to her kneading of the masa. Hours later, when the tamales are done and her cousins have arrived for the Christmas feast, Maria suddenly realizes that her mother's ring is missing and suspects that it was lost in the tamales. In a comedy of errors, the cousins decide to help Maria out by tasting all the tamales in search of the ring. When it is not found, Maria decides it is time to confess, only to discover that her mother is wearing the ring. A story of family, this is an excellent example of realistic fiction in a picture book format for the young.

Another favorite, *Taking Sides*, tells the story of Lincoln Mendoza, a middle school boy who moves to a new neighborhood and a new school. Linc loves to play basketball and when he has to play against his best friend and his former school, things heat up. Soto clearly details the challenges that Lincoln faces when his move from the barrio takes him to the suburbs where life is not the same.

A final discussion relates to *Jesse*, a young adult novel that details the hardships of two brothers who work the fields in the summer in order to pay for college. This poignant novel relates the barriers placed against young Mexican Americans who are desperately trying to get ahead.

Well-known author Rudolfo Anaya gives young readers a lovely story of Christmas traditions and the love of a granddaughter for her grandfather who loses his life to pneumonia after saving his granddaughter's life in *The Farolitos of Christmas*. When the holidays arrive, Luz decides that she will carry on the tradition she shared with her grandfather—the lighting of the farolitos—but this time with a different twist. As Luz decides to place the farolitos on her grandfather's grave, others decide to honor their loved ones as well with farolitos of their own.

Arte Publico Press has offered a number of new releases for such authors as Diane Gonzales Bertrand with *Trino's Time* and *Close to the Heart* and Gloria Velasquez with her Roosevelt High School series, *Ankiza* and *Teen Angel*. Appealing to young people in the middle grades, these are stories of contemporary problems that many teens face.

Recent years have provided Hispanic children and young adults with literature that has moved away from the folktale and migrant workers themes into a broader scheme of issues by which all young people can understand and relate. With the momentum that has been established over the past decade, the literary offerings promise to continue to increase for Hispanic young people.

Native American

Contemporary realistic fiction selections are relatively limited. While readers can find a wealth of folktales and historical fiction about the Native American experiences, we have struggled to find a significant increase in the canon that reflects the contemporary experiences of Native American youth. That said, there are a number of well-written selections that teachers have come to rely on in their classrooms.

One popular selection in schools is *Racing the Sun* by Paul Pitts. In this story, readers meet Brandon Rogers, a twelve-year-old who knows little of his Native American heritage. When his ailing grandfather comes to stay with Brandon's family, they must all adjust to his traditions, and in the process find the meaning of family again.

Janet Campbell Hale has written contemporary realistic fiction for young adults. In *The Owl's Song*, we meet Billy White Hawk who is a desperate teenager in search of a new life. Having lost his mother, his elder, and his best friend, Billy is left with a drunk for a father. When he leaves the reservation in search of a new life, he discovers the pain of racism and more loneliness. A difficult story of loss and heartbreak, readers are brought finally to a sense of hope when Billy returns home to care for his father.

One young adult novel that provides a balance between culture and identity is Susan Power's *The Grass Dancer*. With a hint of the mystery often found in Louise Erdrich's work, *The Grass Dancer* blends the old and the new through a weaving of stories of ancestors and two young teens who are trying to find their way.

One author who writes contemporary realistic fiction for young people is Joseph Bruchac. In *Eagle Song*, readers are introduced to Danny Bigtree. His family has moved to a new city from his Mohawk reservation home, and now Danny just doesn't seem to fit in. He's homesick, and the kids in his class tease him about being an Indian. This is a story of a strong family where the father is able to demonstrate courage that helps Danny to grow into his own level of pride and confidence.

In his 2003 publication of *Warriors*, Bruchac tells the story of Jake Forrest, a young teen who leaves his Iroquois reservation home to live in Maryland with his mother. A lacrosse player, Jake struggles to fit in at his new school. The story is balanced with the challenges any teen would face with a relocation of that magnitude and with the cultural conflicts he endures as a Native American.

CONCLUSIONS

While there is a vast difference in the number of contemporary realistic fiction selections available for different cultures, there remains a significant commitment by authors and illustrators of the cultures to increase the numbers of quality offerings for young people. As we have said throughout this text, it is essential that both the window and the mirror analogies exist for readers. That has never been more important than with the genre of contemporary realistic fiction. Young people need to see themselves in contemporary settings facing contemporary issues, for without that mirror, we are missing the pictures and the stories of today's youth. It is our hope that future resource texts dealing with multicultural literature will be challenged by the abundance of literature choices rather than challenged to find adequate representations.

UNIT PLAN: STORIES REPORTED AS THEY OCCUR IN OUR OWN WORDS
By Karen Adams

Karen I. Adams is dean of the College of Education and Human Services at Central Michigan University. Her professional background includes experience as a classroom reading teacher in the elementary and middle grades, a district reading supervisor, and a university-level teacher in the disciplines of reading, composition, and children's and adolescent literature. In the K–12 realm, her responsibilities were primarily with federal programs provided for students working below grade level and coming primarily from economically disadvantaged homes in rural parts of the southern United States. In her early teaching career, she was shocked to discover that, for her primarily African American students, there were no classroom materials that portrayed them, their families, their rural locale, or their socioeconomic level.

She has been committed ever since this early experience to seeking out and providing literature for all students that portrays the variety of people living in the United States as well as the world beyond. She has traveled widely and attempted to gather information and books from other countries to assist in understanding our world. She authors a regular column of book reviews in a state reading journal and presents frequently on topics of multicultural, multiethnic, and global representation in books for children and adolescents. Her consistent goal is to ensure that teachers are made aware of the very best literature available for use, so that every child will see something of herself or himself in materials used in their classrooms each day.

Rationale

Contemporary realistic fiction can reflect not only the current realities of life facing young readers, but it can go a step further in presenting this reality through the same means of communication used everyday. These means include phone conversations, diary entries, notes passed in class, prayers, newspaper articles, and even police reports. Such varied perspectives of events can assist young readers in making decisions about what actually is reality, in defining characterization, and at times, in making important life choices. These different approaches also broaden young readers' understanding about what the story is and how it can be told.

Goals and Objectives

Students will read two examples of contemporary realistic fiction and identify the various means used to tell the story and the different perspectives or sources represented, determine what is learned from each of these source types, note any sources that seem less than accurate, and respond to the story, either retelling or extending the events through at least two of the source types used. Students will broaden their understanding of storytelling and how different approaches influence our knowledge of events and their influence on us.

Materials Needed

- Draper, Sharon. *Tears of a Tiger*. New York: Simon & Schuster, 1994.
- Myers, Walter Dean. *Monster*. New York: HarperCollins, 1999.
- Samples of local and national newspapers and magazines
- Stories about accidents or deaths and about trials of national prominence
- Video news clips about accidents or deaths and about trials

Assignment One—*Tears of a Tiger*

1. Read the first two pages aloud to the class as an introduction to the book—this amounts to the newspaper report of the automobile accident and death. Introduce the time frame of the book: November 8 to May 15. Initiate student reading of the book by discussing what was learned from the newspaper article and how. Questions may include the following:
   - How do we first learn about the central event in the story?

- How is a newspaper article different from a short story that opens with events being depicted?
- How would you tell this story from a first person perspective if you were Andrew Jackson or if you were BJ or Tyrone?

2. Students will examine and discuss in groups current newspaper accounts of accidents or deaths. Report about how details are presented and if they are presented objectively or subjectively. Try rewriting the stories from a firsthand perspective and from the perspective of a family member.
3. Students will read the book.
4. Students will list, as they read, the main means of telling this story—approximately fifteen broad categories: City newspaper, conversations, phone calls, police statement or interview, prayer, homework assignment, school newspaper, letter, psychologist visit, diary, poetry, school intercom announcement, notes passed in class, thoughts, formal police reports.
5. Students will discuss in groups of three or four specific examples of five of these storytelling approaches and evaluate the appropriateness and effectiveness of each. They can also discuss how they might have changed an approach.
6. Students will discuss what they think Sharon Draper was trying to say in *Tears of a Tiger*. They can also discuss how the different approaches to telling this story may have been important for her.
7. Individually, students will, in writing, either retell or extend the story using at least two of the storytelling approaches used by Draper. Students may choose to place themselves as a key character in the story as they do this.
8. Have students share examples of their writing in class.

Assignment Two—*Monster*

1. Read the first five pages of the book aloud to the class—this is Steve's handwritten letter. Introduce the time frame of the book: July 6 to December 5. Begin student reading of the book by discussing how Steve's note makes us feel about his situation. What will they be hoping to learn from the book on the basis of this introduction?
2. Students will read the book.
3. Students will identify the different means used to tell this story. They include court transcripts; court and jail conversations; use of film-type opening credits; use of long and medium shots and close-ups with staging direction for this Steve Harmon Production; handwritten notes by

Steve; photographs of characters and jail cells; and the design of the book cover and jacket.

4. Students will discuss in groups of four or five how each of these approaches adds to the reality of the story and how they influence the verdict determined in the trial.

5. Students will discuss the topic of Steve's guilt or innocence and what, if anything, they learn about this beyond evidence presented in court? Are there any conversations that *prove* his guilt or innocence? Discuss these conversations. Why do they think Ms. O'Brien turns away from Steve when he is found not guilty?

6. With students, watch video news clips about current major criminal trials. Discuss the cases and, in particular, attorney strategies.

7. In groups, students will read newspaper accounts of current criminal trials and discuss the facts presented, court processes, and verdicts determined.

8. Individually, students will, in writing, state whether or not they believe Steve is guilty or innocent? Then, they will extend the story to make their argument convincing.

9. Have students share examples of their writing in class.

References

Draper, Sharon. *Tears of a Tiger.* New York: Simon & Schuster, 1994.

Johnson, Angela. *The First Part Last.* New York: Simon & Schuster, 2003.

Myers, Walter Dean. *Monster.* New York: HarperCollins, 1999.

Namioka, Lensey. *April and the Dragon Lady.* New York: Harcourt Brace, 1994.

Woodson, Jacqueline. *Hush.* New York: G. P. Putnam's Sons, 2002.

Woodson, Jacqueline. *I Hadn't Meant to Tell You This.* New York: Bantam Doubleday Dell, 1994.

Woodson, Jacqueline. *Lena.* New York: Random House, 1999.

WORKS CITED

Ada, Alma Flor. *My Name Is María Isabel.* New York: Simon & Schuster, 1993.

Anaya, Rudolfo. *The Farolitos of Christmas.* Illustrated by Edward Gonzales. New York: Hyperion Books for Children, 1995.

Banks, Jacqueline Turner. *A Day for Vincent Chin and Me.* Boston: Houghton Mifflin, 2001.

Barnes, Joyce Annette. *Baby Grand, the Moon in July, and Me.* New York: Dial, 1994.

Bertrand, Diane Gonzales. *Close to the Heart.* Houston, Tex.: Pinata Books, 2002.

———. *Trino's Time.* Houston, Tex.: Pinata Books, 2001.

Boyd, Candy Dawson. *Breadsticks, and Blessing Places.* New York: Macmillan, 1985.

————. *Charlie Pippin.* New York: Macmillan, 1987.

————. *Chevrolet Saturdays.* New York: Macmillan, 1993.

————. *Circle of Gold.* New York: Scholastic, 1984.

————. *A Different Beat.* New York: Puffin, 1996.

————. *Fall Secrets.* New York: Puffin, 1994.

————. *Forever Friends.* New York: Penguin, 1986.

Bruchac, Joseph. *Eagle Song.* New York: Puffin, 1999.

————. *Warriors.* Darby Publishing, 2003.

Castañeda, Omar S. *Among the Volcanoes.* New York: Dell Publishing, 1991.

Cofer, Judith Ortiz. *An Island Like You: Stories of the Barrio.* New York: Orchard Books, 1995.

Crew, Linda. *Children of the River.* New York: Delacorte, 1989.

Draper, Sharon. *Tears of a Tiger.* New York: Simon & Schuster, 1994.

Grimes, Nikki. *Bronx Masquerade.* New York: Penguin Group, 2002.

Hale, Janet Campbell. *The Owl's Song.* New York: Bantam, 1991.

Hamilton, Virginia. *Cousins.* New York: Putnam, 1990.

————. *M. C. Higgins the Great.* New York: Macmillan, 1974.

————. *Plain City.* New York: Scholastic, 1993.

————. *Second Cousins.* New York: Scholastic, 1998.

————. *Sweet Whispers, Brother Rush.* New York: Philomel Books, 1982.

Johnson, Angela. *The First Part Last.* New York: Simon & Schuster, 2003.

————. *Toning the Sweep.* New York: Orchard Books, 1995.

Kidd, Diana. *Onion Tears.* Illustrated by Lucy Montgomery. New York: Orchard Books, 1991.

Lee, Marie G. *If It Hadn't Been for Yoon.* New York: Avon Books, 1993.

Mathis, Sharon Bell. *The Hundred Penny Box.* New York: Viking, 1975.

Mead, Alice. *Junebug.* New York: Bantam, 1995.

Mochizuki, Ken. *Beacon Hill Boys.* New York: Scholastic, 2002.

Mohr, Nicholasa. *Felita.* New York: Dial, 1976.

————. *Going Home.* New York: Dial, 1986.

————. *In Nueva York.* Houston, Tex.: Arte Publico Press, 1988.

Myers, Walter Dean. *The Beast.* New York: Scholastic, 2003.

————. *Crystal.* New York: Viking, 1987.

————. *Fast Sam, Cool Clyde, and Stuff.* New York: Viking, 1975.

————. *Hoops.* New York: Delacorte, 1981.

————. *Me, Mop, and the Moondance Kid.* New York: Delacorte, 1988.

————. *Monster.* New York: HarperCollins, 1999.

————. *Mop, Moondance, and the Nagasaki Knights.* New York: Delacorte, 1992.

————. *The Mouse Rap.* New York: Harper & Row, 1990.

————. *The Outside Shot.* New York: Delacorte, 1984.

————. *Scorpions.* New York: Harper & Row, 1988.

————. *SLAM!* New York: Scholastic, 1996.

————. *Somewhere in Darkness.* New York: Scholastic, 1992.

————. *Won't Know Until I Get There.* New York: Viking, 1982.

Namioka, Lensey. *April and the Dragon Lady.* San Diego: Browndeer Press, 1994.

————. *Half and Half.* New York: Delacorte, 2003.

————. *Ties That Bind, Ties That Break.* New York: Delacorte Press, 1999.

————. *Yang the Eldest and His Odd Jobs.* New York: Yearling, 2002.

————. *Yang the Second and Her Secret Admirers.* New York: Little, Brown, 1998.

————. *Yang the Third and Her Impossible Family.* New York: Little, Brown, 1995.

————. *Yang the Youngest and His Terrible Ear.* New York: Little, Brown, 1992.

Pinkney, Andrea Davis. *Hold Fast to Dreams.* New York: William & Morrow, 1995.

Pitts, Paul. *Racing the Sun.* New York: Avon, 1988.

Power, Susan. *The Grass Dancer.* New York: Berkley Books, 1997.

Soto, Gary. *Baseball in April.* New York: Harcourt Brace, 1990.

————. *Jesse.* New York: Harcourt Brace, 1994.

————. *Taking Sides.* New York: Harcourt Brace, 1991.

————. *Too Many Tamales.* Illustrated by Ed Martinez. New York: Putnam, 1993.

Talbert, Marc. *A Sunburned Prayer.* New York: Simon & Schuster, 1995.

Velasquez, Gloria. *Ankiza.* Houston, Tex.: Pinata Books, 2000.

————. *Teen Angel.* Houston, Tex.: Pinata Books, 2003.

Woodson, Jacqueline. *Behind You.* New York: G. P. Putnam's Sons, 2004.

————. *Between Madison and Palmetto.* New York: Penguin, 1993.

————. *The Dear One.* New York: Delacorte Press, 1991.

————. *From the Notebooks of Melanin Sun.* New York: Scholastic, 1995.

————. *The House You Pass on the Way.* New York: Bantam, 1997.

————. *Hush.* New York: Penguin, 2003.

————. *If You Come Softly.* New York: Puffin, 2000.

————. *I Hadn't Meant to Tell You This.* New York: Delacorte Press, 1994.

————. *The Last Summer with Maizon.* New York: Delacorte Press, 1990.

————. *Lena.* New York: Delacorte Press, 1999.

————. *Locomotion.* New York: Putnam, 2003.

————. *Maizon at Blue Hill.* New York: Delacorte Press, 1992.

————. *Miracle's Boys.* New York: Putnam, 2000.

————. *The Other Side.* New York: Putnam, 2001.

Yep, Laurence. *The Case of the Firecrackers.* New York: HarperCollins, 1999.

————. *The Case of the Goblin Pearls.* New York: HarperTrophy, 1998.

————. *The Case of the Lion Dance.* New York: HarperTrophy, 1999.

————. *Child of the Owl.* New York: HarperTrophy, 1977.

————. *Ribbons.* New York: Putnam, 1996.

————. *Sea Glass.* New York: HarperCollins, 1979.

————. *Thief of Hearts.* New York: HarperCollins, 1995.

Chapter Eight

A Journey

A journey is more than a visit or a vacation.
It is more than a time to play, to temporarily leave your
work for another time, another day.

A journey is more than a trip to the home of a nearby relative or friend.
It is more than staying at a hotel, motel, Holiday Inn,
and eating out at the local restaurants.

A journey is more than stopping by for a quick "How do you do?"
It is more than loading up the car and packing a lunch
of fried chicken and bologna sandwiches.

A journey is an adventure to places and sights unknown.
It can be mystical and perhaps mysterious, as you uncover new friends and lost treasures.

Journeys are life-long experiences that have no beginnings or endings.
It is filled with days of joys and wonderment, as well as nights of excitement and dreams.

A journey is a blessing from God.
It is being able to experience life so full of memories—the good, the bad,
or the ugly—and to treasure those memories close to your heart.

A journey is where you are headed.
And although some things may appear a little fuzzy right now,
it will all become clear with each passing day.

Enjoy your journey and cherish your time.
We wish you well as you proceed through this new path of your life.

—Dianne L. H. Mark, 2004

As the stories in the books that we include takes readers on a cultural journey, this poem, *The Journey*, captures the essence of thinking creatively, broadly, and challenges readers and teachers with an opportunity to open up their minds and move beyond the traditional ways of viewing things. The poem, also provides an introduction to this chapter on multicultural poetry.

As in previous chapters, this chapter will highlight literature and poetry written and illustrated by people of color, specifically African Americans, Asian Americans, Hispanic Americans, and Native Americans. Our investigation discovered a disproportionate number of poems written by or about African Americans. And while the number of Hispanic, Asian American, and Native American writers and illustrators has increased over the past two decades, few of them have published children's poetry.

The format for this chapter will consist of four sections. In the first section, we describe the criteria for selecting multicultural poetry. In section two, we discuss the types of poems, giving significant attention to collections and anthologies, while in section three, we highlight individual poets and some of their work. We end this chapter with an example of a unit plan from a teacher in the Denver School District and an infusion of poetry and song from her middle school classroom.

CRITERIA FOR SELECTING MULTICULTURAL POETRY

In evaluating poetry, the richness of language is often defined through the elements of rhythm, imagery, and linguistic patterns that provide colorful word choices that engage young people. In an attempt to apply those same concepts, we suggest the following set of criteria to be used for selecting and evaluating multicultural poetry.

- The sense of rhythm used in poetry for young people should be lively and should contain a clear beat or stylistic movement that is associated and consistent with cultural nuisances.
- The language used in poetry for young people should be linguistically colorful and figurative and should be authentic to the culture and its traditions and backgrounds.
- Imagery is the use of language that is colorful and figurative; it allows children to expand their imaginations and to see the beauty of dialect, language differences, and cultural habitats.
- Language patterns whenever possible, should include words and phrases that create repetition or combinations of words that are found in various cultural environments and are authentic linguistically.

Poetry for very young children should be playful, while poetry for older students should present life events appropriate to their age level. Whatever the level, poetry should provide opportunities to evoke feelings. Award-winning poet and critic Lee Bennett Hopkins suggests that "Life itself is embodied in poetry and each poem reveals a bit of life. . . . Poetry for children should appeal to them and meet their emotional needs and interests" (1987, 9). Whether we embrace that statement or not, it is imperative that we set high standards for the poetry we use in our classrooms for young people, providing good models that present cultures and people fairly and accurately.

ELEMENTS OF POETRY

There are many resource books that provide detailed descriptions of the various types of poetry. While we will discuss a few here, these are not meant to be exclusive. June Hu defines poetry as "a spirit with wings" and as "the inspiration of the spirit / the flames of life, / the sudden flash of the brilliance of humanity" (1994, 9). Poems generally fall into several categories, which can include such stylistic forms as lyrics, narratives, ballads, limericks, concrete, free verse, and haiku. While not all of these forms are found across all cultures, variations of these forms are. A quick review of these forms is described below:

Lyric poetry consists of poems that are usually brief descriptive pieces that emphasize sound and imagery rather than narrative or dramatic movement. Jose Villa envisioned this type of poetry as magical, musical, and flying like a bird in the sky. Many of these poems are songlike and expressive of a single mood. Lyric poems are meant to be read repeatedly. An example can be seen in the poem by Nikki Grimes "Jump Rope Rhyme." This four-line poem is sung repeatedly while jumping a rope, substituting names as a new jumper comes in.

A *narrative poem* tells the reader a story—usually a brief story with a sense of rapid action and generally relayed in chronological order. Some narrative forms also can be found in a collection of short poems that as individual pieces detail a single event but when placed in a collection with other thematic pieces provide a full narrative. One such example is found in the collection *In for Winter, Out for Spring*, written by Arnold Adoff and illustrated by Jerry Pinkney. This collection of short poems provides details in the life of a young girl and her family over a year's span. Although each poem focuses on particular events that occur each month of the year, together they tell a story. The illustrations are done in pencil, watercolor, color pencil, and pastels and present lifelike images that complement the accompanying verse.

Ballad poems are a form of narrative folk songs that are usually read instead of sung. Some type of action is the focus of many ballads, and often there is a particular cultural dialect present in the telling of the story and repeated refrains. Resource books often agree that there are generally two types of ballads: folk and literary. Folk ballads have no identified author and have been passed down from generation to generation. Literary ballads, on the other hand, are authored pieces that have kept the songlike nature found in verse.

Limericks are short and witty poems. They appeal to children because they make fun of things and often make us laugh. In a basic five-line structure of a limerick poem, lines one, two, and five rhyme and lines two and three often rhyme providing readers with a slapstick sense of silliness.

Concrete poems are fun to read and write (see figure 8.1). They are poems with design and shape as essential elements—word constructions form a picture. The actual physical form of the words often describes the subject, illustrating itself as the shapes of words and lines take form.

Free verse poems do not rhyme, nor is there any particular shape or pattern evident. The arrangement on the page, the essence of the subject, and the density of thought distinguish free verse from prose. Impressed by anthologies, which were "nothing like the rhyme-and-meter poetry," Gary Soto writes *A Fire in My Hands*. Each of his twenty-three free verse poems depicts things that were common in his life while growing up.

Haiku is a form of ancient poetry. It usually consists of three lines with five syllables in the first line, seven syllables in the second, and five syllables in the last line. Haiku poems generally relate to something in nature—sun, wind, trees, or seasons. While traditional haiku may not be highly favored by students, many teachers engage their students in the writing of haiku in age-appropriate ways.

Figure 8.1.   Example of a concrete poem.

                                                            at a time.

                                                    one step

                                            requires

                                    our journey

                            knowing that

                    closer to

            brings us

    Each day

Similar to a haiku, *cinquain* poetry consists of five unrhymed lines with the first and last lines having two syllables and lines two, three, and four having six and eight syllables, respectively. Teachers often use cinquain poetry as a means to introduce their students to the writing process of poetry.

Poems can also be parts of a book that may be called *collections* or *anthologies*. Collections are poems that are related by a theme or authorship. Author and poet Demi provides the reader with many haiku-type poems in the collection *In the Eyes of the Cat: Japanese Poetry*. Richard Lewis provides a collection of Chinese and Japanese poetry written by Asian poets. These haiku poems are centered on nature and its aesthetics and on the human experience, which if it were to be analyzed would be analogous to the seasons. However, they still are descriptions of the struggles of Chinese and Japanese Americans.

In *Families: Poems Celebrating the African American Experience*, compiled by Dorothy Strickland and Michael Strickland, John Ward beautifully illustrates the twenty-four-poem collection. Contributors include a host of well-known African American poets and poets who write about African Americans. They include Arnold Adoff ("Big Sister Tells Me That I'm Black"); Nikki Giovanni ("Covers," "The Drum," and "Pretty"); and Eloise Greenfield ("Missing Mama"). Other poets include Gwendolyn Brooks, Langston Hughes, and Lucille Clifton. The book concludes with the song, "Hush, Little Baby" (Anonymous).

Other popular books that contain collections include Michio Mado's *The Animals: Selected Poems*, Virginia Driving Hawk Sneve's *Dancing Teepees: Poems of American Indian Youth*, John Bierhorst's *In the Trail of the Wind: American Indian Poems and Ritual Orations*, and Ashley Bryan's *Sing to the Sun*. Bryan's collection provides the reader with a representation of poems about the Hispanic culture and the ups and downs of life. This book of poetry was written and illustrated by Bryan and is the winner of the 1993 Lee Bennett Hopkins Poetry Award.

Similarly to collections, anthologies are grouped by ideas, themes, or poets. A good example of an anthology grouped by a theme would be the work by Nancy Wood in her book *War Cry on a Prayer Feather*. In this book, Wood provides historical events of the Ute tribe as well as poems that highlight their culture and traditions. Many of her poems focus on generations and the significance of the family. The book provides the reader with many photographs of warriors, lifestyles, children, and adults. Naomi Nye's *This Same Sky: A Collection of Poems from around the World* provides readers with a series of poems that reflect various ethnic groups. Other anthologies include *American Indian Poetry*, edited by George Cronyn, and *Unsettling America: An Anthology of Contemporary Multicultural Poetry*, edited by Maria Gillian and Jennifer Gillian.

SELECTIONS OF MULTICULTURAL POETRY

African American

The pioneers of literature about and by African Americans began early in the United States. Some stemmed from the days of slavery, while others were brought over from Africa, and others yet focused on the current lifestyles of the culture. Because of space consideration, not all of the key African American authors and illustrators of children's poetry can be discussed; however, we are not suggesting that any of them should be overlooked when developing a curriculum for one's classroom. Authors and poets such as Langston Hughes, Gwendolyn Brooks, Dudley Randall, Paul Lawrence Dunbar, and Maya Angelou are recognized for their contributions to literature and the culture; however, much of their work is used within high school and college settings and deemed appropriate for older students.

An author and poet who spent her life creating for children is Nikki Grimes. Award winner for many of her books for younger children, Grimes states that many of her poems were inspired by her childhood as seen in *From a Child's Heart*. The children about whom she writes are dealing with everyday issues that children face—hopes, fears, longings, and God. Brenda Joysmith provides breathtaking pictures for illustration. They are detailed pastels and portray the essence of each poem. The poem that lends its title to the book talks about a child enjoying her time with her friend and wishing that her mom would take her time coming to pick her up. She writes, "I love being with my friend / not having to speak / rubbing a blade of grass to make it squeak / and laying in the sun." The illustration complements the text by showing two girls lying in the grass holding a blade of grass.

With words by Nikki Grimes, Tom Feelings portrays a very warm and elegant book in *Something on My Mind*. The art is reproduced in black and warm yellows. This book has received the Coretta Scott King Award for illustrations, the Saturday Review Children's Books Best of the Season, and the Philadelphia Inquirer Best Book of the Year, and it is distinguished as an ALA Notable Children's Book. Grimes's poems depict the lives of children and young adults and the many struggles, joys, hopes, and fears that they experience in life. In this selection of poems, she writes about waiting— waiting to grow up, waiting for summer to end, waiting for school to begin, waiting for someone to play with, waiting for lunchtime, and waiting for Daddy.

Grimes's *A Pocketful of Poems*, with illustrations by Javaka Steptoe, is a book of poems and haiku verses that provide glimpses of life in a city. Steptoe's inventive collage illustrations are crafted from a wide range of materials, from ribbons and seashells to drinking straws and tin pans. This book provides the readers with many haiku verses. Also describing a young child's life in a city, *My Man Blue* by Grimes introduces a boy living with his working mother and establishing a relationship with Blue, an acquaintance of his mother. This very enriching and inspiring book is illustrated by Jerome Lagarrigue. The poems depict Blue as a positive role model for youngsters. It ends with the poem "Like Blue," where the young boy is talking about why he wants to be like Blue. He says he wants to be like the "other Blue . . . The one that says he cares and shows it."

With illustrations by Angelo, *Stepping Out with Grandma Mac*, also by Grimes, provides us with poems that look at a relationship between a feisty grandmother and her equally spunky granddaughter. It will make you smile and sometimes laugh out loud. In "Keeping Secrets," Tisha, the granddaughter is shocked to find out that her grandmother has a boyfriend. She talks about how she "gave the guy the once-over" when her grandmother was not looking. In "Fences," Tisha comes to the realization that her grandmother does care for her, even it she doesn't show it in the most obvious ways. She says, "So I figure Grandma's chilly words aren't brick walls. . . . They are more like picket fences . . . for me to squeeze through" (2001, 21).

In Grimes's *Come Sunday*, a young girl describes her Sunday from the time that she wakes up, through worship service at her church, to Sunday dinner. Beautifully illustrated by Michael Bryant, who uses bright paints and detailed etchings for his pictures, this is a very spiritual, fun, and motivating set of poems for readers of all ages. Another fun book by Grimes, is *Wild, Wild Hair*. In this rhyming story, an African American girl goes through the challenges of getting her hair combed. She hides from everybody in the house, until her mother finds her. George Ford, whose many drawings were inspired by his grandmother, is credited for his exceptional job of illustrating the evolution of Tisa's ordeal. In the end, her hair is braided and styled very much to her delight as she "eyed herself. She couldn't turn away." Other books of poems by Grimes include *Shoe Magic, Meet Danitra Brown, Hopscotch Love: A Family Treasury of Love Poems*, and *Is It Far to Zanzibar? Poems about Tanzania.*

Arnold Adoff has written several anthologies on poems by African American poets. *I Am the Darker Brother* grew from years of collecting black American poetry for use in his classrooms. He taught in Harlem in the 1950s and 1960s. This anthology was created to present good, interesting, and evocative poems by African Americans. Another anthology, *Black Out Loud: An Anthology of Modern Poems of Black Americans*, was Adoff's attempt to reach African American children who did not have the opportunity to discover the world of their heritage. Similarly, in *The Poetry of Black America: Anthology of the 20th Century*, Adoff shows the diversity and the depth of black American poetry up to its "second renaissance" of today's fine young poets. Again, the author wanted to make black children strong in their knowledge of themselves and their great heritage. He also wanted to give knowledge to white children so that mutual respect and understanding will come from mutual learning. The first anthology of black poetry compiled especially for young readers, *Golden Slippers* by Arna Bontemps, was published in 1941. With drawings by Henrietta Bruce Sharon, this book highlights well-known authors such as James Weldon Johnson, Claude McKay, Countee Cullen, Langston Hughes, and Fenton Johnson. It includes the Black National Athem, "Lift Every Voice and Sing," and the lyrics to a traditional song, "Swing Low, Sweet Chariot." Many of the drawings depict African Americans in stereotypical caricature.

All the Colors of the Race and *Black Is Brown Is Tan* are poetry books that focus on biracial families. *All the Colors*, with illustrations by John Steptoe, is a collection of poems from the point of view of a biracial child whose mother is black and whose father is white. Steptoe, a highly recognized illustrator states, "In my picture books I put all the things I never saw when I was a child" (H. Smith 1994, 105). Similarly, *Black Is Brown*, illustrated by Emily McCully, portrays the life of two children with a black mother and a white father. It plays on words such as *white*, when the father says for example, "I am white, the milk is white. . . . I am not the color of the milk." The book also introduces the concept of extended family members.

Another book by Adoff and illustrated by Steptoe describes how it feels to be young and growing up. *Outside Inside Poems* shares the excitements and disappointments experienced by children. The poems reflect a child's thoughts, inside and outside, describing what he feels and sees. For example, on the outside, he sees "the ketchup and relish are dripping on my shirt . . ." But on the inside he feels, "neatness is all, but if [you] drip don't slip on the ball." Turning his attention to siblings again, Adoff writes a book that consists of poems about a brother and sister and their day at the beach. In *Today We Are Brother and Sister*, the siblings sometimes argue, but usually they are compatible as they play in the water and on the beach. The illustrations were done by Glo Coalson who draws very bright, colorful pictures.

An ALA Notable Children's Book, *Honey, I Love and Love Poems*, is sixteen poems written by Eloise Greenfield, with pictures by Jan Spivey Gilchrist. Gilchrist states, "I wish always to portray a positive and sensitive image for all children, especially African American children" (Smith 1994, 86). Both younger and older students will enjoy these poems and the drawings. The book begins with a poem that talks about all the things that are loved—a cousin, the water hose, the sound of laughter, a family ride, and a mother's kiss. Some of her poems relate to places, both near and far, such as the store around the corner, the beach, and farms. Other poems talk about people such as Aunt Roberta, Reggie, Lessie, Moochie, and Harriet Tubman.

Greenfield is a well-known poet and author of many highly acclaimed books. Several of her other books are also illustrated by Gilchrist. In *For the Love of the Game: Michael Jordan and Me*, she writes about a girl and a boy and their views of the world, both good and bad. They discover the importance of the human spirit and recognize their similarities to Michael Jordan. The illustrations are angelic and spiritual in nature with warm, soft colors. The poetic story ends with a picture of Jordan in a defensive stance. The girl and boy are holding hands and the words follow, "I take my stance, I make my move / For the love of the game of my life, I live."

Another poetry book by Greenfield that is illustrated by Gilchrist is *Nathaniel Talking*, which is about the life of a young boy. It begins with a rap, and throughout the book are poems about family, schooling, and friends. It received the Coretta Scott King Award for Illustrations. The black and white pencil illustrations capture all the intensity of young Nathaniel, especially for the poems "Watching the World Go By" and "My Daddy" in which you see the intensity in his eyes and his face. In *Under the Sunday Tree*, Greenfield provides readers with a collection of poems and paintings that epitomize life in the Bahamas. The illustrator, Amos Ferguson, is a native of the Bahamas. Poems highlight themes on Bahamian traditions, culture, and the family. *Under the Sunday Tree* has received the ALA Notable Children's Book Award and the Coretta Scott King Honor Book for Illustrations.

Greenfield's *Night on Neighborhood Street* is colorfully illustrated in dynamic blends giving a realistic portrayal of African American children. The poems reflect family life in an urban community. Topics include newborns, sleepovers, "fambly" times, and community events. One of the poems, "Karen," is about a sister who has to put her younger sister to bed each night because her mom is at work. The younger sister lies in bed and "waits for her sister to tender a mama's kiss." This is a fun book to read that provides real life experiences in poetry. This book received the National Council of Teachers of English Notable Trade Book Award and the Coretta Scott King Honor Book for both Author and Illustrator Award. Other poems by Greenfield can be found in *Daydreamers* and *Africa Dream*.

Ashley Bryan is the author and illustrator of *Sing to the Sun*, which is a collection of poems and paintings celebrating the ups and downs of life. Bryan is a graduate of Columbia University with a degree in philosophy and is the winner of the 1993 Lee Bennett Hopkins Poetry Award. The colorful mosaic drawings complement the simple language and rhythmic verses.

Ashley Bryan's ABC of African American Poetry was also written and illustrated by Bryan. He uses the alphabet to introduce young children to poetry by letting the letters represent the first name of African American poets or beginning words of a poem. The sketches are of images and finished printings. The poets who are recognized in the book are Robert Hayden, Henry Dumas, Anne Spencer, and Raymond Patterson.

A favorite poet among adults and children alike is Nikki Giovanni who was born in Knoxville, Tenn., June 7, 1943. Giovanni went to an Episcopal school and was a voracious reader of literature from T. S. Eliot to Richard Wright. Her poetry was greatly inspired by the assassination of Malcolm X and the rise of the Black Panthers. She has received a number of awards for her contributions to the field of literature. They include Omega Psi Phi Fraternity Award; an honorary doctorate of literature; an NAACP image award; a Langston Hughes Award for Distinguished Contributions to the Arts and Letters; and being named Woman of the Year by *Essence, Mademoiselle*, and *Ladies Home Journal* magazines.

Giovanni's *Ego-Tripping* captures the essence of the African American experience in ways that have special relevance and appeal for young children. In these thirty-two poems, "young people are taught how to live, to know, and to remember who they are . . . young people [are] made to feel what life is. They weep. . . . They laugh. . . . They are reborn," as written by Virginia Hamilton in her foreword (Giovanni 1993, xi). They learn to love, appreciate, and understand poetry. In "Kidnap Poem," also in *Ego-Tripping*, Giovanni writes about being able to make you understand what poetry is all about. She writes, "i'd kidnap you / put you in my phrases and meter / you to jones beach / . . . lyric you in lilacs / . . . ode you with my love song . . ." (1993, 43). The illustrations are done by George Ford, who received the first Coretta Scott King Award. Other books by Giovanni include *Spin a Soft Black Song: Poems for Children, Knoxville, Tennessee*, and *Vacation Time: Poems for Children*.

Walter Dean Myers has written many highly acclaimed books for children and young adults. Many of his books have been ALA Notable Children's Books and ALA Best Books for Young Adults. In 1991, Myers won a Coretta Scott King Award for his book *Now Is Your Time!* and in 1985, for *Motown and Didi*. In 1994, he was honored with a Margaret Edwards Award for major contributions to the field of literature for young adults. He has also received two Newbery honors. *Brown Angels* is composed of verses and pictures. The pictures are of African American children living around the turn of the twentieth century. The pictures are so wonderful, they just make you feel warm inside. They also provide somewhat of a historical view of African Americans in the United States. The poems and verses are short and rhythmic, such as "Pretty Little Black Girl" and "Jolly, Jolly."

Harlem has illustrations by Christopher Myers, the son of Walter Dean

Myers who authored this picture book of poetry. Father and son boldly assemble collage art and verse that resonate with an attitude that tells us about Harlem. From African ancestors, such as Marcus Garvey and Malcolm X, to the subway trains, readers are captivated by this collection.

Asian American

Minfong Ho grew up on the outskirts of Bangkok, Thailand. Her parents were from China and recited poetry to her nightly at bedtime. As part of the Chinese culture, not only did children learn to read by reading poetry, but adults had to compose poetry as part of the civil service examination. Some of the poems read by her parents can be found in *Maples in the Mist: Children's Poems from the Tang Dynasty*. This book, translated by Ho and illustrated by Jean and Mou-sien Tseng, contains sixteen ancient and timeless poems from the Tang Dynasty, or the Golden Age of China (618–907 AD). They were translated as an effort to bridge the linguistic gap between Ho's mother and her children. They celebrate the precious words of life, from white egrets (birds) to spring blossoms to harvest moons. This book has received recognition from the International Reading Association Notable Book for a Global Society and is an ALA Notable Book.

Another poetry book by Ho is *Hush! A Thai Lullaby*. Rhythmic verses and comical illustrations tell the story of a mother's efforts to quiet various animals so that her baby can sleep. She quiets the monkey, the duck, and the frog only to get it so quiet that she falls asleep instead of the baby. Illustrated by Holly Meade, the work for this book is cut paper and ink. This book is recognized as a Caldecott Honor Book, an ALA Notable Book, and a Horn Book Fanfare.

Janet S. Wong grew up in Los Angeles, Calif. As child of a Chinese immigrant father and a Korean immigrant mother, Janet was often subjected to many forms of prejudice. After graduating from law school and practicing law for a number of years, she decided to devote her time to writing on a full-time basis. Her book *Good Luck Gold* is a collection of poems that children from all cultural arenas will appreciate. Five years after that publication, Wong published *The Rainbow Hand*. This is a collection of eighteen original poems about mothers and motherhood. With illustrations by Jennifer Hewitson, this book was written as a testimony to her mother, and she hopes "to walk in her shadow, bright with hope." The poem "The Rainbow Hand" describes how meticulous mothers are by protecting their children and keeping them safe. "And when lightning flashes bright, too bright, see how she slips her hand over his eyes, her fingers curved / like a rainbow" (1999, 9).

Finally, in her book *Night Garden*, Wong provides the readers with fifteen poems that describe a variety of dreams. Some of these dreams were familiar, such as "Old Friend." Others were strange and disturbing, such as "Turnip Cake"; and still others were beautiful, such as "Gently down the Stream." Illustrations are by Julie Paschkis and the book is suitable to primary and intermediate grades.

Currently a freelance artist, graphic illustrator, and author, Jeanne M. Lee spent her childhood in Vietnam. As a child, she read most of the time and offers this advice, "Read as much as you can afford the time; live, taste the world, then write about it" (Day 1999, 137). As an artist, she has illustrated many books for children, including *The Butterfly Boy* that was written by Laurence Yep. In her book *The Song of Mu Lan*, Lee beautifully portrays the story of a daughter who rides off to war in her father's place.

A native of China and author of *Sojourner*, Jane Hwa Hu writes eighty-four poems that span over several years and many places. It appears that several of these poems were written while traveling. For example, "The Tea House" was written in Ginza, Tokyo; "January Snow" was written in Potomac, Md.; and "City in the Night" was written on a Northwest flight in December 1987.

The Animals: Selected Poems is Michio Mado's first collections of verse to be published in the United States. Originally from Japan, Mado began writing poetry as a teenager. In 1968, he received the prestigious Noma Award for Children's Literature. He has been described as possibly the foremost contemporary Japanese poet writing children's poetry. In *The Animals*, Mado has twenty of his poems about animals translated into English. The animals in the book include the peacock, giraffe, dove, and sea cucumber, and the book is written in both Japanese and English and illustrated in cut-paper decorations by Mitsumasa Anno. Translations were done by the Empress Michiko of Japan.

Latino and Hispanic American

As a child growing up in the San Joaquin Valley of California, Gary Soto experienced many of the disadvantages associated with being poor and being Hispanic. Many of his poems were inspired by his relatives who toiled in the fields. He is considered the best Latino/Chicano poet of his generation, and in 1975, he won the Academy of American Poets Prize and the Nation Award. Much of his poetry is so narrative that it reads like fiction.

In 1990, Soto wrote *A Fire in my Hands*. This collection of twenty-three poems is preceded by an anecdote and ends with a list of questions and answers at the back of the book. Soto first became interested in poetry when he read an anthology in college and changed his major from geography to poetry. In his poems, he tries to write about common-day items such as pets, alleys, his baseball mitt, and the fruit of the valley where he grew up. In 1992, he wrote another book of poems titled *Neighborhood Odes*. These twenty-one poems, many with Spanish titles, are part of a collection of poems, again about common-day experiences. They include poems about soap operas, eating snow cones, playing in the sprinkler, and spending a day in the country. With illustrations by David Diaz, Soto includes a list of English-Spanish translations at the end of the book.

Canto Familiar, written by Soto and illustrated by Annika Nelson, was published in 1995. Again, Soto focuses on the Mexican American children and the world around them as they grow up. With Spanish words sprinkled throughout, these twenty-five poems remind us of many things familiar to all children, no matter what their cultural background.

Cool Salsa: Bilingual Poems on Growing up Latino in the United States, is a book of poems that have been translated from Spanish into English and that highlight many Hispanic authors. Without the help of illustrations, Lori Carlson categorizes these poems into several groups: School Days, Home and Homeland, Memories, Hard Times, and Time to Play.

Pat Mora, who spent most of her life in the desert, is an award-winning poet and author of many books for adults and children. *Confetti: Poems for Children* is her first collection of poetry for children. In 1994, she received a National Endowment for the Arts Creative Writing Fellowship in Poetry. That same year, *Listen to the Desert* was published. Mora provides the reader with poems about the sounds and animals of the desert. Illustrated by Francisco X. Mora, this book is written in both English and Spanish.

Illustrated by Enrique O. Sanchez, *Confetti* contains poems about a Mexican American girl who lives in the Southwest. It contains a glossary for many of the Spanish terms that are infused throughout the book. In "Sun Song," for example, Mora uses the Spanish term *ranitas*, which means frogs that "hear the sun's first song."

Toni de Gerez received a master's degree in literature at Boston University. She has lived all over Latin America and has been a lecturer and writer of Latin American mythology and poetry. Her book *My Song Is a Piece of Jade* is an anthology of fragments of poems originally composed in the Nahuatl language in honor of the gods of ancient Mexico. William Stark is the illustrator and has had a particular interest in Mexico's pre-Columbian arts. *My Song Is a Piece of Jade* is written in both English and Spanish.

Sylvia Cavozos Pena was a faculty member at the University of Houston and a specialist in children's literature. With her collection of literary works published in *Tun-ta-ca-tun*, Pena wants to help the "teachers of Spanish-speaking children bring young readers to the rich world of literature" (1986,

13). This edited book contains poems and short stories that are illustrated by Narciso Pena. The story with the same name as the book title was written by Franklyn P. Varela. It is a tall tale about how Puerto Rico was created. In 1987, Pena edited a book of poetry, titled *Kikiriki: Stories and Poems in English and Spanish for Children*. This book contains poems, short stories, and folktales written by many authors such as Sandra Cisneros, Nicholasa Mohr, Pat Mora, and Lucy Torres. Similar to *Tun-ta-ca-tun*, the first half of the book is written in Spanish and the second half in English.

Charlotte Pomerantz has written several books and has won the Jane Addams Children's Book Award. Her book *The Day They Parachuted Cats on Borneo* was selected by the United Nations for the International Year of the Child. In 1982, she published *If I Had a Paka*. Illustrated by Nancy Tafuri, this book is a collection of twelve poems using eleven languages. Some of the languages that Pomerantz includes are Swahili, Native American dialects, Samoan, Vietnamese, and Spanish. Also by Pomerantz is *The Tamarindo Puppy*, which is a collection of thirteen poems written in English and Spanish. With pictures by Byron Barton, these poems provide the reader with topics about a firehouse (parque de bombas), a fat cat (gata gordo), and of course, the tamarindo puppy.

Although Naomi Shihab Nye is not from the Hispanic culture, she has written many books not only about Mexican culture but also about other cultures around the world. In *The Tree Is Older Than You Are*, she writes, "this may not qualify me to gather writings of a culture not in my blood. I suggest that blood be bigger than what we're born with, that blood keep growing and growing as live . . ." (1995, 7). Nye, whose ancestors originated from Palestine, visited Mexico as a child and fell in love with the country. She is a poet, novelist, and anthologist. She has been a visiting writer-in-the-schools since 1974 and is the recipient of a Guggenheim Fellowship. The selection of writers in *The Tree Is Older Than You Are* represents legendary names as well as young writers. Many of the poems appear in Spanish, with English translations and would fascinate both young and old readers alike. The book also includes over twenty illustrators, including Rodolfo Morales, Julio Lopez Segura, and Leticia Tarrago.

Another selection by Nye is *This Same Sky*, which is a collection of poems from around the world. In this book, she collects writings from 129 poets who represent 68 countries. Countries include India, Canada, Brazil, Mexico, Mozambique, and the Philippines, just to name a few. The book comprises six sections that include topics such as Words and Silences, Dreams and Dreamers, Families, This Earth and Sky in Which We Live, Losses, and Human Mysteries. Similarly, in 1999, Nye selected poems that explore all kinds of losses. With poems primarily intended for the young adult, she deals with emergency situations, custody, and suicide in her book.

In *Salting the Ocean*, Nye provides a venue for young writers. These poems were collected by Nye while visiting schools in Texas, Oregon, Maine, Wyoming, and other places across the country. This book, illustrated by Ashley Bryan, contains one hundred poems of first and second graders. They represent poems that she collected over the past twenty-five years of her life. Also published in 2000, *Come with Me: Poems for a Journey* was written by Nye and has images by Dan Yaccarino, who created collages using mixed media. He is an award-winning artist whose large-scale paintings and sculptures have been exhibited worldwide.

Native American

Joseph Bruchac was the recipient of the 1993 Benjamin Franklin Award "Person of the Year" from the Publishers' Marketing Association. Born in 1942, Bruchac is from the Abenaki Tribe, and his poems, articles, and stories have appeared in over five hundred publications. In the book titled *The Earth Under Sky Bear's Feet*, the author provides twelve lyrical poems and stories to celebrate many stories about the living earth below. Two years later, Bruchac wrote another book *Thirteen Moons on Turtle's Back: A Native American Year of Moons*. A 1993 Notable Children's Book in the Language Arts, this book presents one moon legend for each of the thirteen tribal nations in different regions of the continent. Powered by the turtle who is believed to hold the mystery of the moon on her back, each story is lovingly told through poetry and oil paintings. The illustrator for both of these books was Thomas Locker.

In another book which draws on his Abenaki heritage, Bruchac writes about the many ways of saying thank you. *The Circle of Thanks: Native American Poems and Songs of Thanksgiving* is a collection of thanksgiving prayers of fourteen Native American cultures. They include the following tribes: Micmac, Mohawk, Pawnee, and the Osage, just to name a few. The themes also reflect the appreciation of nature. This book is illustrated by Murv Jacob, a descendant of the Cherokees. The notes at the end of the book provide an explanation of the tribal traditions for each of the poems.

Nancy Wood has been fascinated by the heritage and culture of the Native American people for a long time. She has spent many years in the State of Colorado and was invited to write a libretto for a symphony. She chose the Ute Indians as the subject of her poems and as a result, *War Cry on a Prayer Feather* was published in 1979. This collection contains many photographs of the Ute tribe and is accompanied by many free verse poems. In 1993, Wood published a book of poetry that reflected the deep spirituality and values of the Taos Pueblo Indians and their interconnectedness to nature. *Spirit Walker* is beautifully illustrated with breathtaking paintings by Frank Howell. Two of the poems from this book "All As It Was in This Place Timeless" and "My Help Is in the Mountain," also appear in an earlier book of poetry by Wood, entitled *Hollering Sun*.

When Shonto Begay was still very young, he realized and respected nature and its beauty. He says that "teaching of the elders made it clear that this land is sacred and we belong to it; it does not belong to us . . ." (Day 1999, 23). His love for art led him to pursue it in college, and his work has appeared in dozens of exhibitions. In his volume of *Navajo: Visions and Voices across the Mesa*, Begay assembles twenty of his celebrated paintings with his original poetry. Throughout the collection, there is a keen awareness of the need to balance harmony between two cultures: the natural world and the high-tech world.

Illustrated with photographs by Edward S. Curtis, *Earth Always Endures*, edited by Neil Philip is an anthology that gives a vivid insight into the world of Native Americans. This combination of sixty poems and photographs brings us closer to the realities of the traditions and heritage of this culture. Curtis used a poet's eye to take over forty thousand photographs of Native Americans to partially contribute to this book. Some of these poems were translated from various lyrics in Native American song, representing many tribes (for example, Navajo, Osage, Sioux, Omaha, and Zuni).

Along with some of her own poems, Virginia Sneve includes a sample of contemporary tribal poets, as well as selections that have been passed down through generations for the book, *Dancing Teepees: Poems of American Indian Youth*. Stephen Gammell provides the artwork for each of the poems, which are very colorful and representative of the Native American culture. The book includes songs and free verse poems that represent tribes such as the Lakota Sioux, Ute-Navajo, and the Apache.

CONCLUSIONS

Poetry can be a very creative, interesting, and fun strategy for introducing a multicultural curriculum to children and young adults. There are many opportunities for students to reflect, analyze, and create their own language of expression, and the use of poetry in Language Arts classes can reduce the amount of perceived or real stress that is often evident when teaching from a multicultural perspective. Poetry offers an opportunity for students to use their critical thinking skills as they attempt to understand, reflect, and analyze, while it provides a great venue for creativity and expression that most students thoroughly enjoy when given the chance.

UNIT PLAN: THE EXPANSION OF RIGHTS
By Vicki Martizna

Vicki Martizna is an African American whose Spanish grandfather married a slave and, using the Underground Railroad, made their home in Iowa. Currently a social studies teacher in Denver, Colo., in the Cherry Creek School District, Martizna spent several years in the Des Moines School District as an elementary and middle school teacher of Language Arts. Prairie Middle School, her present school, is in the suburb of Aurora, outside of Denver. Also, she serves on the WEB (Welcome Everybody) Program. This program strives to decrease the fear of incoming fifth graders when they make their transition into middle school. Prairie Middle School is very diverse with students representing fourteen different languages.

Multicultural literature plays an important role in her curriculum. Along with integration of respect for all cultures all year, there is an emphasis in their curriculum on cultural awareness. The unit called The Expansion of Rights Unit touches on many different ethnic groups; it touches on the oppression each group has suffered throughout the years of our country's growth. The unit consists of the history and knowledge of how African Americans became the target of slavery and the cruel and inhumane treatment that was set upon this specific group of people. It continues with the Japanese Americans and how they were mistreated after the bombing of Pearl Harbor. Finally, the unit covers the Jewish Americans and how their ancestors became targets for terrible catastrophes during World War II. Martizna's goal as an educator is to have her students love not only themselves but also others, even if they are different in race, creed, and color.

In 2007–2008, Ms. Martizna was honored with the Cherry Creek School District Teacher of the Year Award based upon her master teacher skills and her connections and relationships with her students. She was also recognized in the district as being highly qualified by passing the National Praxis Test.

Lesson One

Rationale

Students should know how citizens exercise their rights and become aware of the characteristics of U.S. political culture.

Goals and Objectives

- Students will read and understand a variety of materials of multicultural information.
- Students will apply thinking skills to reading.
- Students will read and recognize literature as a record of human experiences.

Materials Needed

- Poems: On the Picket Line (Buelah Amidon) and Free Elections (Anonymous)
- Reading: "Ain't I a Woman?" (Sojourner Truth)
- Song/CD: "Ain't I a Woman?" (Ropy Block)

Activities and Time Frame (Approximately Four Forty-five-Minute Class Periods)

- Day starters are to be put on the board and read aloud by the teacher. Students will then respond in their "books of knowledge."
- Day #1 Day Starter (5 min.): Think of a time in your life when you had to stand up for something you believed in. Tell me about it.
- Day #2 Day Starter (10 min.): How did it make you feel? Why was this so important to you? Was it a difficult choice to make? Did it involve risk? Were you satisfied with the outcome?
- Day #3 Day Starter (10 min.): Play the song, "Ain't I a Woman?" for students. They should listen for emotion, purpose, audience, and content.
- Day #4 Day Starter (20 min.): Pass out a copy of the poem "Ain't I a Woman?" by Sojourner Truth. Read background information to large group. Discuss and define vocabulary. Read the passage again as large group points out subject, occasion, audience, purpose, and source. Discuss the following: How much of a risk was it for Sojourner Truth to make this speech? Would you have done it?

Assessments and Evaluations

Using emotion, purpose, and content of the poem, write a two-paragraph paper telling me about the poem and the influence it has on you. Think about punctuation, spelling, and content while writing the paper. You will need an introduction and a closing.

Lesson Two

Rationale

Reading and writing skills will be emphasized for the purpose of analyzing main ideas and using reading strategies, as well as activating background knowledge and the coding of text, inferring and synthesizing to build knowledge of freedom and liberty.

Goals and Objectives

- Students will know and understand what government is and what purpose it serves.
- Students will know the distinctive characteristics of U.S. political culture.
- Students will know how citizens can exercise their rights.

Materials Needed

- The emancipation proclamation (Primary Resource)
- Poem: "Refugee in America" (Langston Hughes)
- Readings: "I Have a Dream" speech (Martin Luther King Jr.) and Blanche K. Bruce, 1876 speech in the senate

Activities and Time Frame (Approximately Five Forty-Five-Minute Class Periods)

- Read and discuss with class the emancipation proclamation.
- Read Blanche K. Bruce's speech in the senate. List the opportunities the speaker visualizes for the African Americans in the future.
- Read Langston Hughes's "Refugee in America" and have students code the text with "I wonder . . ." Emphasize the difference between liberty and freedom.
- Read Martin Luther King Jr.'s "I Have a Dream" speech. List opportunities the speaker visualizes for African American in the future.

- Using a Venn diagram, compare Bruce's speech with King's speech.
- Add a circle to the Venn diagram for students' picture, indicating equality for all people in America today.

Assessments and Evaluations

According to you and according to these writers, what must change if people are to gain more equality in America? Write your response in a well-structured expository paragraph.

Activities and Strategies

These activities and strategies will center on the elements of poetry: rhythm, language, imagery, and patterns.

1. To analyze rhythms in poetry, students can bring in examples of "jump rope rhymes" or lyrics to rap songs. After discussing the materials they brought to class, instruct students to develop their own rhythmic poem that could focus on a specific topic. Examples of how lyrics can be similar to poetry can be seen in Will Smith's book *Just the Two of Us*. Smith, an actor, musician, and father, along with illustrator Kadir Nelson, captures the intense relations between a loving father and his son.
2. Study in detail, the rhythms and lyrics of contemporary music that students enjoy. Decide on one or two songs that can be agreed upon by the class. Instruct students to write a rhythmic stanza that could be included in the song. Share the fun by having students sing their new versions of the song, possibly like karaoke.

WORKS CITED

Adoff, Arnold. *All the Colors of the Race*. Illustrated by John Steptoe. New York: Lothrop, Lee & Shepard Books, 1982.

———. *Black Is Brown Is Tan*. Illustrated by Emily McCully. New York: Harper & Row, 1973.

———. *Black Out Loud: An Anthology of Modern Poems by Black Americans*. New York: Macmillan, 1970.

———. *Eats*. Illustrated by Susan Russo. New York: Mulberry Books, 1979.

———, ed. *I Am the Darker Brother: An Anthology of Modern Poems by Negro Americans*. Illustrated by Benny Andrews. New York: Macmillan, 1968.

———. *In for Winter, Out for Spring*. Illustrated by Jerry Pinkney. New York: Harcourt Brace Jovanovich, 1991.

————. *Outside Inside Poems*. Illustrated by John Steptoe. New York: Lothrop, Lee & Shepard Books, 1981.

————, ed. *The Poetry of Black America: Anthology of the 20th Century*. Introduction by Gwendolyn Brooks. New York: Harper & Row, 1973.

————. *Today We Are Brother and Sister*. Illustrated by Glo Coalson. New York: Lothrop, Lee & Shepard Books, 1981.

Begay, Shonto. *Navajo Visions and Voices across the Mesa*. New York: Scholastic, 1995.

Bierhorst, John, ed. *In the Trail of the Wind: American Indian Poems and Ritual Orations*. New York: Farrar, Straus and Giroux, 1971.

Bontemps, Arna. *Golden Slippers: An Anthology of Negro Poetry for Young Readers*. Illustrated by Henrietta Bruce Sharon. New York: Harper, 1941.

Bruchac, Joseph. *The Circle of Thanks: Native American Poems and Songs of Thanksgiving*. Illustrated by Murv Jacob. Mahwah, N.J.: Bridgewater Books, 1996.

————. *The Earth Under Sky Bear's Feet: Native American Poems of the Land*. Illustrated by Thomas Locker. New York: Philomel Books, 1995.

————. *Thirteen Moons on Turtle's Back: A Native American Year of Moons*. Illustrated by Thomas Locker. New York: Putnam, 1997.

Bryan, Ashley. *Ashley Bryan's ABC of African American Poetry*. New York: Atheneum Books for Young Readers, 1997.

————. *Sing to the Sun*. New York: HarperCollins, 1992.

Carlson, Lori, ed. *Cool Salsa: Bilingual Poems on Growing up Latino in the United States*. New York: Henry Holt, 1994.

Cronyn, George W., ed. *American Indian Poetry*. New York: Ballantine Books, 1962.

Cullinan, Bernice E., and Lee Galda. *Literature and the Child*. 3rd ed. New York: Harcourt Brace College, 1994.

Day, Frances Ann. *Multicultural Voices in Contemporary Literature: A Resource for Teachers*. Portsmouth, N.H.: Heinemann, 1999.

de Gerez, Toni. *My Song Is a Piece of Jade: Poems of Ancient Mexico in English and Spanish*. Illustrated by William Stark. Boston: Little, Brown, 1984.

Demi. *In the Eyes of the Cat: Japanese Poetry for all Seasons*. Trans. Tze-Si Huang. Illustrated by Demi. New York: Henry Holt, 1994.

Gillian, Maria M., and Jennifer Gillian, eds. *Unsettling America: An Anthology of Contemporary Multicultural Poetry*. New York: Penguin Books, 1994.

Giovanni, Nikki. *Ego-Tripping and Other Poems for Young People*. Illustrated by George Ford. New York: Lawrence Hill Books, 1993.

————. *Knoxville, Tennessee*. Illustrated by Larry Johnson. New York: Scholastic Books for Children, 1994.

————. *Spin a Soft Black Song: Poems for Children*. New York: Hill and Wang, 1971.

————. *Vacation Time: Poems for Children*. New York: Morrow, 1980.

Greenfield, Eloise. *Africa Dream*. Illustrated by Carole Byard. New York: HarperCollins, 1977.

————. *Daydreamers*. Illustrated by Tom Feelings. New York: Dial Books for Young Readers, 1981.

————. *For the Love of the Game: Michael Jordan and Me*. New York: HarperCollins, 1997.

————. *Honey, I Love*. New York: HarperCollins, 1978.

————. *Nathaniel Talking.* New York: Black Butterfly Children's Books, 1988.

————. *Night on Neighborhood Street.* New York: Dial Books for Young Readers, 1991.

————. *Under the Sunday Tree.* New York: Harper & Row, 1988.

Grimes, Nikki. *Come Sunday.* Illustrated by Michael Bryant. Grand Rapids, Mich.: W. B. Eerdmans, 1996.

————. *From a Child's Heart.* Illustrated by Brenda Joysmith. Orange, N.J.: Just Us Books, 1993.

————. *Hopscotch Love: A Family Treasury of Love Poems.* New York: Lothrop, Lee & Shepard Books, 1999.

————. *Is It Far to Zanzibar? Poems about Tanzania.* New York: Lothrop, Lee & Shepard Books, 2000.

————. *Meet Danitra Brown.* New York: Lothrop, Lee & Shepard Books, 1994.

————. *My Man Blue.* Illustrated by Jerome Lagarrigue. New York: Dial Books for Young Readers, 1999.

————. *A Pocketful of Poems.* Illustrated by Javaka Steptoe. New York: Clarion Books, 2001.

————. *Shoe Magic.* New York: Orchard Books, 2000.

————. *Something on My Mind.* Illustrated by Tom Feelings. New York: Dial Books for Young Readers, 1999.

————. *Stepping Out with Grandma Mac.* Illustrated by Angelo. New York: Orchard Books, 2001.

————. *Wild, Wild Hair.* Illustrated by George Ford. New York: Scholastic, 1997.

Ho, Minfong. *Hush! A Thai Lullaby.* Illustrated by Holly Meade. New York: Scholastic, 1996.

————. *Maples in the Mist: Children's Poems from the Tang Dynasty.* Illustrated by Jean Tseng and Mou-sien Tseng. New York: Lothrop, Lee & Shepard Books, 1996.

Hopkins, Lee Bennett. *Pass the Poetry, Please!* New York: Harper & Row, 1987.

Hu, Jane Hwa. *Sojourner.* Baltimore, Md.: Noble House, 1994.

Lee, Jeanne M. *The Song of Mu Lan.* Arden, N.C.: Front Street, 1995.

Lewis, Richard. *Miracles: Poems by Children of the English-Speaking World.* New York: Simon & Schuster, 1984.

Mado, Michio. *The Animals: Selected Poems.* New York: McElderry Books, 1992.

McKissack, Patricia, and Fredrick McKissack. *Sojourner Truth: Ain't I a Woman?* New York: Scholastic, 1994.

Mora, Pat. *Confetti: Poems for Children.* Illustrated by Enrique O. Sanchez. New York: Lee & Low Books, 1996.

————. *Listen to the Desert.* Illustrated by Francisco X. Mora. New York: Clarion Books, 1994.

Myers, Walter Dean. *Brown Angels: An Album of Pictures and Verses.* New York: Harper-Collins, 1993.

————. *Harlem.* Illustrated by Christopher Myers. New York: Scholastic Press, 1997.

————. *Motown and Didi.* New York: Laurel Leaf, 1987.

————. *Now Is Your Time: The African-American Struggle for Freedom.* New York: HarperCollins, 1991.

Nye, Naomi Shihab. *Come with Me: Poems for a Journey.* Illustrated by Dan Yaccarino. New York: Greenwillow Books, 2000.

——. *Salting the Ocean: 100 Poems by Young Poets*. Illustrated by Ashley Bryan. New York: Greenwillow Books, 2000.

——. *This Same Sky: A Collection of Poems from around the World*. New York: Aladdin Paperbacks, 1992.

——. *The Tree Is Older Than You Are: A Bilingual Gathering of Poems and Stories from Mexico with Paintings by Mexican Artists*. New York: Aladdin Paperbacks, 1995.

——, comp. *What Have You lost?* New York: Greenwillow Books, 1999.

Pena, Sylvia Cavozos, ed. *Kikiriki: Stories and Poems in English and Spanish for Children*. Illustrated by Narciso Pena. Houston, Tex.: Arte Publico Press, 1987.

——. *Tun-ta-ca-tun: More Stories and Poems in English and Spanish*. Houston, Tex.: Arte Publico Press, 1986.

Philip, Neil. *Earth Always Endures*. Illustrated by Edward S. Curtis. New York: Penguin Books, 1996.

Pomerantz, Charlotte. *The Day They Parachuted Cats on Borneo*. Boston, Mass.: Addison-Wesley, 1971.

——. *If I Had a Paka: Poems in Eleven Languages*. Illustrated by Nancy Tafuri. New York: Greenwillow Books, 1982.

——. *The Tamarindo Puppy and Other Poems*. Illustrated by Byron Barton. New York: Greenwillow Books, 1980.

Schneider, Reissa, Gary Gottfriedson, and George Littlechild. *In Honour of Our Grandmothers*. Penticton, B.C.: Theytus Books, 1994.

Smith, Henrietta M., ed. *The Coretta Scott King Awards Book: From Vision to Reality*. Chicago: American Library Association, 1994.

Smith, Will. *Just the Two of Us*. New York: Scholastic Press, 1980.

Sneve, Virginia Driving Hawk. *Dancing Teepees: Poems of American Indian Youth*. Illustrated by Stephen Gammell. New York: Holiday House, 1989.

Soto, Gary. *Canto Familiar*. Illustrated by Annika Nelson. New York: Harcourt Brace, 1995.

——. *A Fire in My Hands: A Book of Poems*. New York: Scholastic, 1990.

——. *Neighborhood Odes*. Illustrated by David Diaz. New York: Scholastic, 1992.

Strickland, Dorothy S., and Michael R. Strickland, comps. *Families: Poems Celebrating the African American Experience*. Illustrated by John Ward. Honesdale, Pa.: Wordsong Boyds Mills Press, 1994.

Wong, Janet. *Good Luck Gold and Other Poems*. New York: McElderry Books, 1994.

——. *Night Garden: Poems from the World of Dreams*. Illustrated by Julie Paschkis. New York: McElderry Books, 2000.

——. *The Rainbow Hand: Poems about Mothers and Children*. Illustrated by Jennifer Hewitson. New York: McElderry Book, 1999.

Wood, Nancy. *Hollering Sun*. Illustrated by Myron Wood. New York: Simon & Schuster, 1972.

——. *Spirit Walker*. New York: Doubleday Books for Young Readers, 1993.

——. *War Cry on a Prayer Feather: Prose and Poetry of the Ute Indians*. Illustrated by Frank Howell. Garden City, N.Y.: Doubleday, 1979.

Yep, Laurence. *American Dragons: Twenty-five Asian American Voices*. New York: HarperCollins, 1993.

——. *The Butterfly Boy*. Illustrated by Jeanne M. Lee. New York: Farrar Straus and Giroux, 1993.

Chapter Nine

Creating the Climate for Success

As a teacher of literature for children and young adults, I have prided myself with the wealth of good books I have been able to share with my own children as they grew from toddlers to teens. Now as young adults beginning careers and families of their own, we sometimes talk about their favorite books and what books they can take from my shelves for their own budding home and classroom libraries. The stories that touched them and hold favorite spots in their hearts are not always the ones that I expected would have the greatest influence on their lives, but they are, nonetheless, stories that provided windows into their past and mirrors that reflected images of who they were as children, learning about new worlds and other peoples.

Throughout the process of writing this text, Dianne and I have discovered that our own histories and our own life experiences have often entered into our thinking about what we would say next, how we would say it, and if what we said would have the kind of influence we intended to have. As the book developed over the years of writing, rewriting, and reexamining texts, new books have been published and old favorites have been set aside to make room for new and important discussions. Our roles as teachers have changed; we no longer find ourselves as full-time faculty, and instead we find ourselves mentoring new faculty who have joined our respective colleges. While we wrestle with time constraints, fulfilling all of our new roles as administrators and maintaining ourselves as scholars in our individual fields, we remain grounded in our commitment to literature, to literacy, and to the education of young people in their own journeys to become teachers of the children. To that end, we have given you our mirrors and our windows so that you might have the opportunity to glance through our lenses into the world of books that we love and travel with us as we continue to grow in our knowledge of, and commitment to, the field of multicultural literature. One major change for us on this journey is related to the new experiences of another significant minority group in our country—those whose ethnic culture is based in the Middle East. In our own state of Michigan, one finds that nearly one-quarter of all Arabic people in the United States reside in the Dearborn area—2.4 million in all. When we began this book, there was little discussion of this ethnic group and its role for children in our classrooms; that all changed, however, with the tragedy of September 11. From that time forth, we have seen images of a people most of us did not know or understand. The negative stereotypes and fears of another generation and another war suddenly and firmly had been replaced with a different culture and different faces. What George Santayana, a twentieth-century poet and philosopher, had once stated a century ago now threatened us anew: *"those who do not remember the past are condemned to repeat it."* In response to the fears expressed by some of our students and the realization of our responsibilities as teachers of multicultural literature, we discussed the need to add a fifth division to our text. We found quickly, however, that there were very few literature selections for children and young adults that did not contain some element of stereotype casting. Much of what we have found has been in either the area of informational texts related to religious observances or in the genre of folktales and fairy tales—both, while providing knowledge or archetypal humor, are limited in providing a window into the universality of the human experiences to which those children outside the culture can relate. While the limited selection of quality examples of literature representing this culture is a current problem, it is our hope that authors of this culture will begin to answer the need by writing for the children who need to see their faces and their cultures represented fairly and authentically in the literature they read. While it was our intent to present a resource for the major minority cultures in our country, we acknowledge and apologize for the lack of adequate discussion across the genres for those whose cultural identities reside with Middle Eastern countries. It is our hope that any future revisions and reprints of this resource text will be able to include a healthy representation of quality selections of literature for children and young adults in all our major minority groups. In response to our lack of depth in the area of Arabic American literature for children and young adults and as a helpful resource for teachers, we have provided the appendix, which lists books that are available and some of the resources one might use to gain knowledge of this group. It also provides information about other key cultural groups that were not discussed within the main areas of our text. We hope you will find it useful and supportive of your work as teachers.

Appendix

Additional Cultural Resources and Unit Plans

BIBLIOGRAPHY OF MIDDLE EASTERN LITERATURE FOR CHILDREN AND YOUNG ADULTS

Ahsan, M. M. *Muslim Festivals.* Illustrated by M. M. Ahsan. Vero Beach, Fla.: Rourke Enterprises, 1987.

Burns, Khephra. *Mansa Musa.* Illustrated by Leo and Diane Dillon. San Francisco: Harcourt Brace, 2001.

Carmi, Daniella, and Yael Lotan. *Samir and Yonatan.* New York: Scholastic, 2002.

Chalfonte, Jessica. *I Am Muslim.* New York: PowerKids Press, 1996.

Clark, Emma. *Sinan: Architect of Istanbul.* Illustrated by Emma Alcock. London: Hood Hood Books,

Cohen, Barbara, and Bahia Lovejoy. *Seven Daughters and Seven Sons.* New York: Atheneum, 1982.

Durkee, Noura. *Animals of Paradise.* Illustrated by Simon Trethewey. London: Hood Hood Books, 1997.

Ellis, Deborah. *The Breadwinner.* Toronto: Groundwood Books, 2000.

———. *Mud City.* Toronto: Groundwood Books, 2003.

———. *Parvana's Journey.* Toronto: Groundwood Books, 2002.

Ghazi, Suhaib Hamid. *Ramadan.* Illustrated by Omar Rayyan. New York: Holiday House, 1996.

Heide, Florence Parry, and Judith Gilliland. *The Day of Ahmed's Secret.* Illustrated by Ted Lewin. New York: Lothrop, Lee & Shepard Books, 1990.

———. *The House of Wisdom.* Illustrated by Mary Grandpre. New York: Dorling Kindersley, 1999.

———. *Sami and the Time of the Troubles.* Illustrated by Ted Lewin. New York: Clarion Books, 1992.

Husain, Shahrukh. *What Do We Know about Islam?* Illustrated by Celia Hart. New York: Peter Bedrick Books, 1995.

Johnson-Davies, Denys. *Rumi: Poet and Sage.* Illustrated by Laura De La Mare. London: Hood Hood Books, 1996.

Kessler, Cristina. *One Night: A Story from the Desert.* Illustrated by Ian Schoenherr. New York: Philomel Books, 1995.

Khan, Rukhsana. *The Roses in My Carpets.* Illustrated by Ronald Himler. New York: Holiday House, 1998.

Kimmel, Eric. *The Three Princes: A Middle Eastern Tale.* Illustrated by Leonard Everett Fisher. New York: Holiday House, 1994.

Kurtz, Jane. *Pulling the Lion's Tale.* Illustrated by Floyd Cooper. New York: Simon & Schuster, 1995.

Levine, Anna. *Running on Eggs.* New York: Cricket Books, 1999.

Lewin, Ted. *The Storytellers.* Illustrated by Ted Lewin. New York: Lothrop, Lee & Shepard Books, 1998.

Maalouf, Amin, and Jon Rothschild. *The Crusades through Arab Eyes.* London: Schocken Books, 1989.

MacDonald, Fiona. *A 16th Century Mosque.* Illustrated by Mark Bergin. New York: P. Bedrick Books, 1994.

Marshall, Julia. *Suleiman the Magnificent: The Story of Istanbul.* London: Hood Hood Books, 2002.

Matthews, Mary. *Magid Fasts for Ramadan.* Illustrated by E. B. Lewis. New York: Clarion Books, 1996.

McMane, Fred. *Hakeem Olajawon.* New York: Chelsea Books, 1999.

Naff, Alixa. *The Arab Americans.* New York: Chelsea House, 1988.

Nye, Naomi Shihab. *The Flag of Childhood: Poems from the Middle East.* New York: Aladdin Paperbacks, 2002.

———. *Habibi.* New York: Simon & Schuster, 1997.

———. *19 Varieties of Gazelle: Poems of the Middle East.* New York: Greenwillow Books, 2002.

———. *Sitti's Secrets.* Illustrated by Nancy Carpenter. New York: Simon & Schuster, 1994.

———. *The Space Between Our Footsteps: Poems and Paintings from the Middle East.* New York: Simon & Schuster, 1998.

Oppenheim, Shulamith Levey. *The Hundredth Name.* Illustrated by Michael Hays. Honesdale, Pa.: Boyds Mills Press, 1995.

Rumford, James. *Traveling Man: The Journey of Ibn Battuta, 1325–1354.* Illustrated by James Rumford. Boston, Mass.: Houghton Mifflin, 2001.

Shah, Idries. *The Boy without a Name.* Illustrated by Mona Caron. Cambridge, Mass.: Hoopoe Books, 2000.

Staples, Suzanne Fisher. *Haveli.* New York: Knopf, 1993.

———. *Shabanu.* New York: Knopf, 1989.

———. *Shiva's Fire.* New York: Farrar, Straus and Giroux, 2000.

Weiss-Armush, Anne Marie. *Arabian Cuisine.* Illustrated by John Berry. Beirut, Lebanon: Dar An-nafaés, 1984.

Wormser, Richard. *American Islam: Growing Up Muslim in America.* New York: Walker, 1994.

Zeman, Linda. *Sindbad.* Illustrated by Linda Zeman. Toronto: Tundra Books, 1999.

OTHER RESOURCES

Bloom, Jonathan, and Sheila S. Blair. *Islam: A Thousand Years of Faith and Power.* New Haven, Conn., and London: Yale University Press, 2002.

———. *Islamic Arts. Art and Ideas.* London: Phaidon Press, 1997.

Esposito, John, ed. *The Oxford History of Islam.* New York: Oxford University Press, 2000.

Goodwin, Jan. *Price of Honor: Muslim Women Lift the Veil of Silence on the Islamic World.* New York: Plume, 1995.

Lunde, Paul. *Islam.* London: Dorling Kindersley, 2002.

UNIT PLAN: CHINESE LITERATURE
By Renee Flennoy

Renee Flennoy is presently a sixth-grade language arts, social studies, and reading teacher at Derby Middle School of Birmingham, Mich. Birmingham is a suburban area of Metropolitan Detroit. Flennoy began her teaching career in Detroit public schools, where she taught second through fifth grade in a span of fifteen years. In her twenty-second year of teaching, Flennoy continues to enhance her teaching skills by serving as Derby's sixth-grade teacher representative on the District's Language Arts Curriculum Committee, the District's Cultural Diversity Committee, and Derby's School Improvement Plan Committee.

Flennoy sees that the incorporation of culturally diverse literature in the classroom not only extends learning but also enriches it. Furthermore, it reduces the possibility for attitudes to be underdeveloped toward people who are not part of society's majority. Culturally diverse literature allows respect to grow toward people of different cultural and ethnic backgrounds. Also, it can be used to display, in the United States, how it takes the contributions of those born here and elsewhere to shape our present-day society.

By being both a social studies and a language arts teacher, Flennoy perceives the opportunity to bridge these two curricular areas with materials that bring far-away places into the classroom. Also, having students, or their parents, who were born in various parts of the world gives a sense of self-respect, pride, and appreciation to them and to all students in general.

Lesson One

Rationale

This lesson is part of our sixth-grade Black Teachers' China "Round-Robin" teaching unit. Each teacher takes a subject area that goes beyond our social studies textbook to extend the students' knowledge of China. Using literature to broaden this unit is not only fascinating but also enriching and fun, and we are able to make cultural connections with the similarities and differences in various ways of living.

Goals and Objectives

Students will be able to understand the evolution of Chinese literature; they will create a one-to-two-page story, or rewrite a known tale set in the Chinese culture, using folklore, Confucianism, Taoism, or a combination of either. Students will work their tale with a partner; the partners will include an illustration relating to their written piece.

Activities and Time Frame (Approximately Two Forty-Five-Minute Class Periods)

- Introduce or discuss notes of how Chinese literature has evolved through cultural beliefs, teachings, philosophies, and religions.
- As students enter, take a seat, and settle down, have taped music of plucked stringed instruments playing in the background (two to three minutes).
- Begin the lesson with a brief overview of what is to take place during the next two class periods. Start the students by having them brainstorm some of their all-time favorite fiction stories (the teacher shares too).
- Introduce the following information that you will have written out on the board beforehand. The students are to listen and ask questions only. They are not to write notes on any of this.
- 1100 BC—Earliest known writings, "Classic of Songs"—poems, stories, songs about love, farming, and war.
- Folklore—Stories honoring the ancestors, persons of nobility, royalty, and the wealthy.
- Confucianism—Teachings of the ancient philosopher Confucius, teaching moral lessons such as the ideal life is service to others.
- Taoism—Teachings of the ancient sage and philosopher Lao-tzu; beautiful poetry of stories about the wonders of nature.
- 700 AD—Tu Fu, a great poet of ancient China whose writings criticized the government or rulers of China (dynasties).
- 1800s—Writers were exposed to Western ideas.
- 1900s—Many writers were critical of life in China.

- 1949: Communism—Writers could only write about peasants, soldiers, and workers.
- 1960: Mao's Cultural Revolution—Many writers were jailed who were critical of China's government.
- 1976—Some restrictions were lifted. Writers were allowed more freedom of expression.
- Briefly retell the story *The Five Chinese Brothers* (Bishop 1996/1938). Compare it with *The Seven Chinese Brothers* (Mahy 1990). Relate these stories to Chinese folklore, honoring family, and families working together to overcome obstacles.
- Briefly retell the story, *Yeh Shen: A Cinderella Story from China* (Ai-Ling 1982). Relate it to the honoring of ancestors and nature. Compare or contrast it with European, American, and African versions of the Cinderella story.

Extensions

Assign to a partner the task of brainstorming a story idea based on the Chinese culture. The story must be typed or handwritten in cursive writing. The story must have an illustration with it that relates to the story. The story will be due five days from the day the class meets for this session. Stories will be collected and displayed on a hallway bulletin board as an extension of the sixth grade's social studies unit on China

References

Ai-Ling, L. *Yeh-Shen: A Cinderella Story from China.* New York: Philomel Books, 1982.
Bishop, Claire H. *Five Chinese Brothers.* Illustrated by Kurt Wiese. New York: Putnam Juvenile, 1996. (Org. pub. 1938.)
Demi. *A Chinese Zoo, Fables, and Proverbs.* New York: Harcourt, 1987.
Flack, Marjorie. *The Story of Ping.* Illustrated by Kurt Weise. New York: Puffin, 1977.
Gerstein, Mordicai. *The Mountains of Tibet.* New York: HarperTrophy, 1989.
Lee, Wong Herbert. *A Drop of Rain.* Boston: Houghton Mifflin, 1995.
Mahy, Margaret. *Seven Chinese Brothers.* New York: Scholastic, 1992.
Osborne, Mary Pope. *One World, Many Religions: The Way We Worship.* New York: Knopf Books for Young Readers, 1996.
Shepard, Sandy. *Myths and Legends: Around the World.* New York: Simon & Schuster Children's Publishing, 1995.
Tan, Amy. *The Chinese Siamese Cat.* Illustrated by Gretchen Schields. New York: Aladdin Books, 2001.
Tao, Wang. *Exploration into China.* New York: Chelsea House Publications, 2000.

Yep, Laurence. *Dragonwings*. New York: HarperTrophy, 1975.
Yolen, Jane. *The Emperor and the Kite*. New York: Putnam Juvenile, 1998.

Lesson Two

Rationale

Using literature to extend students' understanding of the Chinese culture.

Goals and Objectives

- Students will be able to do a Directed Reading Thinking Activity (DRTA).
- Students will be able to read and discuss a selected novel to gain an understanding of the Chinese culture.

Materials needed

Dragonwings (Laurence Yep)

Activities and Time Frame (Approximately Three to Four Weeks)

- This lesson should be implemented after studying Ancient China through modern-day China, including the dynasty periods, nationalism to communism to the present. Present the novel *Dragonwings*.
- Students will read the novel during the daily twenty-two-minute reading class periods as an organized reading activity, with the DRTA using teacher-selected activity sheets from the study guide.
- Discuss what students learned about China during the later 1800s to the early 1900s: the changing traditions of China, the ending of dynasties, foreign trade, opium wars, foreign travel, and so on.
- Discuss why Chinese men were sent or traveled to America. (They were sent or they traveled to work during the American gold rush and railroad expansion to earn money to send back home to their families.)
- Discuss why Chinese wives and children remained in China. (U.S. immigration laws restricted work in the United States to men to limit the Chinese population in the U.S.)
- Introduce the main characters and their respective dreams.
- Discuss Windrider's talent as an excellent kite maker and a handyman or repairman.
- Read chapters aloud to the students. Discuss why America is called the

"Land of the Demons" and the "Land of the Golden Mountains." Have the students illustrate on drawing paper what Moonshadow's idea may have been of these two descriptions. Have students share their ideas.

- Alternate the use of the study guide activities with class discussions and questions after each chapter.
- Relate information that the students have learned from social studies China unit as it fits with the time period of the story: What is going on in China while the characters are in the United States?
- This novel contains twelve chapters. Upon finishing the final chapter, discuss the events that unfolded, the problems, resolutions, and the ending.

Extension Activities

- Assign to the students the task of making a kite (provide a sheet of directions). Give students a drawing of a dragon, which is to be colored and placed on the finished kite, along with four scenes from the story. Any four of the scenes that the students select will be explained. The students will then take the kites to the playing field and fly them.
- Provide a pictorial summary of the novel to be explained to the class as an oral book summary.

Bibliography

READER'S RESOURCES

Aardema, Verna. *Oh, Kojo! How Could You!* Illustrated by Marc Brown. New York: Dial Books for Young Readers, 1984.

————. *Sebgugugu, the Glutton: A Bantu Tale from Rwanda.* Illustrated by Nancy Clouse. Grand Rapids, Mich.: W. B. Eerdmans, 1993.

————. *Why Mosquitoes Buzz in People's Ears.* Illustrated by Leo and Diane Dillon. New York: Dial Books for Young Readers, 1984.

Ada, Alma Flor. *My Name Is María Isabel.* New York: Simon & Schuster, 1993.

Adler, David. *A Picture Book of George Washington Carver.* Illustrated by Dan Brown. New York: Holiday House, 1999.

————. *A Picture Book of Jesse Owens.* Illustrated by Robert Casilla. New York: Holiday House, 1992.

Adoff, Arnold. *All the Colors of the Race.* Illustrated by John Steptoe. New York: Lothrop, Lee & Shepard Books, 1982.

————. *Black Is Brown Is Tan.* Illustrated by Emily McCully. New York: Harper & Row, 1973.

————. *Black Out Loud: An Anthology of Modern Poems by Black Americans.* New York: Macmillan, 1970.

————. *Eats.* Illustrated by Susan Russo. New York: Mulberry Books, 1979.

————. *I Am the Darker Brother: An Anthology of Modern Poems by Negro Americans.* Illustrated by Benny Andrews. New York: Macmillan, 1968.

————. *In for Winter, Out for Spring.* Illustrated by Jerry Pinkney. New York: Harcourt Brace Jovanovich, 1991.

————. *Outside Inside Poems.* Illustrated by John Steptoe. New York: Lothrop, Lee & Shepard Books, 1981.

————, ed. *The Poetry of Black America: Anthology of the 20th Century.* Introduction by Gwendolyn Brooks. New York: Harper & Row, 1973.

Ahsan, M. M. *Muslim Festivals.* Illustrated by M. M. Ahsan. Vero Beach, Fla.: Rourke Enterprises, 1987.

Ai-Ling, L. *Yeh-Shen: A Cinderella Story from China.* Illustrated by Ed Young. New York: Philomel Books, 1982.

Albert, Burton. *Where Does the Trail Lead?* Illustrated by Brian Pinkney. New York: Simon & Schuster Books for Young Readers, 1991.

American Heritage Dictionary. 2nd ed. Boston, Mass: Houghton Mifflin, 1982.

Anaya, Rudolfo. *Farolitos of Christmas.* Illustrated by Edward Gonzales. New York: Hyperion Books for Children, 1995.

Ancona, George. *Barrio: Jose's Neighborhood.* New York: Harcourt Brace, 1998.

———. *Fiesta, U.S.A.* New York: Lodestar Books, 1995.

———. *Pablo Remembers: The Fiesta of the Day of the Dead.* New York: Lothrop, Lee & Shepard Books, 1993.

Anderson, David A. *The Origin of Life on Earth: An African Creation Myth.* Illustrated by Kathleen Atkins Wilson. Mt. Airy, Md.: Sights Productions, 1991.

Bandon, Alexandra. *Chinese Americans.* New York: New Discovery Books, 1994.

———. *Korean Americans.* New York: New Discovery Books, 1994.

———. *Vietnamese Americans.* New York: New Discovery Books, 1994.

Banks, Jacqueline Turner. *A Day for Vincent Chin and Me.* Boston: Houghton Mifflin, 2001.

Bannerman, Helen. *Little Black Sambo.* New York: Buccaneer Books, 1976. (Orig. pub. 1899.)

Barnes, Joyce Annette. *Baby Grand, the Moon in July, and Me.* New York: Dial Books for Young Readers, 1994.

Beals, Melba P. *Warriors Don't Cry: A Searing Memoir of the Battle to Integrate Little Rock's Central High.* New York: Archway, 1995.

Begay, Shonto. *Ma'ii and Cousin Toad.* New York: Scholastic, 1992.

———. *Navajo Visions and Voices across the Mesa.* New York: Scholastic, 1995.

Berry, James. *Ajeemah and His Son.* New York: Willa Perlman, 1991.

Bertrand, Diane Gonzales. *Close to the Heart.* Houston, Tex.: Pinata Books, 2002.

———. *Trino's Time.* Houston, Tex.: Pinata Books, 2001.

Bierhorst, John, ed. *In the Trail of the Wind: American Indian Poems and Ritual Orations.* New York: Farrar, Straus and Giroux, 1971.

———, ed. *The Red Swan.* New York: Farrar, Straus and Giroux, 1976.

Bishop, Claire. *The Five Chinese Brothers.* Illustrated by Kurt Wiese. New York: Putnam, 1996. (Orig. pub. 1938.)

Bolden, Tonya. *And Not Afraid to Dare.* New York: Scholastic, 1998.

Bontemps, Arna. *Golden Slippers: An Anthology of Negro Poetry for Young Readers.* New York: Harper, 1941.

Borden, Louise, and Mary Kay Kroeger. *Fly High! The Story of Bessie Coleman.* Illustrated by Teresa Flavin. New York: McElderry Books, 2001.

Boyd, Candy Dawson. *Breadsticks, and Blessing Places.* New York: Macmillan, 1985.

———. *Charlie Pippin.* New York: Macmillan, 1987.

———. *Chevrolet Saturdays.* New York: Macmillan, 1993.

———. *Circle of Gold.* New York: Scholastic, 1984.

———. *A Different Beat.* New York: Puffin, 1996.

———. *Fall Secrets.* New York: Puffin, 1994.

———. *Forever Friends.* New York: Puffin, 1986.

Bradshaw, Douglas. *Shaquille O'Neal: Man of Steel.* New York: Grosset & Dunlap, 2001.

Bredeson, Carmen. *Henry Cisneros: Building a Better America.* Berkeley Heights, N.J.: Enslow, 1995.

Bridges, Ruby. *Through My Eyes.* New York: Scholastic, 1999.

Brill, Marlene T. *The Trail of Tears: The Cherokee Journey.* Brookfield, Conn.: Millbrook Press, 1995.

Brown, Dee. *Wounded Knee.* (Adapted by Amy Ehrlich.) New York: Random House Children's Books, 1978.

Browne, Maggie. *Wanted—A King.* London: Cassell & Co., 1890.

Bruchac, Joseph. *Between Earth and Sky: Legends of Native American Sacred Places.* Illustrated by Thomas Locker. New York: Harcourt Brace, 1996.

———. *A Boy called Slow.* Illustrated by Rocco Baviera. New York: Putnam, 1994.

———. *The Boy Who Lived with the Bears.* Illustrated by Mury Jacob. New York: Harper-Collins, 1995.

———. *Children of the Longhouse.* New York: Dial Books for Young Readers, 1996.

———. *The Circle of Thanks: Native American Poems and Songs of Thanksgiving.* Mahwah, N.J.: Bridgewater Books, 1996.

———. *Eagle Song.* New York: Puffin, 1999.

———. *The Earth Under Sky Bear's Feet: Native American Poems of the Land.* Illustrated by Thomas Locker. New York: Philomel Books, 1995.

———. *The First Strawberries: A Cherokee Story.* Illustrated by Anna Vojtech. New York: Puffin Books, 1993.

———. *Four Ancestors: Stories, Songs, and Poems from Native North America.* Illustrated by S.S. Burrus. Duke Sine, and Mury, Jacob. Mahwah, N.J.: Bridgewater Books, 1996.

———. *Fox Song.* Illustrated by Paul Morin. New York: Paper Star Book, 1993.

———. *Skeleton Man.* New York: HarperCollins, 2001.

———. *Thirteen Moons on Turtle's Back: A Native American Year of Moons.* New York: Putnam, 1997.

———. *Warriors.* Plain City, Ohio: Darby Publishing, 2003.

Bruchac, Joseph, and James Bruchac. *Between Earth and Sky: Legends of Native American Sacred Places.* Illustrated by Thomas Locker. New York: Harcourt Brace, 1996.

———. *How Chipmunk Got His Stripes.* Illustrated by Jose Aruego and Ariane Dewey. New York: Dial Books for Young Readers, 2001.

Bryan, Ashley. *Ashley Bryan's ABC of African American Poetry.* New York: Atheneum Books for Young Readers, 1997.

———. *The Cat's Purr.* New York: Atheneum, 1985.

———. *Sing to the Sun.* New York: HarperCollins, 1992.

Burks, Brian. *Runs with Horses.* New York: Harcourt Brace, 1995.

Burns, Khephra. *Mansa Musa.* Illustrated by Leo and Diane Dillon. San Francisco: Harcourt Brace, 2001.

Caduto, Michael J., and Joseph Bruchac. *Keepers of Life: Discovering Plants through Native American Stories and Earth Activities for Children.* Golden, Colo.: Fulcrum Publishing, 1994.

Calhoun, Mary. *Tonio's Cat.* Illustrated by Ed Martinez. New York: Morrow Junior Books, 1996.

Calvino, Italo. *Italian Folktales.* Translated by George Martin. New York: Pantheon, 1981.

Cameron, Ann. *The Kidnapped Prince: The Life of Olaudah Equiano.* New York: Random House, 2000.

Carlson, Lori, ed. *Cool Salsa: Bilingual Poems on Growing up Latino in the United States.* New York: Henry Holt, 1994.

Carmi, Daniella, and Yael Lotan. *Samir and Yonatan.* New York: Scholastic, 2002.

Cassedy, Sylvia, and Kunihiro Suetake (translators). *Red Dragonfly on My Shoulder.* Illustrated by Molly Bang. New York: HarperCollins, 1992.

Castañeda, Omar S. *Among the Volcanoes.* New York: Dell Publishing, 1991.

Chalfonte, Jessica. *I Am Muslim.* New York: PowerKids Press, 1996.

Chang, Margaret, and Raymond Chang. *The Cricket Warrior: A Chinese Tale.* Illustrated by Warwick Hutton. New York: McElderry Books, 1994.

Choi, Sook-Nyul. *Echoes of the White Giraffe.* Boston: Houghton Mifflin, 1993.

———. *Year of the Impossible Goodbyes.* Boston: Houghton Mifflin, 1991.

Clark, Emma. *Sinan: Architect of Istanbul.* Illustrated by Emma Alcock. London: Hood Hood Books.

Clifton, Lucille. *Everett Anderson's Goodbye.* Illustrated by Ann Grifalconi. New York: Holt, Rinehart and Winston, 1983.

Climo, Shirley. *The Egyptian Cinderella.* New York: HarperCollins, 1989.

———. *The Irish Cinderlad.* New York: HarperCollins, 1996.

———. *The Korean Cinderella.* New York: HarperCollins, 1993.

———. *The Persian Cinderella.* New York: HarperCollins, 1999.

Coerr, Eleanor. *Sadako.* Illustrated by Ed Young. New York: Putman, 1993.

Cohen, Barbara, and Bahia Lovejoy. *Seven Daughters and Seven Sons.* New York: Atheneum, 1982.

Cohen, Caron Lee. *Mud Pony.* Illustrated by Shonto Begay. New York: Scholastic, 1988.

Cole, Judith. *The Moon, the Sun, and the Coyote.* Illustrated by Cecile Scholberle. New York: Simon & Schuster, 1991.

Collier, James L. *Duke Ellington.* New York: Macmillan, 1987.

Cooper, Floyd. *Coming Home.* New York: Putnam, 1994.

Cormier, Robert. *We All Fall Down.* New York: Delacorte Press, 1991.

Cox, Clinton. *Come All You Brave Soldiers: Blacks in the Revolutionary War.* New York: Scholastic Press, 1999.

———. *Undying Glory: The Story of the Massachusetts 54th Regiment.* New York: Scholastic, 1991.

Creech, Sharon. *Walk Two Moons.* New York: HarperCollins, 1994.

Crew, Linda. *Children of the River.* New York: Delacorte, 1989.

Cronyn, George W., ed. *American Indian Poetry.* New York: Ballantine Books, 1962.

Cruz Martinez, Alejandro. *The Woman Who Outshone the Sun.* Illustrated by Fernando Olivera. San Francisco: Children's Book Press, 1991.

Culleton, Beatrice. *April Raintree.* Winnipeg: Pemmican, 1984.

———. *In Search of April Raintree.* Winnipeg: Peguis, 1995.

Cullinan, Bernice E., and Lee Galda. *Literature and the Child.* 3rd ed. New York: Harcourt Brace College, 1994.

Cummings, Pat. *Purrrrr.* New York: HarperFestival, 1999.

Cumpian, Carlos. *Latino Rainbow: Poems about Latino Americans.* Chicago: Children's Press, 1994.

Curtis, Christopher Paul. *Bud, Not Buddy.* New York: Delacorte, 1999.

———. *The Watsons Go to Birmingham—1963.* New York: Delacorte, 1995.

Davis, Ossie. *Just Like Martin.* New York: Simon & Schuster, 1992.

Day, Frances Ann. *Multicultural Voices in Contemporary Literature: A Resource for Teachers.* Portsmouth, N.H.: Heinemann, 1999.

de Gerez, Toni. *My Song Is a Piece of Jade: Poems of Ancient Mexico in English and Spanish.* Illustrated by William Stark. Boston: Little, Brown, 1984.

DeGross, Monalisa. *Granddaddy's Street Songs.* Illustrated by Floyd Cooper. New York: Hyperion, 1999.

Dell, Pamela. *I.M. Pei: Designer of Dreams.* Chicago: Children's Press, 1993.

Demi. *A Chinese Zoo: Fables and Proverbs.* New York: Harcourt Brace, 1987.

———. *The Empty Pot.* New York: Henry Holt, 1990.

———. *The Greatest Treasure.* New York: Scholastic Press, 1998.

———. *In the Eyes of the Cat: Japanese Poetry.* Trans. Tze-Si Huang. Illustrated by Demi. New York: Henry Holt, 1994.

———. *The Magic Boat.* New York: Henry Holt, 1990.

dePaola, Tomie. *The Legend of the Bluebonnet: An Old Tale of Texas.* New York: G. P. Putnam's Sons, 1983.

De Ruiz, Dana, and Richard Larios. *La Causa: The Migrant Farmworkers' Story.* Illustrations by Rudy Gutierrez. Austin, Tex.: Raintree Steck-Vaughn, 1993.

De Sauza, James. *Brother Anansi and the Cattle Ranch.* Adapted by Harriet Rohmer. Illustrated by Stephen Von Mason. San Francisco and Emeryville, Calif.: Children's Book Press, 1989.

Dorris, Michael. *Guests.* New York: Hyperion Books for Children, 1994.

———. *Morning Girl.* New York: Hyperion Books for Children, 1992.

———. *Sees Behind Trees.* New York: Hyperion Books for Children, 1996.

Dorros, Arthur. *Abuela.* Illustrated by Elisa Kleven. New York: Dutton, 1991.

———. *Radio Man.* Translated by Sandra Marulanda Dorros. New York: HarperCollins, 1993.

Draper, Sharon. *Tears of a Tiger.* New York: Simon & Schuster, 1994.

Durkee, Noura. *Animals of Paradise.* Illustrated by Simon Trethewey. London: Hood Hood Books, 1997.

Echewa, T. Obinkaram. *The Magic Tree: A Folktale from Nigeria.* Illustrated by E. B. Lewis. New York: Morrow Junior Books, 1999.

Ehrlich, Amy. *Wounded Knee: An Indian History of the American West.* New York: Random House Children's Books, 1978.

Ellis, Deborah. *The Breadwinner.* Toronto: Groundwood Books, 2000.

———. *Mud City.* Toronto: Groundwood Books, 2003.

———. *Parvana's Journey.* Toronto: Groundwood Books, 2002.

English, Karen. *Francie.* New York: Farrar, Straus and Giroux, 1999.

Erdrich, Louise. *The Birchbark House.* New York: Hyperion Books for Children, 1999.

Esbensen, Barbara Juster. *The Star Maiden.* Illustrated by Helen K. Davie. Boston: Little, Brown, 1988.

Fang, Linda. *The Ch'i-Lin Purse: A Collection of Ancient Chinese Stories.* Illustrated by Jeanne M. Lee. New York: Farrar, Straus and Giroux, 1995.

Farmer, Nancy. *Casey Jones's Fireman: The Story of Sim Webb.* Illustrated by James Bernardin. New York: Phyllis Fogelman Books, 1999.

Flack, Marjorie. *The Story of Ping.* Illustrated by Kurt Weise. New York: Puffin, 1977.

Flake, Sharon. *The Skin I'm In.* New York: Hyperion, 1998.

Flournoy, Valerie. *Patchwork Quilt.* Illustrated by Jerry Pinkney. New York: Dial Books for Young Readers, 1985.

Forrester, Sandra. *Sound of Jubilee.* New York: Puffin, 1995.

Fox, Mary V. *Bette Bao Lord: Novelist and Chinese Voice for Change.* Chicago: Children's Press, 1993.

Freedman, Russell. *The Life and Death of Crazy Horse.* Illustrated by Amos Bad Heart Bull. New York: Holiday House, 1996.

Garland, Sherry. *Indio.* New York: Harcourt Brace, 1995.

———. *Song of the Buffalo Boy.* San Diego: Harcourt Brace Jovanovich, 1992.

Gates, Pamela S., Susan B. Steffel, and Francis J. Molson. *Fantasy Literature for Children and Young Adults.* Lanham, Md.: Scarecrow Press, 2003.

George, Jean C. *Julie of the Wolves.* New York: Harper & Row, 1972.

Gerson, Mary-Joan. *Fiesta Femenina: Celebrating Women in Mexican Folktale.* Illustrated by Maya Christina Gonzalez. New York: Barefoot Books, 2001.

Gerstein, Mordicai. *The Mountains of Tibet.* New York: Trumpet Club, 1987.

Ghazi, Suhaib Hamid. *Ramadan.* Illustrated by Omar Rayyan. New York: Holiday House, 1996.

Gillian, Maria M., and Jennifer Gillian, eds. *Unsettling America: An Anthology of Contemporary Multicultural Poetry.* New York: Penguin Books, 1994.

Giovanni, Nikki. *Ego-Tripping and Other Poems for Young People.* Illustrated by George Ford. New York: Lawrence Hill Books, 1993.

———. *Grand Fathers.* New York: Henry Holt, 1999.

———. *Knoxville, Tennessee.* Illustrated by Larry Johnson. New York: Scholastic Books for Children, 1994.

———. *Spin a Soft Black Song: Poems for Children.* New York: Hill and Wang, 1971.

———. *Vacation Time: Poems for Children.* New York: Morrow, 1980.

Goble, Paul. *Adopted by the Eagles.* New York: Aladdin Paperbacks, 1994.

———. *Buffalo Woman.* New York: Aladdin Books, 1984.

———. *The Gift of the Sacred Dog.* New York: Bradbury Press, 1985.

———. *The Great Race of the Birds and Animals.* New York: Aladdin Books, 1985.

———. *Iktomi and the Boulder.* New York: Orchard Books, 1988.

———. *Remaking the Earth: A Creation Story from the Great Plains of North America.* New York: Orchard Books, 1996.

———. *Star Boy.* New York: Aladdin Books, 1983.

Goldin, Barbara. *Red Means Good Fortune: A Story of San Francisco's Chinatown.* New York: Viking, 1994.

Graff, Nancy P. *Where the River Runs: A Portrait of a Refugee Family.* Photographs by Richard Howard. Boston: Little, Brown, 1993.

Greaves, Nick. *When Lion Could Fly and Other Tales from Africa.* Illustrated by Rod Clement. Hauppauge, N.Y.: Barron Educational Series, 1993.

Greenfield, Eloise. *Africa Dream.* Illustrated by Carole Byard. New York: HarperCollins, 1977.

———. *Daydreamers.* Illustrated by Tom Feelings. New York: Dial Books for Young Readers, 1981.

———. *For the Love of the Game: Michael Jordan and Me.* New York: HarperCollins, 1997.

———. *Grandpa's Face*. Illustrated by Floyd Cooper. New York: Philomel Books, 1988.

———. *Honey, I Love*. New York: HarperCollins, 1978.

———. *Nathaniel Talking*. New York: Black Butterfly Children's Books, 1988.

———. *Night on Neighborhood Street*. New York: Dial Books for Young Readers, 1991.

———. *Under the Sunday Tree*. New York: Harper & Row, 1988.

Grimes, Nikki. *Bronx Masquerade*. Illustrated by Javaka Steptoe. New York: Penguin Group, 2002.

———. *Come Sunday*. Illustrated by Michael Bryant. Grand Rapids, Mich.: W. B. Eerdmans, 1996.

———. *From a Child's Heart*. Illustrated by Brenda Joysmith. Orange, N.J.: Just Us Books, 1993.

———. *My Man Blue*. Illustrated by Jerome Lagarrigue. New York: Dial Books for Young Readers, 1999.

———. *A Pocketful of Poems*. Illustrated by Javaka Steptoe. New York: Clarion Books, 2001.

———. *Something on My Mind*. Illustrated by Tom Feelings. New York: Dial Books for Young Readers, 1999.

———. *Stepping Out with Grandma Mac*. Illustrated by Angelo. New York: Orchard Books, 2001.

———. *Wild, Wild Hair*. Illustrated by George Ford. New York: Scholastic, 1997.

Grossman, Virginia. *Ten Little Rabbits*. Illustrated by Sylvia Long. New York: Chronicle, 1998.

Hade, Daniel D. "Reading Multiculturally." In *Using Multiethnic Literature in the K-8 Classroom*. Ed. Violet Harris. Norwood, Mass.: Christopher-Gordon, 1997.

Hale, Janet Campbell. *The Owl's Song*. New York: Bantam, 1991.

Haley, Gail E. *A Story, A Story: An African Tale*. New York: Aladdin Books, 1970.

———. *Two Bad Boys: A Very Old Cherokee Tale*. New York: Dutton Children's Books, 1996.

Hamanaka, Sheila. *Screen of Frogs*. New York: Orchard Books, 1993.

Hamilton, Virginia. *Cousins*. New York: Putnam, 1990.

———. *The Dark Way: Stories from the Spirit World*. Illustrated by Lambert Davis. San Diego: Harcourt Brace Jovanovich, 1990.

———. *The Girl Who Spun Gold*. Illustrated by Leo and Diane Dillon. New York: Blue Sky Press, 2000.

———. *Her Stories: African American Folktales, Fairy Tales, and True Tale*. New York: Blue Sky Press, 1995.

———. *In the Beginning: Creation Stories from around the World*. Illustrated by Barry Moser. San Diego: Harcourt Brace Jovanovich, 1988.

———. *The Magical Adventures of Pretty Pearl*. New York: Harper & Row, 1983.

———. *M. C. Higgins the Great*. New York: Macmillan, 1974.

———. *The People Could Fly: American Black Folktales*. Illustrated by Leo and Diane Dillon. New York: Knopf, 1985.

———. *Plain City*. New York: Scholastic, 1993.

———. *Second Cousins*. New York: Scholastic, 1998.

———. *Sweet Whispers, Brother Rush*. New York: Philomel Books, 1982.

———. *When Birds Could Talk and Bats Could Sing*. Illustrated by Barry Moser. New York: Blue Sky Press, 1996.

Hamilton, Virginia, and Leo and Diane Dillon. *Drylongso*. Illustrated by Jerry Pinkney. New York: Harcourt Brace, 1992.

Han, Oki S. *Kongi and Potgi: A Cinderella Story from Korea*. New York: Dial Books, 1996.

Hansen, Joyce. *The Captive*. New York: Scholastic, 1994.

Hargrove, Jim. *Dr. An Wang: Computer Pioneer (People of Distinction)*. Chicago: Children's Press, 1993.

Harris, Violet, ed. *Using Multiethnic Literature in the K-8 Classroom*. Norwood, Mass.: Christopher-Gordon, 1997.

Haskins, James. *Against All Opposition: Black Explorers in America*. New York: Haskins, 1992.

———. *One More River to Cross: The Stories of Twelve Black Americans*. New York: Scholastic, 1992.

———. *Outward Dreams: Black Inventors and Their Inventions*. New York: Walker, 1991.

Heide, Florence Parry, and Judith Gilliland. *The Day of Ahmed's Secret*. Illustrated by Ted Lewin. New York: Lothrop, Lee & Shepard Books, 1990.

———. *The House of Wisdom*. Illustrated by Mary Grandpre. New York: Dorling Kindersley, 1999.

———. *Sami and the Time of the Troubles*. Illustrated by Ted Lewin. New York: Clarion Books, 1992.

Heyer, Marilee. *The Weaving of a Dream*. New York: Puffin Books, 1986.

Hickox, Rebecca. *The Golden Sandal: A Middle Eastern Cinderella Story*. Illustrated by Will Hillenbrand. New York: Holiday House, 1999.

Ho, Minfong, and Saphan Ros. *Brother Rabbit: A Cambodian Tale*. Illustrated by Jennifer Hewitson. New York: Lothrop, Lee & Shepard Books, 1997.

———. *The Clay Marble*. New York: Farrar, Straus and Giroux, 1991.

———. *Hush! A Thai Lullaby*. Illustrated by Holly Meade. New York: Scholastic, 1996.

———. *Maples in the Mist: Children's Poems from the Tang Dynasty*. Illustrated by Jean Tseng and Mou-sien Tseng. New York: Lothrop, Lee & Shepard Books, 1996.

Hoobler, Dorothy, and Thomas Hoobler. *The Chinese American Family Album*. London: Oxford University Press, 1994.

Hopkins, Lee Bennett. *Pass the Poetry, Please!* New York: Harper & Row, 1987.

Hopkinson, Deborah. *Sweet Clara and the Freedom Quilt*. New York: Knopf, 1993.

Houston, Gloria. *Bright Freedom's Song: A Story of the Underground Railroad*. New York: Harcourt Brace, 1998.

Houston, Jeanne Wakatsuki. *Farewell to Manzanar*. San Francisco: Bantam, 1973.

Hoyt-Goldsmith, Diane. *Celebrating Chinese New Year*. Illustrated by Lawrence Migdale. New York: Holiday House, 1998.

———. *Celebrating Hanukkah*. Illustrated by Lawrence Migdale. New York: Holiday House, 1996.

———. *Celebrating Kwanza*. Illustrated by Lawrence Migdale. New York: Holiday House, 1994.

———. *Day of the Dead*. Illustrated by Lawrence Migdale. New York: Holiday House, 1994.

———. *Las Posadas*. Illustrated by Lawrence Migdale. New York: Holiday House, 1999.

———. *Mardi Gras: A Cajun Celebration.* Illustrated by Lawrence Migdale. New York: Holiday House, 1995.

Hu, Jane Hwa. *Sojourner.* Baltimore, Md.: Noble House, 1994.

Hudson, Jan. *Sweetgrass.* New York: Scholastic, 1984.

Husain, Shahrukh. *What Do We Know about Islam?* Illustrated by Celia Hart. New York: Peter Bedrick Books, 1995.

Isadora, Rachel. *City Seen from A to Z.* New York: Greenwillow, 1983.

Jaffe, Nina. *The Golden Flower: A Taino Myth from Puerto Rico.* Illustrated by Enrique O. Sanchez. New York: Simon & Schuster Books for Young Readers, 1996.

Jeffers, Susan. *Brother Eagle, Sister Sky.* New York: Dial Books, 1991.

Jimenez, Francisco. *The Circuit.* New York: Houghton Mifflin, 1997.

Johnson, Angela. *The First Part Last.* New York: Simon & Schuster, 2003.

———. *Toning the Sweep.* New York: Orchard Books, 1995.

Johnson-Davies, Denys. *Rumi: Poet and Sage.* Illustrated by Laura De La Mare. London: Hood Hood Books, 1996.

Johnston, Tony. *The Tale of Rabbit and Coyote.* Illustrated by Tomie dePaola. New York: G. P. Putnam's Sons, 1994.

Kessler, Cristina. *One Night: A Story from the Desert.* Illustrated by Ian Schoenherr. New York: Philomel Books, 1995.

Khan, Rukhsana. *The Roses in My Carpets.* Illustrated by Ronald Himler. New York: Holiday House, 1998.

Kidd, Diana. *Onion Tears.* New York: Orchard Books, 1991.

Kimmel, Eric. *The Three Princes: A Middle Eastern Tale.* Illustrated by Leonard Everett Fisher. New York: Holiday House, 1994.

———. *Anansi and the Talking Melon.* Illustrated by Janet Stevens. New York: Holiday House, 1994.

King, Sandra. *Shannon: An Ojibway Dancer.* New York: Lerner, 1993.

Koram, Jamal, and Demba Mbengue. *Aesop: Tales of Aethiop the African,* vol. 1. Silver Spring, Md.: Sea Island Information Group, 1989.

Krull, Kathleen. *The Other Side: How Kids Live in a California Latino Neighborhood.* New York: Lodestar Books, 1994.

Kudlinski, Kathleen. *Rosa Parks: Young Rebel.* Illustrated by Meryl Henderson. New York: Aladdin Paperbacks, 2001.

Kurtz, Jane. *Pulling the Lion's Tail.* Illustrated by Floyd Cooper. New York: Simon & Schuster, 1995.

Kurtz, Jane. *Fire on the Mountain.* Illustrated by E. B. Lewis. New York: Simon & Schuster Books for Young Readers, 1994.

Lankford, Mary D. *Quinceanera: A Latina's Journey to Womanhood.* Brookfield, Conn.: Millbrook Press, 1994.

Lasky, Kathryn. *True North.* New York: Scholastic, 1996.

———. *Vision of Beauty: The Story of Sarah Breedlove Walker.* Illustrated by Nneka Bennett. New York: Candlewick, 2000.

Lee, Huy Voun. *At the Beach.* New York: Henry Holt, 1994

Lee, Jeanne M. *The Legend of the Li River: An Ancient Chinese Tale.* New York: Holt, Rinehart and Winston, 1983.

———. *The Song of Mu Lan.* Arden, N.C.: Front Street, 1995.

Lee, Marie G. *If It Hadn't Been for Yoon*. New York: Avon Books, 1993.

Lee, Wong Herbert. *A Drop of Rain*. Boston, Mass.: Houghton Mifflin, 1995.

Lester, Julius. *John Henry*. Illustrated by Jerry Pinkney. New York: Dial Books, 1994

————. *Sam and the Tigers: A New Telling of Little Black Sambo*. Illustrated by Jerry Pinkney. New York: Puffin Books, 1996.

————. *Uncle Remus: The Complete Tales*. Illustrated by Jerry Pinkney. New York: Dial Books for Young Readers, 1999.

Levine, Anna. *Running on Eggs*. New York: Cricket Books, 1999.

Lewin, Ted. *The Storytellers*. Illustrated by Ted Lewin. New York: Lothrop, Lee & Shepard Books, 1998.

Lewis, Richard. *Miracles: Poems by Children of the English-Speaking World*. New York: Simon & Schuster, 1984.

Lord, Bette Bao. *In the Year of the Boar and Jackie Robinson*. New York: HarperCollins, 1984.

Louie, Ai-Ling. *Yeh-Shen: A Cinderella Story from China*. Illustrated by Ed Young. New York: Philomel Books, 1982.

Lunge-Larsen, Lise, and Margi Preus. *The Legend of the Lady Slipper: An Ojibwe Tale*. Illustrated by Andrea Arroyo. Boston: Houghton Mifflin, 1999.

Lyons, Mary E. *Letters from a Slave Girl: The Story of Harriet Jacobs*. New York: Scribner, 1992.

————. *Sorrow's Kitchen: The Life and Folklore of Zora Neale Hurston*. New York: Charles Scribner's Sons, 1990.

Maalouf, Amin, and Jon Rothschild. *The Crusades Through Arab Eyes*. London: Schocken Books, 1989.

MacDonald, Fiona. *A 16th Century Mosque*. Illustrated by Mark Bergin. New York: P. Bedrick Books, 1994.

Mado, Michio. *The Animals: Selected Poems*. New York: McElderry Books, 1992.

Mah, Adeline Y. *Chinese Cinderella*. New York: Delacorte Press, 1999.

————. *Falling Leaves: The Memoir of an Unwanted Chinese Daughter*. New York: Wiley, 1998.

Mahy, Margaret. *Seven Chinese Brothers*. New York: Scholastic Paperbacks, 1992.

Malone, Mary. *Maya Lin: Architect and Artist*. Berkeley Heights, N.J.: Enslow, 1995.

Malotki, Ekkehart. *The Mouse Couple*. Illustrated by Michael Lacapa. Flagstaff, Ariz.: Northland Press, 1988.

Marshall, Julia. *Suleiman the Magnificent: The Story of Istanbul*. London: Hood Hood Books, 2002.

Martin, Francesca. *Clever Tortoise: A Traditional African Tale*. Cambridge, Mass.: Candlewick Press, 2000.

Martin, Rafe. *The Boy Who Lived with the Seals*. Illustrated by David Shannon. New York: G. P. Putnam's Sons, 1993.

————. *Mysterious Tales of Japan*. Illustrated by Tatsuro Kiuchi. New York: G. P. Putnam's Sons, 1996.

————. *The Rough-Face Girl*. New York: Scholastic, 1992.

Martinez, Elizabeth Coonrod. *Coming to America: The Mexican-American Experience*. Brookfield, Conn.: Millbrook Press, 1995.

Mathis, Sharon Bell. *The Hundred Penney Box*. New York: Viking, 1975.

Matthews, Mary. *Magid Fasts for Ramadan.* Illustrated by E. B. Lewis. New York: Clarion Books, 1996.

McDermott, Gerald. *Arrow to the Sun: A Pueblo Indian Tale.* New York: Puffin Books, 1974.

———. *Coyote: Trickster Tale from the American Southwest.* San Diego: Harcourt Brace, 1994.

———. *Raven: Trickster Tale from the Pacific Northwest.* San Diego: Harcourt Brace, 1993.

———. *Zomo, The Rabbit: Trickster Tale from West Africa.* San Diego: Harcourt Brace, 1993.

McKissack, Fredrick. *Black Hoops: The History of African Americans in Basketball.* New York: Scholastic, 1999.

McKissack, Patricia. *The Dark-Thirty: Southern Tales of the Supernatural.* Illustrated by Brian Pinkney. New York: Knopf, 1992.

———. *A Million Fish . . . More or Less.* Illustrated by Dena Schutzer. New York: Knopf, 1992.

———. *Mirandy and Brother Wind.* Illustrated by Jerry Pinkney. New York: Knopf, 1988.

McKissack, Patricia, and Fredrick McKissack. *Black Hands, White Sails: The Story of African American Whalers.* New York: Scholastic Press, 1999.

———. *Christmas in the Big House, Christmas in the Quarters.* New York: Scholastic, 1994.

———. *Rebels against Slavery.* New York: Scholastic, 1996.

———. *Sojourner Truth: Ain't I a Woman?* New York: Scholastic, 1992.

McMane, Fred. *Hakeem Olajawon.* New York: Chelsea Books, 1999.

Mead, Alice. *Junebug.* New York: Bantam, 1995.

Medearis, Angela Shelf. *Too Much Talk.* Illustrated by Stefano Vitale. Cambridge, Mass.: Candlewick Press, 1995.

Miller, William. *Zora Hurston and the Chinaberry Tree.* New York: Lee & Low Books, 1994.

Mochizuki, Ken. *Baseball Saved Us.* Illustrated by Dom Lee. New York: Scholastic, 1993.

———. *Beacon Hill Boys.* New York: Scholastic, 2002.

———. *Heroes.* Illustrated by Dom Lee. New York: Lee & Low Books, 1995.

Mohr, Nicholasa. *All for the Better: A Story of El Barrio.* Austin, Tex.: Raintree Steck-Vaughn, 1993.

———. *Felita.* New York: Dial Press, 1976.

———. *Going Home.* New York: Dial Books for Young Readers, 1986.

———. *In Nueva York.* Houston, Tex.: Arte Publico Press, 1988.

———. *Nilda.* New York: Harper & Row, 1973.

———. *Old Letivia and the Mountain of Sorrows.* Illustrated by Rudy Gutierrez. New York: Penguin Books, 1996.

Monceaux, Morgan, and Ruth Katcher. *My Heroes, My People: African Americans and Native Americans in the West.* Illustrated by Morgan Monceaux. New York: Farrar, Straus and Giroux 1999.

Mora, Pat. *Confetti: Poems for Children.* New York: Lee & Low Books, 1996.

———. *Listen to the Desert.* New York: Clarion Books, 1994.

Myers, Walter Dean. *The Beast.* New York: Scholastic, 2003.

————. *Brown Angels: An Album of Pictures and Verses.* New York: HarperCollins, 1993.

————. *Crystal.* New York: Viking, 1987.

————. *Fast Sam, Cool Clyde, and Stuff.* New York: Viking, 1975.

————. *The Greatest—Muhammad Ali.* New York: Scholastic, 2001.

————. *Harlem.* New York: Scholastic Press, 1997.

————. *Hoops.* New York: Delacorte, 1981.

————. *Malcolm X: A Fire Burning Brightly.* Illustrated by Leonard Jenkins. New York: HarperCollins, 2000.

————. *Malcolm X: By Any Means Necessary.* New York: Scholastic Trade, 1993.

————. *Me, Mop, and the Moondance Kid.* New York: Delacorte, 1988.

————. *Monster.* New York: HarperCollins, 1999.

————. *Mop, Moondance, and the Nagasaki Knights.* New York: Delacorte, 1992.

————. *The Mouse Rap.* New York: Harper & Row, 1990.

————. *Now Is Your Time! The African-American Struggle for Freedom.* New York: HarperCollins, 1991.

————. *The Outside Shot.* New York: Delacorte, 1984.

————. *Scorpions.* New York: Harper & Row, 1988.

————. *SLAM!* New York: Scholastic, 1996.

————. *Somewhere in Darkness.* New York: Scholastic, 1992.

————. *Won't Know until I Get There.* New York: Viking, 1982.

Naff, Alixa. *The Arab Americans.* New York: Chelsea House, 1988.

Namioka, Lensey. *April and the Dragon Lady.* New York: Harcourt Brace, 1994

————. *Half and Half.* New York: Delacorte, 2003.

————. *Ties That Bind, Ties That Break.* New York: Delacorte Press, 1999.

————. *Yang the Eldest and His Odd Jobs.* New York: Yearling, 2002.

————. *Yang the Second and Her Secret Admirers.* New York: Little, Brown, 1998.

————. *Yang the Third and Her Impossible Family.* New York: Little, Brown, 1995.

————. *Yang the Youngest and His Terrible Ear.* New York: Little, Brown, 1992.

Nye, Naomi Shihab. *Come with Me: Poems for a Journey.* New York: Greenwillow Books, 2000.

————. *The Flag of Childhood: Poems from the Middle East.* New York: Aladdin Paperbacks, 2002.

————. *Habibi.* New York: Simon & Schuster, 1997.

————. *19 Varieties of Gazelle: Poems of the Middle East.* New York: Greenwillow Books, 2002.

————. *Salting the Ocean: 100 Poems by Young Poets.* New York: Greenwillow Books, 2000.

————. *Sitti's Secrets.* Illustrated by Nancy Carpenter. New York: Simon & Schuster, 1994.

————. *The Space between Our Footsteps: Poems and Paintings from the Middle East.* New York: Simon & Schuster, 1998.

————. *This Same Sky: A Collection of Poems from around the World.* New York: Aladdin Paperbacks, 1992.

————. *The Tree Is Older Than You Are: A Bilingual Gathering of Poems and Stories from Mexico with Paintings by Mexican Artists.* New York: Aladdin Paperbacks, 1995.

————, comp. *What Have You Lost?* New York: Greenwillow Books, 1999.

O'Dell, Scott. *Carlota.* Boston: Houghton Mifflin, 1981.

Opie, Iona, and Peter Opie. *The Classic Fairy Tales.* London: Oxford University Press, 1974.

Oppenheim, Shulamith Levey. *The Hundredth Name.* Illustrated by Michael Hays. Honesdale, Pa.: Boyds Mills Press, 1995.

Ortiz, Simon. *The People Shall Continue.* Illustrated by Sharol Graves. San Francisco: Children's Book Press, 1988.

Osborne, Mary Pope. *One World, Many Religions: The Way We Worship.* New York: Knopf Books for Young Readers, 1996.

Osofsky, Audrey. *Dreamcatcher.* Illustrated by Ed Young. New York: Orchard Books, 1992.

Oughton, Jerrie. *How the Stars Fell into the Sky.* Illustrated by Lisa Desmini. Boston: Houghton Mifflin, 1992.

Parks, Rosa, and Jim Haskins. *Rosa Parks: My Story.* New York: Dial Books, 1992.

Parks, Van Dyke. *Jump Again! More Adventures of Brer Rabbit.* Illustrated by Barry Moser. San Diego: Harcourt Brace Jovanovich, 1987.

Parks, Van Dyke, and Malcolm Jones. *Jump!* Illustrated by Barry Moser. San Diego: Harcourt Brace Jovanovich, 1986.

Patterson, Katherine. *Jip: His Story.* New York: Lodestar Books, 1996.

Paulsen, Gary. *Harris and Me.* New York: Yearling, 1995.

———. *Nightjohn.* New York: Delacorte Press, 1993.

———. *Sarny.* New York: Delacorte Press, 1997.

Pena, Sylvia Cavozos, ed. *Kikiriki: Stories and Poems in English and Spanish for Children.* Houston, Tex.: Arte Publico Press, 1987.

———. *Tun-ta-ca-tun: More Stories and Poems in English and Spanish.* Houston: Arte Publico Press, 1986.

Philip, Neil. *Earth Always Endures.* New York: Penguin, 1996.

Piggott, Juliet. *Mexican Folk Tales.* Illustrated by John Spencer. New York: Crane Russak, 1976.

Pinkney, Andrea Davis. *Duke Ellington.* Illustrated by Brian Pinkney. New York: Hyperion, 1998.

———. *Hold Fast to Dreams.* New York: William Morrow, 1995.

———. *Silent Thunder: A Civil War Story.* New York: Hyperion, 1999

Pinkney, Brian. *Cosmo and the Robot.* New York: HarperCollins, 2000.

Pitcher, Diana. *Tokoloshi: African Folk Tales.* Illustrated by Meg Rutherford. Millbrae, Calif.: A Dawne-Leigh Book, 1980.

Pitre, Felix. *Paco and the Witch.* Illustrated by Christy Hale. New York: Lodestar Books, 1995.

Pitts, Paul. *Racing the Sun.* New York: Avon, 1988.

Polacco, Patricia. *Pink and Say.* New York: Philomel Books, 1994.

Pomerantz, Charlotte. *If I Had a Paka: Poems in Eleven Languages.* New York: Greenwillow Books, 1982.

———. *The Tamarindo Puppy and Other Poems.* New York: Greenwillow Books, 1980.

Poole, Amy Lowry. *How the Rooster Got His Crown.* New York: Holiday House, 1999.

Porter, A. P. *Jump at de Sun: The Story of Zora Neale Hurston.* Minneapolis, Minn.: Carolrhoda Books, 1992.

Power, Susan. *The Grass Dancer.* New York: Berkley Books, 1997.

Ramirez, Michael Rose. *The Legend of the Hummingbird: A Tale from Puerto Rico.* Illustrated by Magaret Sanfilippo. Greenvale, N.Y.: Mondo Publishing, 1998.

Rappaport, Doreen. *Freedom River.* Illustrated by Bryan Collier. New York: Hyperion, 2000.

Reiser, Lynn. *Tortillas and Lullabies.* Illustrated by Corazones Valientes. New York: Greenwillow Books, 1998.

Riley, Gail. B. *Wah Ming Chang: Artist and Master of Special Effects.* Berkeley Heights, N.J.: Enslow, 1995.

Ringgold, Faith. *If a Bus Could Talk: The Story of Rosa Parks.* New York: Simon & Schuster, 1999.

Roessel, Monty. *Kinaalda: A Navajo Girl Grows Up.* Minneapolis, Minn.: Lerner, 1993.

Rohmer, Harriet. *The Legend of Food Mountain.* Illustrated by Graciela Carrillo. San Francisco: Children's Book Press, 1982.

———. *Uncle Nacho's Hat.* Illustrated by Mira Reisberg. San Francisco: Children's Book Press, 1989.

Ruffin, Frances E. *Martin Luther King, Jr. and the March on Washington.* Illustrated by Stephen Marchesi. New York: Grosset & Dunlap, 2001.

Rumford, James. *Traveling Man: The Journey of Ibn Battuta, 1325–1354.* Illustrated by James Rumford. Boston, Mass.: Houghton Mifflin, 2001.

Sabin, Louis. *Roberto Clemente: Young Baseball Hero.* Illustrated by Marie Dejohn. New York: Troll, 1997.

Salisbury, Graham. *Under the Blood Red Sun.* New York: Delacorte Press, 1994.

Sanford, William R. *Chief Joseph: Nez Percé Warrior.* Berkeley Heights, N.J.: Enslow, 1994.

———. *Crazy Horse: Sioux Warrior.* Berkeley Heights, N.J.: Enslow, 1994.

———. *Osceola: Seminole Warrior.* Berkeley Heights, N.J.: Enslow, 1994.

———. *Quannah Parker: Comanche Warrior.* Berkeley Heights, N.J.: Enslow, 1994.

———. *Sitting Bull: Sioux Warrior.* Berkeley Heights, N.J.: Enslow, 1994.

San Souci, Robert. *Cendrillon: A Caribbean Cinderella.* Illustrated by Brian Pinkney. New York: Simon & Schuster Books for Young Readers, 1998.

———. *Sootface: An Ojibwa Cinderella Story.* Illustrated by Daniel San Souci. New York: Bantam Doubleday Dell Books for Young Readers, 1994.

———. *Sukey and the Mermaid.* Illustrated by Brian Pinkney. New York: Four Winds Press, 1992.

———. *The Talking Eggs.* Illustrated by Jerry Pinkney. New York: Dial Books for Young Readers, 1989.

Santiago, Esmeralda. *Almost a Woman.* New York: Vintage Books, 1998.

———. *When I Was Puerto Rican.* New York: Vintage Books, 1993.

Say, Allen. *El Chino.* Boston: Houghton Mifflin, 1990.

———. *Emma's Rug.* Boston: Houghton Mifflin, 1996.

———. *Grandfather's Journey.* Boston: Houghton Mifflin, 1993.

———. *Kamishibai.* Boston: Houghton Mifflin, 2005.

———. *Music for Alice.* Boston: Houghton Mifflin, 2004.

———. *The Sign Painter.* Boston: Houghton Mifflin, 2000.

———. *Stranger in the Mirror.* Boston: Houghton Mifflin, 1998.

————. *Tea with Milk.* Boston: Houghton Mifflin, 1999.

————. *Under the Cherry Blossom Tree.* Boston: Houghton Mifflin, 2005.

Schmidt, Jeremy. *Two Lands, One Heart: An American Boy's Journey to His Mother's Vietnam.* Illustrated by Ted Wood. New York: Walker, 1995.

Schroeder, Alan. *Lily and the Wooden Bowl.* Illustrated by Yoriko Ito. New York: Bantam Doubleday Dell Books for Young Readers, 1994.

Scott, Ann Herbert. *In My Mother's Lap.* Illustrated by Glo Coalson. New York: Clarion, 2000.

Sebestyen, Ouida. *Words by Heart.* New York: Little, Brown, 1979.

Shah, Idries. *The Boy without a Name.* Illustrated by Mona Caron. Cambridge, Mass.: Hoopoe Books, 2000.

Shepard, Aaron. *Master Man: A Tall Tale of Nigeria.* Illustrated by David Wisniewski. New York: HarperCollins, 2001.

Shepard, Sandy. *Myths and Legends: Around the World.* New York: Simon & Schuster Children's Publishing, 1995.

Siegelson, Kim L. *In the Time of the Drums.* Illustrated by Brian Pinkney. New York: Hyperion Books for Children, 1999.

Sierra, Judy. *Wiley and the Hairy Man.* Illustrated by Brian Pinkney. New York: Lodestar Books, 1996.

Silverstein, Shel. *The Giving Tree.* New York: Harper & Row, 1964.

Slipperjack, Ruby. *Honour the Sun.* Winnipeg: Pemmican, 1987.

Sloat, Teri. *The Eye of the Needle.* New York: Dutton Children's Books, 1990.

Smith, David. *If the World Were a Village.* Illustrated by Shelagh Armstrong. Toronto: Kids Can Press, 2002.

Smith, Henrietta M., ed. *The Coretta Scott King Awards Book: From Vision to Reality.* Chicago: American Library Association, 1994.

Smith, Will. *Just the Two of Us.* New York: Scholastic Press, 1980.

Sneve, Virginia Driving Hawk. *Dancing Teepees: Poems of American Indian Youth.* New York: Holiday House, 1989.

————. *The Hopis.* Illustrated by Ronald Himler. New York: Holiday House, 1995.

————. *The Iroquois.* Illustrated by Ronald Himler. New York: Holiday House, 1995.

————. *The Navajos.* Illustrated by Ronald Himler. New York: Holiday House, 1993.

————. *The Nez Percé.* Illustrated by Ronald Himler. New York: Holiday House, 1994.

————. *The Sioux.* Illustrated by Ronald Himler. New York: Holiday House, 1994.

————. *The Trickster and the Troll.* Lincoln: University of Nebraska Press, 1997.

————. *The Twelve Moons.* New York: Houghton Mifflin, 1977.

Snyder, Dianne. *The Boy of the Three-Year Nap.* Illustrated by Allen Say. Boston: Houghton Mifflin, 1988.

Soto, Gary. *Baseball in April.* New York: Harcourt Brace, 1990.

————. *Canto Familiar.* New York: Harcourt Brace, 1995.

————. *A Fire in My Hands: A Book of Poems.* New York: Scholastic, 1990.

————. *Jesse.* New York: Harcourt Brace, 1994.

————. *Neighborhood Odes.* New York: Scholastic, 1992.

————. *Taking Sides.* New York: Harcourt Brace, 1991.

————. *Too Many Tamales.* Illustrated by Ed Martinez. New York: Putnam, 1993.

Souhami, Jessica. *The Leopard's Drum: An Asante Tale from West Africa.* Boston: Little, Brown, 1995.

Stamm, Claus. *Three Strong Women: A Tall Tale from Japan.* Illustrated by Jean Tseng, Mou-sien Tseng, and Kazue Mizumura. New York: Viking, 1990.

Staples, Suzanne Fisher. *Haveli.* New York: Knopf, 1993.

———. *Shabanu.* New York: Knopf, 1989.

———. *Shiva's Fire.* New York: Farrar, Straus and Giroux, 2000.

Steptoe, John. *Mufaro's Beautiful Daughters: An African Tale.* New York: Lothrop, Lee & Shepard Books, 1987.

———. *The Story of Jumping Mouse: A Native American Legend.* New York: Lothrop, Lee & Shepard Books, 1972.

Sterling, Shirley. *My Name Is Seepeetza.* Vancouver: Groundwood Press, 1992.

Stevens, Janet. *Coyote Steals the Blanket: A Ute Tale.* New York: Holiday House Book, 1993.

Stolz, Mary. *Cezanne Pinto: A Memoir.* New York: Knopf: Distributed by Random House, 1994.

———. *Storm in the Night.* Illustrated by Pat Cummings. New York: Harper & Row, 1988.

Strickland, Dorothy S., and Michael R. Strickland, comps. *Families: Poems Celebrating the African American Experience.* Honesdale, Pa.: Wordsong Boyds Mills Press, 1994.

Surat, Michele Marie. *Angel Child, Dragon Child.* Illustrated by Mai Vo-Dinh. New York: Scholastic, 1989.

Talbert, Marc. *A Sunburned Prayer.* New York: Simon & Schuster, 1995.

Talltree, Robert. *The Legend of Spinoza: The Bear Who Speaks from the Heart.* St. Paul, Minn.: Universal Tradewinds, 1995.

Tan, Amy. *The Chinese Siamese Cat.* Illustrated by Gretchen Schields. New York: Aladdin Books, 2001.

Tao, Wang. *Exploration into China.* New York: Chelsea House Publications, 2000.

Tapahonso, Luci. *Navajo ABC: A Diné Alphabet Book.* Las Vegas: Sagebrush Press, 1999.

Taylor, Ann. *Baby Dance.* New York: HarperFestival, 1999.

Taylor, Harriet Peck. *Brother Wolf: A Seneca Tale.* New York: Farrar, Straus and Giroux, 1996.

Taylor, Mildred. *The Friendship.* New York; Puffin, 1987.

———. *Let the Circle Be Unbroken.* New York: Dial Press, 1981.

———. *The Mississippi Bridge.* New York: Dial Books for Young Readers, 1990.

———. *Roll of Thunder, Hear My Cry.* New York: Dial Press, 1976.

———. *Song of the Trees.* New York: Bantam Skylark, 1975.

———. *The Well: David's Story.* New York: Dial Books for Young Readers, 1995.

Temple, Frances. *Tiger Soup: An Anansi Story from Jamaica.* New York: Orchard Books, 1994.

Uchida, Yoshiko. *The Dancing Kettle and Other Japanese Folk Tales.* Illustrated by Richard C. Jones. New York: Harcourt, Brace & World, 1949.

———. *The Invisible Thread: An Autobiography.* Englewood Cliffs, N.J.: Messner, 1991.

———. *Journey Home.* New York: McElderry Books, 1978.

———. *Journey to Topaz: A Story of the Japanese American Evacuation.* Berkeley, Calif.: Creative Arts, 1985.

———. *The Magic Listening Cap: More Folk Tales from Japan.* New York: Harcourt, Brace, 1955.

————. *The Magic Purse.* Illustrated by Keiko Narahashi. New York: McElderry Books, 1993.

————. *The Sea of Gold and Other Tales from Japan.* Illustrated by Marianne Yamaguchi. New York: Charles Scribner's Sons, 1965.

————. *The Two Foolish Cats: Suggested by a Japanese Folktale.* Illustrated by Margo Zemach. New York: McElderry Books, 1987.

————. *The Wise Old Woman.* Illustrated by Martin Springett. New York: McElderry Books, 1994.

Velasquez, Gloria. *Ankiza.* Houston, Tex.: Pinata Books, 2000.

————. *Teen Angel.* Houston, Tex.: Pinata Books, 2003.

Wade, Mary D. *Guadalupe Quintanilla: Leader of the Hispanic Community.* Springfield, N.J.: Enslow, 1995.

Walker, Paul R. *Pride of Puerto Rico: The Life of Roberto Clemente.* San Diego: Harcourt Brace Jovanovich, 1988.

Wallis, Velma. *Bird Girl.* New York: HarperCollins, 1996.

Walter, Mildred P. *Mississippi Challenge.* New York: Aladdin Paperbacks, 1992.

Wargin, Kathy-jo. *The Legend of Mackinac Island.* Illustrated by Gijsbert van Frankenhuyzen. Chelsea, Mich.: Sleeping Bear Press, 1999.

————. *The Legend of Sleeping Bear.* Illustrated by Gijsbert van Frankenhuyzen. Chelsea, Mich.: Sleeping Bear Press, 1998.

Waters, Kate, and Madeline Slovenz-Low. *Lion Dancer: Ernie Wan's Chinese New Year.* New York: Scholastic, 1990.

Watkins, Yoko Kawashima. *Tales from the Bamboo Grove.* Illustrated by Jean Tseng and Mou-sien Tseng. New York: Bradbury Press, 1992.

Weidt, Maryann N. *Voice of Freedom: A Story about Frederick Douglass.* Illustrated by Jeni Reeves. New York: Carolrhoda Books, 2001.

Weiss-Armush, Anne Marie. *Arabian Cuisine.* Illustrated by John Berry. Beirut, Lebanon : Dar An-nafaés, 1984

Whelan, Gloria. *Goodbye, Vietnam.* New York: Dell Yearling, 2000.

White Deer of Autumn. *Ceremony—In the Circle of Life.* Illustrated by Daniel San Souci. Hillsboro, Ore.: Beyond Words Publishing, 1983.

White, Elwyn B. *Charlotte's Web.* New York: Harper, 1952.

Winter, Janette. *Follow the Drinking Gourd.* New York: Knopf, 1988.

Wolkstein, Diane. *Bouki Dances the Kokioko: A Comical Tale from Haiti.* Illustrated by Jesse Sweetwater. New York: Gulliver Books, Harcourt Brace, 1997.

Wong, Janet. *Good Luck Gold and Other Poems.* New York: McElderry Books, 1994.

————. *Night Garden: Poems from the World of Dreams.* New York: McElderry Books, 2000.

————. *The Rainbow Hand: Poems about Mothers and Children.* New York: McElderry Books, 1999.

Wood, Nancy. *Hollering Sun.* New York: Simon & Schuster, 1972.

————. *Spirit Walker.* New York: Doubleday Books for Young Readers, 1993.

————. *War Cry on a Prayer Feather: Prose and Poetry of the Ute Indians.* Garden City, N.Y.: Doubleday, 1979.

Wood, Ted. *A Boy Becomes a Man at Wounded Knee.* New York: Walker, 1992.

Woodson. Jacqueline. *Behind You.* New York: Puffin, 2004.

————. *Between Madison and Palmetto*. New York: Penguin, 1993.

————. *The Dear One*. New York: Delacorte, 1991.

————. *From the Notebooks of Melanin Sun*. New York: Scholastic, 1995.

————. *The House You Pass on the Way*. New York: Bantam, 1997.

————. *Hush*. New York: Penguin, 2003.

————. *If You Come Softly*. New York: Puffin, 2000.

————. *I Hadn't Meant to Tell You This*. New York: Delacorte, 1994.

————. *The Last Summer with Maizon*. New York: Delacorte, 1990.

————. *Lena*. New York: Delacorte, 1999.

————. *Locomotion*. New York: Putnam, 2003.

————. *Maizon at Blue Hill*. New York: Delacorte, 1992.

————. *Miracle's Boys*. New York: Putnam, 2000.

————. *The Other Side*. New York: Putnam, 2001.

Wormser, Richard. *American Islam: Growing Up Muslim in America*. New York: Walker, 1994.

Yacowitz, Caryn. *The Jade Stone: A Chinese Folktale*. Illustrated by Ju-Hong Chen. New York: Holiday House, 1992.

Yep, Laurence. *American Dragons: Twenty-five Asian American Voices*. New York: HarperCollins, 1993.

————. *The Case of the Firecrackers*. New York: HarperCollins, 1999.

————. *The Case of the Goblin Pearls*. New York: HarperTrophy, 1998.

————. *The Case of the Lion Dance*. New York: HarperTrophy, 1999.

————. *Child of the Owl*. New York: HarperTrophy, 1977.

————. *The Dragon Prince: A Chinese Beauty and the Beast Tale*. Illustrated by Kam Mak. New York: HarperCollins, 1997.

————. *Dragon's Gate*. New York: HarperCollins, 1993.

————. *Dragonwings*. New York: Harper, 1975.

————. *Ghost Fox*. Illustrated by Jean Tseng and Mou-sien Tseng. New York: Scholastic Books, 1994.

————. *The Junior Thunder Lord*. Illustrated byRobert Van Nutt. New York: Bridgewater Books, 1994.

————. *The Khan's Daughter: A Mongolian Folktale*. Illustrated by Mou-sien Tseng. New York: Scholastic Press, 1997.

————. *The Lost Garden*. Englewood Cliffs, N.J.: Messner, 1991.

————. *The Man Who Tricked a Ghost*. Illustrated by Isadore Seltzer. Mahwah, N.J.: Bridgewater Press, 1993.

————. *The Rainbow People*. Illustrated by David Wiesner. New York: Harper & Row, 1989.

————. *Ribbons*. New York: Putnam, 1996.

————. *Sea Glass*. New York: HarperCollins, 1979.

————. *The Shell Woman and the King*. Illustrated by Yang Ming-Yi. New York: Dial Books for Young Readers, 1993.

————. *The Star Fisher*. New York: Morrow Junior Books, 1991.

————. *Thief of Hearts*. New York: HarperCollins, 1995.

————. *Tongues of Jade*. New York: HarperCollins, 1991.

Yolen, Jane. *The Devil's Arithmetic*. New York: Viking Kestrel, 1988.

―――. *The Emperor and the Kite*. New York: Putnam Juvenile, 1998.

―――. *Encounter.* Illustrated by David Shannon. New York: Harcourt, 1993.

Yopp, Ruth, and Hallie K. Yopp. *Literature-Based Reading Activities*. 3rd ed. Boston, Mass.: Allyn and Bacon, 2001.

Young, Ed. *Lon Po Po: A Red-Riding Hood Story from China*. New York: Philomel Books, 1989.

―――. *Night Visitors*. New York: Philomel Books, 1995.

Zeman, Linda. *Sindbad*. Illustrated by Linda Zeman. Toronto: Tundra Books, 1999.

Zhang, Song Nan. *The Children of China*. Illustrated by Song Nan Zhang. Plattsburgh, N.Y.: Tundra Books, 1995.

Ziner, Feenie. *Cricket Boy: A Chinese Tale*. Illustrated by Ed Young. Garden City, N.Y.: Doubleday, 1977.

PROFESSIONAL RESOURCES

Banks, J. A. "Multicultural Citizenship Education." In *Teaching and Learning in the New Millennium*, Ed. Barbara Day, 54–61. Indianapolis, Ind.: Kappa Delta Pi, 1999.

Bishop, Rudine S. "Multicultural Literature for Children: Making Informed Choices." In *Teaching Multicultural Literature in Grades K–8*. Ed. V. J. Harris, 37–54. Norwood, Mass.: Christopher-Gordon, 1993.

Bloom, Jonathan, and Sheila S. Blair. *Islam: A Thousand Years of Faith and Power*. New Haven, Conn., and London: Yale University Press, 2002.

―――. *Islamic Arts: Art and Ideas*. London: Phaidon Press, 1997.

Cai, Mingshui. *Multicultural Literature for Children and Young Adults*. London: Greenwood Press, 2002.

Cianciolo, Patricia, and M. E. VanCamp. *The Analysis of Commonly Used Curriculum Materials*. East Lansing: Michigan State University Center for Learning and Teaching Elementary Subjects, 1991.

Cullinan, Bernice. *Literature and the Child*. New York: Harcourt Brace Jovanovich, 1989, 1994, 1998, 2001.

Esposito, John., ed. *The Oxford History of Islam*. New York. Oxford University Press, 2000.

Gates, Pamela S., Susan B. Steffel, and Francis J. Molson. *Fantasy Literature for Children and Young Adults*. Lanham, Md.: Scarecrow Press, 2003.

Gates-Duffield, Pamela. *A Qualitative Analysis of the Use of Language Arts Instruction in Two Sixth-Grade Classrooms to Develop Awareness and Understanding of Cultural Diversity*. PhD Diss. East Lansing: Michigan State University, 1993.

Goodwin, Jan. *Price of Honor: Muslim Women Lift the Veil of Silence on the Islamic World*. New York: Plume, 1995.

Grant, Carl A., and Mary Louise Gomez, eds. *Campus and Classroom: Making Schooling Multicultural*. 2nd ed. Upper Saddle River, N.J.: Merrill-Prentice, 2001.

Harris, Violet J., ed. *Using Multiethnic Literature in the K-8 Classroom*. Norwood, Mass.: Christopher-Gordon, 1997.

Hawisher, Gail, and Anna O. Soter, eds. *On Literacy and Its Teaching: Issues in English Education*. Albany: State University of New York Press, 1990.

Keats, Ezra Jack. *Snowy Day*. New York: Viking, 1962.

Klein, T. "Facing History at South Boston High School." *English Journal* 82, no. 2 (1993).

Larrick, Nancy. "The All-White World of Children's Books." *Saturday Review* 11 (September 1965).

Lunde, Paul. *Islam*. London: Dorling Kindersley, 2002.

Naidoo, Beverley. *Through Whose Eyes? Exploring Racism: Reader, Text, and Context*. Staffordshire, England: Trentham Books, 1992.

Nieto, Sonia. *Affirming Diversity: The Sociopolitical Context of Multicultural Education*. New York: Longman, 1992.

Probst, Robert. *Response and Analysis: Teaching Literature in Junior and Senior High School*. Portsmouth, N.H.: Heinemann, 1988.

Rosenblatt, Louise M. *The Reader, the Text, the Poem: The Transactional Theory of the Literary Work*. Carbondale: Southern Illinois University Press, 1978.

Talbert, Marc. "What Is a Mirror to Do?" *ALAN Review* 24, no. 1 (1996): 2–6.

Terrill, Margueritte, and Dianne L. H. Mark. "Preservice Teachers' Expectations for Schools with Children of Color and Second-Language Learners." *Journal of Teacher Education* 51, no. 2 (2000): 149–55.

Yolen, Jane. "Taking Time: Or How Things Have Changed in the Thirty-five Years of Children's Publishing." *New Advocate* 1997.

REFERENCES BY CULTURAL GROUP

African American

Aardema, Verna, and Marc Brown. *Oh, Kojo! How Could You!* New York: Dial Books for Young Readers, 1984.

Aardema, Verna, and Nancy Clouse. *Sebgugugu, The Glutton: A Bantu Tale from Rwanda*. Grand Rapids, Mich.: W. B. Eerdmans, 1993.

Adler, David. *A Picture Book of George Washington Carver*. New York: Holiday House, 1999.

———. *A Picture Book of Jesse Owens*. New York: Holiday House, 1992.

Adoff, Arnold. *All the Colors of the Race*. New York: Lothrop, Lee & Shepard Books, 1982.

———. *Black Is Brown Is Tan*. New York: Harper & Row, 1973.

———. *Black Out Loud: An Anthology of Modern Poems by Black Americans*. New York: Macmillan, 1970.

———. *Eats*. Illustrated by Susan Russo. New York: Mulberry Books, 1979.

———. *I Am the Darker Brother: An Anthology of Modern Poems by Negro Americans*. New York: Macmillan, 1968.

———. *In for Winter, Out for Spring*. New York: Harcourt Brace Jovanovich, 1991.

———. *Outside Inside Poems*. New York: Lothrop, Lee & Shepard Books, 1981.

———, ed. *The Poetry of Black America: Anthology of the 20th Century*. New York: Harper & Row, 1973.

Albert, Burton. *Where Does the Trail Lead?* Illustrated by Brian Pinkney. New York: Simon & Schuster Books for Young Readers, 1991.

Anderson, David A., and Kathleen Atkins Wilson. *The Origin of Life on Earth: An African Creation Myth.* Mt. Airy, Md.: Sights Productions, 1991.

Barnes, Joyce Annette. *Baby Grand, the Moon in July, and Me.* New York: Dial Books for Young Readers, 1994.

Beals, Melba P. *Warriors Don't Cry: A Searing Memoir of the Battle to Integrate Little Rock's Central High.* New York: Archway, 1995.

Berry, James. *Ajeemah and His Son.* New York: Willa Perlman, 1991.

Bolden, Tonya. *And Not Afraid to Dare.* New York: Scholastic, 1998.

Bontemps, Arna. *Golden Slippers: An Anthology of Negro Poetry for Young Readers.* New York: Harper, 1941.

Boyd, Candy Dawson. *Breadsticks, and Blessing Places.* New York: Macmillan, 1985.

———. *Charlie Pippin.* New York: Macmillan, 1987.

———. *Chevrolet Saturdays.* New York: Macmillan, 1993.

———. *Circle of Gold.* New York: Scholastic, 1984.

———. *A Different Beat.* New York: Puffin, 1996.

———. *Fall Secrets.* New York: Puffin, 1994.

———. *Forever Friends.* New York: Penguin, 1986.

Bradshaw, Douglas. *Shaquille O'Neal: Man of Steel.* New York: Grosset & Dunlap, 2001.

Bryan, Ashley. *Ashley Bryan's ABC of African American Poetry.* New York: Atheneum Books for Young Readers, 1997.

———. *Sing to the Sun.* Hong Kong: HarperCollins, 1992.

Burns, Khephra. *Mansa Musa.* Illustrated by Leo and Diane Dillon. San Francisco: Harcourt Brace, 2001.

Cameron, Ann. *The Kidnapped Prince: The Life of Olaudah Equiano.* New York: Random House, 2000.

Clifton, Lucille. *Everett Anderson's Goodbye.* Illustrated by Ann Grifalconi. New York: Henry Holt, 1983

Collier, James L. *Duke Ellington.* New York: Macmillan, 1987.

Cooper, Floyd. *Coming Home.* New York: Putnam, 1994.

Cox, Clinton. *Come All You Brave Soldiers: Blacks in the Revolutionary War.* New York: Scholastic Press, 1999.

———. *Undying Glory: The Story of the Massachusetts 54th Regiment.* New York: Scholastic, 1991.

Cummings, Pat. *Purrrrr.* New York: HarperFestival, 1999.

Curtis, Christopher P. *Bud, Not Buddy.* New York: Delacorte, 1999.

———. *The Watsons Go to Birmingham—1963.* New York: Delacorte, 1995.

Davis, Ossie. *Just Like Martin.* New York: Simon & Schuster, 1992.

DeGross, Monalisa. *Granddaddy's Street Songs.* Illustrated by Floyd Cooper. New York: Hyperion, 1999.

Echewa, T. Obinkaram. *The Magic Tree: A Folktale from Nigeria.* Illustrated by E. B. Lewis. New York: Morrow Junior Books, 1999.

English, Karen. *Francie.* New York: Farrar, Straus and Giroux, 1999.

Farmer, Nancy. *Casey Jones's Fireman: The Story of Sim Webb.* Illustrated by Bernardin James. New York: Phyllis Fogelman Books, 1999.

Flake, Sharon. *The Skin I'm In.* New York: Hyperion, 1998.

Flournoy, Valerie. *Patchwork Quilt.* Illustrated by Jerry Pinkney. New York: Dial Books for Young Readers, 1985.

Forrester, Sandra. *Sound of Jubilee*. New York: Puffin, 1995.

Giovanni, Nikki. *Ego-Tripping and Other Poems for Young People*. New York: Lawrence Hill Books, 1993.

———. *Grand Fathers*. New York: Henry Holt, 1999.

———. *Knoxville, Tennessee*. Illustrated by Larry Johnson. New York: Scholastic Books for Children, 1994.

———. *Spin a Soft Black Song: Poems for Children*. New York: Hill and Wang, 1971.

———. *Vacation Time: Poems for Children*. New York: Morrow, 1980.

Graff, Nancy P. *Where the River Runs: A Portrait of a Refugee Family*. Boston: Little, Brown, 1993.

Greenfield, Eloise. *Africa Dream*. Illustrated by Carole Byard. New York: HarperCollins, 1977.

———. *Daydreamers*. Illustrated by Tom Feelings. New York: Dial Books for Young Readers, 1981.

———. *For the Love of the Game: Michael Jordan and Me*. New York: HarperCollins, 1997.

———. *Grandpa's Face*. Illustrated by Floyd Cooper. New York: Philomel Books, 1988.

———. *Honey, I Love*. New York: HarperCollins, 1978.

———. *Nathaniel Talking*. New York: Black Butterfly Children's Books, 1988.

———. *Night on Neighborhood Street*. New York: Dial Books for Young Readers, 1991.

———. *Under the Sunday Tree*. New York: Harper & Row, 1988.

Grimes, Nikki. *Bronx Masquerade*. Illustrated by Javaka Steptoe. New York: Penguin Group, 2002.

———. *Come Sunday*. Grand Rapids, Mich.: W. B. Eerdmans, 1996.

———. *From a Child's Heart*. Orange, N.J.: Just Us Books, 1993.

———. *My Man Blue*. New York: Dial Books for Young Readers, 1999.

———. *A Pocketful of Poems*. New York: Clarion Books, 2001.

———. *Something on My Mind*. Illustrated by Tom Feelings. New York: Dial Books for Young Readers, 1999.

———. *Stepping Out with Grandma Mac*. New York: Orchard Books, 2001.

———. *Wild, Wild Hair*. New York: Scholastic, 1997.

Haley, Gail E. *A Story, A Story: An African Tale*. New York: Aladdin Books, 1970.

Hamilton, Virginia. *Cousins*. New York: Putnam, 1998.

———. *Drylongso*. Illustrated by Jerry Pinkney. New York: Harcourt Brace, 1992.

———. *M. C. Higgins the Great*. New York: Macmillan, 1974.

———. *Plain City*. New York: Scholastic, 1993.

———. *Second Cousins*. New York: Scholastic, 1998.

———. *Sweet Whispers, Brother Rush*. New York: Philomel Books, 1982.

Hansen, Joyce. *The Captive*. New York: Scholastic, 1994.

Haskins, James. *Against All Opposition: Black Explorers in America*. New York: Walker, 1992.

———. *One More River to Cross: The Stories of Twelve Black Americans*. New York: Scholastic, 1992.

———. *Outward Dreams: Black Inventors and Their Inventions*. New York: Walker, 1991.

Hopkins, Lee Bennett. *Pass the Poetry, Please!* New York: Harper & Row, 1987.

Hopkinson, Deborah. *Sweet Clara and the Freedom Quilt.* New York: Knopf, 1993.

Houston, Gloria. *Bright Freedom's Song: A Story of the Underground Railroad.* New York: Harcourt Brace, 1998.

Isadora, Rachel. *City Seen from A to Z.* New York: Greenwillow Books, 1983.

Johnson, Angela. *The First Part Last.* New York: Simon & Schuster, 2003.

———. *Toning the Sweep.* New York: Orchard Books, 1995.

Keats, Ezra Jack. *Snowy Day.* New York: Viking, 1962.

Kudlinski, Kathleen. *Rosa Parks: Young Rebel.* Illustrated by Meryl Henderson. New York: Aladdin Paperbacks, 2001.

Kurtz, Jane. *Pulling the Lion's Tail.* Illustrated by Floyd Cooper. New York: Simon & Schuster, 1995.

Lasky, Kathryn. *True North.* New York: Scholastic, 1996.

Lester, Julius. *John Henry.* Illustrated by Jerry Pinkney. New York: Dial Books for Young Readers, 1994.

———. *Sam and the Tigers.* Illustrated by Jerry Pinkney. New York: Puffin, 1996.

———. *Uncle Remus: The Complete Tales.* Illustrated by Jerry Pinkney. New York: Dial Books for Young Readers, 1999.

Littlechild, George. *In Honor of Our Grandmothers.* New York: Theytus Books, 1994.

Lyons, Mary E. *Letters from a Slave Girl: The Story of Harriet Jacobs.* New York: Scribner, 1992.

———. *Sorrow's Kitchen: The Life and Folklore of Zora Neale Hurston.* New York: Charles Scribner's Sons, 1990.

Martin, Francesca. *Clever Tortoise: A Traditional African Tale.* Cambridge, Mass.: Candlewick Press, 2000.

Mathis, Sharon. *The Hundred Penny Box.* New York: Viking, 1975.

McKissack, Fredrick. *Black Hoops: The History of African Americans in Basketball.* New York: Scholastic, 1999.

McKissack, Patricia. *The Dark-Thirty: Southern Tales of the Supernatural.* Illustrated by Brian Pinkney. New York: Knopf, 1992.

———. *A Million Fish—More or Less.* Illustrated by Dena Schutzer. New York: Knopf, 1992.

———. *Mirandy and Brother Wind.* Illustrated by Jerry Pinkney. New York: Knopf, 1988.

McKissack, Patricia, and Fredrick McKissack. *Black Hands, White Sails: The Story of African American Whalers.* New York: Scholastic Press, 1999.

———. *Christmas in the Big House, Christmas in the Quarters.* New York: Scholastic, 1994.

———. *Mirandy and Brother Wind.* Illustrated by Jerry Pinkney. New York: Knopf, 1988.

———. *Rebels against Slavery.* New York: Scholastic, 1996.

———. *Sojourner Truth: Ain't I a Woman?* New York: Scholastic, 1992.

Mead, Alice. *Junebug.* New York: Bantam, 1995.

Miller, William. *Zora Hurston and the Chinaberry Tree.* New York: Lee & Low Books, 1994.

Monceaux, Morgan, and Ruth Katcher. *My Heroes, My People: African Americans and Native Americans in the West.* Illustrated by Morgan Monceaux. New York: Farrar, Straus and Giroux, 1999.

Myers, Walter Dean. *The Beast.* New York: Scholastic, 2003.

———. *Brown Angels: An Album of Pictures and Verses.* New York: HarperCollins, 1993.

———. *Crystal.* New York: Viking, 1987.

———. *Fast Sam, Cool Clyde, and Stuff.* New York: Viking, 1975.

———. *The Greatest—Muhammad Ali.* New York: Scholastic, 2001.

———. *Harlem.* New York: Scholastic Press, 1997.

———. *Hoops.* New York: Delacorte, 1981.

———. *Malcolm X: A Fire Burning Brightly.* New York: HarperCollins, 2000.

———. *Malcolm X: By Any Means Necessary.* New York: Scholastic Trade, 1993.

———. *Me, Mop, and the Moondance Kid.* New York: Delacorte, 1988.

———. *Monster.* New York: HarperCollins, 1999.

———. *Mop, Moondance, and the Nagasaki Knights.* New York: Delacorte, 1992.

———. *The Mouse Rap. New York:* Harper & Row, 1990.

———. *Now Is Your Time! The African-American Struggle for Freedom.* New York: HarperCollins, 1991.

———. *The Outside Shot.* New York: Delacorte, 1984.

———. *Scorpions.* New York: Harper & Row, 1988.

———. *SLAM!* New York: Scholastic, 1996.

———. *Somewhere in Darkness.* New York: Scholastic, 1992.

———. *Won't Know until I Get There.* New York: Viking, 1982.

Parks, Rosa, and Jim Haskins. *Rosa Parks: My Story.* New York: Dial Books, 1992.

Parks, Van Dyke. *Jump Again! More Adventures of Brer Rabbit.* Illustrated by Barry Moser. San Diego: Harcourt Brace Jovanovich, 1987

Parks, Van Dyke, and Malcolm Jones. *Jump!* Illustrated by Barry Moser. San Diego: Harcourt Brace Jovanovich, 1986.

Patterson, Katherine. *Jip: His Story.* New York: Lodestar Books, 1996.

Paulsen, Gary. *Nightjohn.* New York: Delacorte Press, 1993.

———. *Sarny.* New York: Delacorte Press, 1997.

Pinkney, Andrea Davis. *Duke Ellington.* Illustrated by Brian Pinkney. New York: Hyperion, 1998.

———. *Hold Fast to Dreams.* New York: William Morrow, 1995.

———. *Silent Thunder: A Civil War Story.* New York: Hyperion, 1999.

Pinkney, Brian. *Cosmo and the Robot.* New York: HarperCollins, 2000.

Pitcher, Diana. *Tokoloshi: African Folk Tales.* Illustrated by Meg Rutherford. Millbrae, Calif.: A Dawne-Leigh Book, 1980.

Polacco, Patricia. *Pink and Say.* New York: Philomel Books, 1994.

Porter, A. P. *Jump at de Sun: The Story of Zora Neale Hurston.* Minneapolis, Minn.: Carolrhoda Books, 1992.

Rappaport, Doreen. *Freedom River.* Illustrated by Bryan Collier. New York: Hyperion, 2000.

Ringgold, Faith. *If a Bus Could Talk: The Story of Rosa Parks.* New York: Simon & Schuster Books for Young People, 1999.

Ruffin, Frances E. *Martin Luther King, Jr. and the March on Washington.* Illustrated by Stephen Marchesi. New York: Grosset and Dunlap, 2001.

San Souci, Robert. *Cendrillon.* Illustrated by Brian Pinkney. New York: Simon & Schuster Books for Young People, 1998.

———. *Sukey and the Mermaid.* New York: Four Winds Press, 1992.

———. *The Talking Eggs.* Illustrated by Jerry Pinkney. New York: Dial Books, 1989.

Sebestyen, Ouida. *Words by Heart.* New York: Little, Brown, 1979.

Shepard, Aaron. *Master Man: A Tall Tale of Nigeria.* Illustrated by David Wisniewski. New York: HarperCollins, 2001.

Siegelson, Kim. *In the Time of the Drums.* Illustrated by Brian Pinkney. New York: Hyperion, 1999.

Sierra, Judy. *Wiley and the Hairy Man.* Illustrated by Brian Pinkney. New York: Lodestar Books, 1996.

Souhami, Jessica. *The Leopard's Drum: An Asante Tale from West Africa.* New York: Little, Brown, 1995.

Steptoe, John. *Mufaro's Beautiful Daughters: An African Tale.* New York: Lothrop, Lee & Shepard Books, 1987.

Stolz, Mary. *Storm in the Night.* Illustrated by Pat Cummings. New York: Harper & Row, 1988.

Strickland, Dorothy S., and Michael R., comps. *Families: Poems Celebrating the African American Experience.* Honesdale, Pa.: Wordsong Boyds Mills Press, 1994.

Taylor, Ann. *Baby Dance.* New York: HarperFestival, 1999.

Taylor, Mildred. *The Friendship.* New York: Puffin, 1987.

———. *Let the Circle Be Unbroken.* New York: Dial Press, 1981.

———. *The Mississippi Bridge.* New York: Dial Books for Young Readers, 1990.

———. *Roll of Thunder, Hear My Cry.* New York: Dial Press, 1976.

———. *The Song of the Trees.* New York: Bantam Skylark, 1975.

———. *The Well: David's Story.* New York: Dial Books for Young Readers, 1995.

Temple, Frances. *Tiger Soup: An Anansi Story from Jamaica.* New York: Orchard Books, 1994.

Walter, Mildred P. *Mississippi Challenge.* New York: Aladdin Paperbacks, 1992.

Weidt, Maryann N. *Voice of Freedom: A Story about Frederick Douglass.* Illustrated by Jeni Reeves. New York: Carolrhoda Books, 2001.

Winter, Janette. *Follow the Drinking Gourd.* New York: Knopf, 1988.

Wolkstein, Diane. *Bouki Dances the Kokioko: A Comical Tale from Haiti.* Illustrated by Jesse Sweetwater. New York: Gulliver Books, Harcourt Brace, 1997.

Woodson, Jacqueline. *Behind You.* New York: Puffin, 2004.

———. *Between Madison and Palmetto.* New York: Penguin, 1993.

———. *The Dear One.* New York: Delacorte Press, 1991.

———. *From the Notebooks of Melanin Sun.* New York: Scholastic, 1995.

———. *The House You Pass on the Way.* New York: Bantam, 1997.

———. *Hush.* New York: Penguin, 2003.

———. *If You Come Softly.* New York: Puffin, 2000.

———. *I Hadn't Meant to Tell You This.* New York: Delacorte Press, 1994.

———. *The Last Summer with Maizon.* New York: Delacorte Press, 1990.

———. *Lena.* New York: Delacorte Press, 1999.

———. *Locomotion.* New York: Putnam, 2003.

———. *Maizon at Blue Hill.* New York: Delacorte Press, 1992.

———. *Miracle's Boys.* New York: Putnam, 2000.

———. *The Other Side.* New York: Putnam, 2001.

Asian American

Bandon, Alexandra. *Chinese Americans*. New York: New Discovery Books, 1994.

———. *Korean Americans*. New York: New Discovery Books, 1994.

———. *Vietnamese Americans*. New York: New Discovery Books, 1994.

Banks, Jacqueline Turner. *A Day for Vincent Chin and Me*. Boston: Houghton Mifflin, 2001.

Bishop, Claire H., *Five Chinese Brothers*. Illustrated by Kurt Wiese. New York: Putnam Juvenile; 1938 Reissue edition, 1996.

Cassedy, Sylvia, and Kunihiro Suetake (translators). *Red Dragonfly on My Shoulder*. Illustrated by Molly Bang. New York: HarperCollins, 1992.

Chang, Margaret, and Raymond Chang. *The Cricket Warrior: A Chinese Tale*. Illustrated by Warwick Hutton. New York: McElderry Books, 1994..

Choi, Sook-Nyul. *Echoes of the White Giraffe*. Boston, Houghton Mifflin, 1993.

———. *Year of the Impossible Goodbyes*. Boston, Houghton Mifflin, 1991.

Climo, Shirley. *The Korean Cinderella*. New York: HarperCollins, 1993.

Coerr, Eleanor. *Sadako*. Illustrated by Ed Young. New York: Putnam, 1993.

Crew, Linda. *Children of the River*. New York: Delacorte Press, 1989.

Dell, Pamela. *I.M. Pei: Designer of Dreams*. Chicago: Children's Press, 1993

Demi. *A Chinese Zoo: Fables and Proverbs*. New York: Harcourt Brace, 1987.

———. *The Empty Pot*. New York: Henry Holt, 1990.

———. *The Greatest Treasure*. New York: Scholastic Press, 1998.

———. *The Magic Boat*. New York: Henry Holt, 1990.

———. *In the Eyes of the Cat: Japanese Poetry*. Trans. Tze-Si Huang. Illustrated by Demi. New York: Henry Holt, 1994.

Fang, Linda. *The Ch'i-Lin Purse: A Collection of Ancient Chinese Stories*. Illustrated by Jeanne M. Lee. New York: Farrar, Straus and Giroux, 1995.

Flack, Marjorie. *The Story of Ping*. Illustrated by Kurt Weise. New York: Puffin, 1977.

Fox, Mary. *Bette Bao Lord: Novelist and Chinese Voice for Change*. Chicago: Children's Press, 1993.

Gerstein, Mordicai. *Mountain of Tibet*. New York: Trumpet Club, 1987.

Goldin, Barbara. *Red Means Good Fortune: A Story of San Francisco's Chinatown*. New York: Viking, 1994.

Graff, Nancy P. *Where the River Runs: A Portrait of a Refugee Family*. Photographs by Richard Howard. Boston, Mass: Little, Brown, 1993.

Hamanaka, Sheila. *Screen of Frogs*. New York: Orchard Books, 1993.

Han, Oki S. *Kongi and Potgi: A Cinderella Story from Korea*. New York: Dial Books, 1996.

Hargrove, Jim. *Dr. An Wang: Computer Pioneer (People of Distinction)*. Chicago: Children's Press, 1993.

Ho, Minfong, and Saphan Ros. *Brother Rabbit: A Cambodian Tale*. Illustrated by Jennifer Hewitson. New York: Lothrop, Lee & Shepard Books, 1997.

———. *The Clay Marble*. New York: Farrar, Straus and Giroux, 1991.

———. *Hush! A Thai Lullaby*. Illustrated by Holly Meade. New York: Scholastic, 1996.

———. *Maples in the Mist: Children's Poems from the Tang Dynasty*. New York: Lothrop, Lee, & Shepard Books, 1996.

Hoobler, Dorothy, and Thomas Hoobler. *The Chinese American Family Album.* London: Oxford University Press, 1994.

Houston, Jeanne Wakatsuki. *Farewell to Manzanar.* Boston: Houghton Mifflin, 1973.

Hoyt-Goldsmith, Diane. *Celebrating Chinese New Year.* Illustrated by Lawrence Migdale. New York: Holiday House, 1998.

Hu, Jane Hwa. *Sojourner.* Baltimore, Md.: Noble House, 1994.

Kidd, Diana. *Onion Tears.* Illustrated by Lucy Montgomery. New York: Orchard Books, 1991.

Lee, Huy Voun. *At the Beach.* New York: Henry Holt, 1994.

Lee, Jeanne M. *The Legend of the Li River: An Ancient Chinese Tale.* New York: Holt, Rinehart and Winston, 1983.

———. *The Song of Mu Lan.* Arden, N.C.: Front Street, 1995.

Lee, Marie G. *If It Hadn't Been for Yoon.* New York: Avon Books, 1993.

Lee, Wong Herbert. *A Drop of Rain.* Boston, Mass.: Houghton Mifflin, 1995.

Lord, Bette Bao. *In the Year of the Boar and Jackie Robinson.* New York: HarperCollins, 1984.

Louie, Ai-Ling. *Yeh-Shen: A Cinderella Story from China.* New York: Philomel Books, 1982.

Mado, Michio. *The Animals: Selected Poems.* New York: McElderry Books, 1992.

Mah, Adeline Y. *Chinese Cinderella.* New York: Delacorte Press, 1999.

———. *Falling Leaves: The Memoir of an Unwanted Chinese Daughter.* New York: Wiley, 1998.

Mahy, Margaret. *Seven Chinese Brothers.* New York: Scholastic Paperbacks, 1992.

Malone, Mary. *Maya Lin: Architect and Artist.* Berkeley Heights, N.J.: Enslow, 1995.

Martin, Rafe. *Mysterious Tales of Japan.* Illustrated by Tatsuro Kiuchi. New York: G. P. Putnam and Sons, 1993.

Mochizuki, Ken. *Baseball Saved Us.* New York: Scholastic, 1993.

———. *Beacon Hill Boys.* New York: Scholastic, 2002.

———. *Heroes.* Illustrated by Dom Lee. New York: Lee & Low Books, 1995.

Namioka, Lensey. *April and the Dragon Lady.* San Diego: Browndeer Press, 1994.

———. *Half and Half.* New York: Delacorte, 2003.

———. *Ties That Bind, Ties That Break.* New York: Delacorte Press, 1999.

———. *Yang the Eldest and His Odd Jobs.* New York: Yearling, 2002.

———. *Yang the Second and Her Secret Admirers.* New York: Little, Brown, 1998.

———. *Yang the Third and Her Impossible Family.* New York: Little, Brown, 1995.

———. *Yang the Youngest and His Terrible Ear.* New York: Little, Brown, 1992.

Osborne, Mary Pope. *One World, Many Religions, The Way We Worship.* New York: Knopf Books for Young Readers, 1996.

Poole, Amy Lowry. *How the Rooster Got His Crown.* New York: Holiday House, 1999.

Riley, Gail B. *Wah Ming Chang: Artist and Master of Special Effects.* Berkeley Heights, N.J.: Enslow, 1995.

Salisbury, Graham. *Under the Blood Red Sun.* New York: Delacorte Press, 1994.

Say, Allen. *El Chino.* Boston: Houghton Mifflin, 1990.

———. *Emma's Rug.* Boston: Houghton Mifflin, 1996.

———. *Grandfather's Journey.* Boston: Houghton Mifflin, 1993.

———. *Kamishibai.* Boston: Houghton Mifflin, 2005.

———. *Music for Alice.* Boston: Houghton Mifflin, 2004.

———. *The Sign Painter.* Boston: Houghton Mifflin, 2000.

———. *Stranger in the Mirror.* Boston: Houghton Mifflin, 1998.

———. *Tea with Milk.* Boston: Houghton Mifflin, 1999.

———. *Under the Cherry Blossom Tree.* Boston: Houghton Mifflin, 2005.

Schmidt, Jeremy. *Two Lands, One Heart: An American Boy's Journey to His Mother's Vietnam.* New York: Walker, 1995.

Schroeder, Alan. *Lily and the Wooden Bowl.* Illustrated by Yoriko Ito. New York: Bantam Doubleday Dell Books for Young Readers, 1994.

Shepard, Sandy. *Myths and Legends: Around the World.* New York: Simon & Schuster Children's Publishing, 1995.

Snyder, Dianne. *The Boy of the Three-Year Nap.* Illustrated by Allen Say. Boston: Houghton Mifflin, 1988.

Stamm, Claus. *Three Strong Women: A Tall Tale from Japan.* Illustrated by Jean Tseng, Mou-sien Tseng, and Kazue Misumura. New York: Viking, 1990.

Surat, Michele Marie. *Angel Child, Dragon Child.* Illustrated by Mai Vo-Dinh. New York: Scholastic, 1989.

Tan, Amy. *The Chinese Siamese Cat.* Illustrated by Gretchen Schields. New York: Aladdin Books, 2001.

Tao, Wang. *Exploration into China.* New York: Chelsea House Publications, 2000.

Uchida, Yoshiko. *The Dancing Kettle and Other Japanese Folk Tales.* Illustrated by Richard C. Jones. New York: Harcourt, Brace, & World, 1949.

———. *The Invisible Thread: An Autobiography.* Englewood Cliffs, N.J.: Messner, 1991.

———. *Journey Home.* New York: McElderry Books, 1978.

———. *Journey to Topaz: A Story of the Japanese American Evacuation.* Berkeley, Calif.: Creative Arts, 1985.

———. *The Magic Listening Cap: More Folk Tales from Japan.* New York: Harcourt, Brace, 1955.

———. *The Magic Purse.* Illustrated by Keiko Narahashi. New York: McElderry Books, 1993.

———. *The Sea of Gold and Other Tales from Japan.* Illustrated by Marianne Yamaguchi. New York: Charles Scribner's Sons, 1965.

———. *The Two Foolish Cats: Suggested by a Japanese Folktale.* Illustrated by Margo Zemach. New York: McElderry Books, 1987.

———. *The Wise Old Woman.* Illustrated by Martin Springett. New York: McElderry Books, 1994.

Waters, Kate, and Madeline Slovenz-Low. *Lion Dancer: Ernie Wan's Chinese New Year.* New York: Scholastic, 1990.

Watkins, Yoko Kawashima. *Tales from the Bamboo Grove.* Illustrated by Jean Tseng and Mou-sien Tseng. New York: Bradbury Press, 1992.

Whelan, Gloria. *Goodbye, Vietnam.* New York: Dell Yearling, 2000.

Wong, Janet. *Good Luck Gold and Other Poems.* New York: McElderry Books, 1994.

———. *Night Garden: Poems from the World of Dreams.* New York: McElderry Books, 2000.

———. *The Rainbow Hand: Poems about Mothers and Children.* New York: McElderry Books, 1999.

Yacowitz, Caryn. *The Jade Stone: A Chinese Folktale*. Illustrated by Ju-Hong Chen. New York: Holiday House, 1992.

Yep, Laurence. *American Dragons: Twenty-five Asian American Voices*. New York: HarperCollins, 1993.

———. *The Case of the Firecrackers*. New York: HarperCollins, 1999.

———. *The Case of the Goblin Pearls*. New York: HarperTrophy, 1998.

———. *The Case of the Lion Dance*. New York: HarperTrophy, 1999.

———. *Child of the Owl*. New York: HarperTrophy, 1977.

———. *The Dragon Prince: A Chinese Beauty and the Beast Tale*. Illustrated by Kam Mak. New York: HarperCollins, 1997.

———. *Dragon's Gate*. New York: HarperCollins, 1993.

———. *Dragonwings*. New York: Harper, 1975.

———. *The Ghost Fox*. Illustrated by Jean Tseng and Mou-sien Tseng. New York: Scholastic, 1994.

———. *The Junior Thunder Lord*. Illustrated by Robert Van Nutt. Mahwah, NJ: Bridgewater Books, 1994.

———. *The Khan's Daughter: A Mongolian Folktale*. Illustrated by Mou-sien Tseng. New York: Scholastic Press, 1997

———. *The Lost Garden*. Englewood Cliffs, N.J.: Messner, 1991.

———. *The Man Who Tricked a Ghost*. Illustrated by Isadore Seltzer. New York: Bridgewater Books, 1993.

———. *The Rainbow People*. Illustrated by David Wiesner. New York: Harper & Row, 1989.

———. *Ribbons*. New York: Putnam, 1996.

———. *Sea Glass*. New York: HarperCollins, 1979.

———. *The Shell Woman and the King*. Illustrated by Yan Ming-Yi. New York: Dial Books for Young Readers, 1993.

———. *The Star Fisher*. New York: Morrow Junior Books, 1991.

———. *Thief of Hearts*. New York: HarperCollins, 1995.

———. *Tongues of Jade*. New York: HarperCollins, 1991.

Yolen, Jane. *The Emperor and the Kite*. New York: Putnam Juvenile, 1998.

Young, Ed. *Lon Po Po: A Red-Riding Hood Story from China*. New York: Philomel Books, 1989.

———. *Night Visitors*. New York: Philomel Books, 1995.

Zhang, Song Nan, *The Children of China*. Illustrated by Song Nan Zhang. Plattsburgh, N.Y.: Tundra Books, 1995.

Ziner, Feenie. *Cricket Boy: A Chinese Tale*. Illustrated by Ed Young. Garden City, N.Y.: Doubleday, 1977.

Latino and Hispanic American

Ada, Alma Flor. *My Name Is Maria Isabel*. New York: Atheneum, 1993.

Anaya, Rudolfo. *Farolitos of Christmas*. Illustrated by Edward Gonzales. New York: Hyperion Books for Children, 1995.

Ancona, George. *Barrio: Jose's Neighborhood*. New York: Harcourt Brace, 1998.

———. *Fiesta, U.S.A.* New York: Lodestar Books, 1995.

————. *Pablo Remembers: The Fiesta of the Day of the Dead.* New York: Lothrop, Lee, & Shepard Books, 1993.

Bertrand, Diane Gonzales. *Close to the Heart.* Houston, Tex.: Pinata Books, 2002.

————. *Trino's Time.* Houston, Tex.: Pinata Books, 2001.

Bredeson, Carmen. *Henry Cisneros: Building a Better America.* Berkeley Heights, N.J.: Enslow, 1995.

Calhoun, Mary. *Tonio's Cat.* Illustrated by Ed Martinez. New York: Morrow Junior Books, 1996.

Carlson, Lori, ed. *Cool Salsa: Bilingual Poems on Growing up Latino in the United States.* New York: Henry Holt, 1994.

Castañeda, Omar S. *Among the Volcanoes.* New York: Dell Publishing, 1991.

Cruz Martinez, Alejandro. *The Woman Who Outshone the Sun.* Illustrated by Fernando Olivera. San Francisco: Children's Book Press, 1991.

Cumpian, Carlos. *Latino Rainbow: Poems about Latino Americans.* Chicago: Children's Press, 1994.

De Gerez, Toni. *My Song Is a Piece of Jade: Poems of Ancient Mexico in English and Spanish.* Illustrated by William Stark. Boston: Little, Brown, 1984.

De Ruiz, Dana, and Richard Larios. *La Causa: The Migrant Farmworkers' Story.* Illustrated by Rudy Gutierrez. Austin, Tex.: Raintree Steck-Vaughn, 1993.

De Sauza, James. *Brother Anansi and the Cattle Ranch.* Adapted by Harriet Rohmer. Illustrated by Stephen Von Mason. San Francisco and Emeryville, Calif.: Children's Book Press, 1989.

Dorros, Arthur. *Abuela.* Illustrated by Elisa Kleven. New York: Dutton, 1991.

————. *Radio Man.* Translated by Sandra Marulanda Dorros. New York: HarperCollins, 1993.

Garland, Sherry. *Indio.* New York: Harcourt Brace, 1995.

————. *Song of the Buffalo Boy.* San Diego: Harcourt Brace Jovanovich, 1992.

Gerson, Mary-Joan. *Fiesta Femenina: Celebrating Women in Mexican Folktale.* Illustrated by Maya Christina Gonzalez. New York: Barefoot Books, 2001.

Hoyt-Goldsmith, Diane. *Day of the Dead.* Illustrated by Lawrence Migdale. New York: Holiday House, 1994.

————. *Las Posadas.* Illustrated by Lawrence Migdale. New York: Holiday House, 1999.

Jaffe, Nina. *The Golden Flower: A Taino Myth from Puerto Rico.* Illustrated by Enrique O. Sanchez. New York: Simon & Schuster Books for Young Readers, 1996.

Jimenez, Francisco. *The Circuit.* New York: Houghton Mifflin, 1997.

Krull, Kathleen. *The Other Side: How Kids Live in a California Latino Neighborhood.* New York: Lodestar Books, 1994.

Lankford, Mary D. *Quinceanera: A Latina's Journey to Womanhood.* Brookfield, Conn.: Millbrook Press, 1994.

Martinez, Elizabeth C. *The Mexican-American Experience.* Brookfield, Conn.: Millbrook Press, 1995.

Mohr, Nicholasa. *All for the Better: A Story of El Barrio.* Austin, Tex.: Raintree Steck-Vaughn, 1993.

————. *Felita.* New York: Dial Press, 1976.

————. *Going Home.* New York: Dial Books for Young Readers, 1986.

————. *In Nueva York.* Houston, Tex.: Arte Publico Press, 1988.

———. *Nilda.* New York: Harper Row, 1973.

———. *Old Letivia and the Mountain of Sorrows.* Illustrated by Ruy Gutierrez. New York: Penguin Books, 1996.

Mora, Pat. *Confetti: Poems for Children.* New York: Lee & Low Books, 1996.

———. *Listen to the Desert.* New York: Illustrated by Francisco X. Mora. Clarion Books, 1994.

Nye, Naomi Shihab. *The Tree Is Older Than You Are: A Bilingual Gathering of Poems and Stories from Mexico with Paintings by Mexican Artists.* New York: Aladdin Paperbacks, 1995.

O'Dell, Sandra. *Carlotta.* Boston: Houghton Mifflin, 1981.

Ortiz, Simon. *The People Shall Continue.* Illustrated by Sharol Graves. San Francisco, Calif.: Children's Book Press, 1988.

Pena, Sylvia Cavozos, ed. *Kikiriki: Stories and Poems in English and Spanish for Children.* Houston, Tex.: Arte Publico Press, 1987.

———. *Tun-ta-ca-tun: More Stories and Poems in English and Spanish.* Houston, Tex.: Arte Publico Press, 1986.

Piggott, Juliet, and John Spencer. *Mexican Folk Tales.* New York: Crane Russak, 1976.

Pitre. Felix. *Paco and the Witch.* Illustrated by Christy Hale. New York: Loestar Books, 1995.

Pitre, Felix, and Christy Hale. *Paco and the Witch.* New York: Lodestar Books, 1995.

Pomerantz, Charlotte. *The Tamarindo Puppy and Other Poems.* Illustrated by Byron Barton. New York: Greenwillow Books, 1980.

Ramirez, Michael Rose. *The Legend of the Hummingbird: A Tale from Puerto Rico.* Illustrated by Margaret Sanfilippo. Greenvale, N.Y.: Mondo Publishing, 1998.

Reiser, Lynn. *Tortillas and Lullabies.* Illustrated by Corazones Valientes. New York: Greenwillow Books, 1998.

Rohmer, Harriet. *The Legend of Food Mountain.* Illustrated by Graciela Carrillo. San Francisco: Children's Book Press, 1982.

———. *Uncle Nacho's Hat.* Illustrated by Mira Reisberg. San Francisco: Children's Book Press, 1989.

Sabin, L. *Roberto Clemente: Young Baseball Hero.* New York: Troll Associates, 1992.

Santiago, Esmeraldo. *Almost a Woman.* New York: Vintage Books, 1998.

———. *When I Was Puerto Rican.* New York: Vintage Books 1993.

Soto, Gary. *Baseball in April.* New York: Harcourt Brace, 1990.

———. *Canto Familiar.* New York: Harcourt Brace, 1995.

———. *A Fire in My Hands: A Book of Poems.* New York: Scholastic, 1990.

———. *Jesse.* New York: Harcourt Brace, 1994.

———. *Neighborhood Odes.* New York: Scholastic, 1992.

———. *Taking Sides.* New York: Harcourt Brace, 1991.

———. *Too Many Tamales.* Illustrated by Ed Martinez. New York: Putnam, 1993.

Velasquez, Gloria. *Ankiza.* Houston, Tex.: Pinata Books, 2000.

———. *Teen Angel.* Houston, Tex.: Pinata Books, 2003.

Wade, Mary D. *Guadalupe Quintanilla: Leader of the Hispanic Community.* Springfield, N.J.: Enslow, 1995.

Walker, Paul R. *Pride of Puerto Rico: The Life of Roberto Clemente.* San Diego: Harcourt Brace Jovanovich, 1988.

Middle Eastern

Ahsan, M. M. *Muslim Festivals*. Illustrated by M. M. Ahsan. Vero Beach, Fla.: Rourke Enterprises, 1987.

Bloom, Jonathan, and Sheila S. Blair. *Islam: A Thousand Years of Faith and Power*. New Haven, Conn., and London: Yale University Press, 2002.

———. *Islamic Arts. Art and Ideas*. London: Phaidon Press, 1997.

Burns, Khephra. *Mansa Musa*. Illustrated by Leo and Diane Dillon. San Francisco: Harcourt Brace, 2001.

Carmi, Daniella, and Yael Lotan. *Samir and Yonatan*. New York: Scholastic, 2002.

Chalfonte, Jessica. *I Am Muslim*. New York: PowerKids Press, 1996.

Cohen, Barbara, and Bahia Lovejoy. *Seven Daughters and Seven Sons*. New York: Atheneum, 1982.

Ellis, Deborah. *The Breadwinner*. Toronto: Groundwood Books, 2000.

———. *Mud City*. Toronto: Groundwood Books, 2003.

———. *Parvana's Journey*. Toronto: Groundwood Books, 2002.

Esposito, John., ed. *The Oxford History of Islam*. New York: Oxford University Press, 2000.

Ghazi, Suhaib Hamid. *Ramadan*. Illustrated by Omar Rayyan. New York: Holiday House, 1996.

Goodwin, Jan. *Price of Honor: Muslim Women Lift the Veil of Silence on the Islamic World*. New York: Plume, 1995.

Heide, Florence Parry, and Judith Gilliland. *The Day of Ahmed's Secret*. Illustrated by Ted Lewin. New York: Lothrop, Lee & Shepard Books, 1990.

———. *The House of Wisdom*. Illustrated by Mary Grandpre. New York: Dorling Kindersley, 1999.

———. *Sami and the Time of the Troubles*. Illustrated by Ted Lewin. New York: Clarion Books, 1992.

Husain, Shahrukh. *What Do We Know about Islam?* Illustrated by Celia Hart. New York: Peter Bedrick Books, 1995.

Johnson-Davies, Denys. *Rumi: Poet and Sage*. Illustrated by Laura De La Mare. London: Hood Hood Books, 1996.

Kessler, Cristina. *One Night: A Story from the Desert*. Illustrated by Ian Schoenherr. New York: Philomel Books, 1995.

Khan, Rukhsana. *The Roses in My Carpets*. Illustrated by Ronald Himler. New York: Holiday House, 1998.

Kimmel, Eric A. *The Three Princes: A Middle Eastern Tale*. Illustrated by Leonard Everett Fisher. New York: Holiday House, 1994.

Levine, Anna. *Running on Eggs*. New York: Cricket Books, 1999.

Lewin, Ted. *The Storytellers*. Illustrated by Ted Lewin. New York: Lothrop, Lee & Shepard, 1998.

Lunde, Paul. *Islam*. London: Dorling Kindersley, 2002.

Maalouf, Amin, and Jon Rothschild. *The Crusades through Arab Eyes*. London: Schocken Books, 1989.

MacDonald, Fiona. *A 16th Century Mosque*. Illustrated by Mark Bergin. New York: P. Bedrick Books, 1994.

Matthews, Mary. *Magid Fasts for Ramadan*. Illustrated by E. B. Lewis. New York: Clarion Books, 1996.

McMane, Fred. *Hakeem Olajawon*. New York: Chelsea Books, 1999.

Naff, Alixa. *The Arab Americans*. New York: Chelsea House, 1988.

Nye, Naomi Shihab. *The Flag of Childhood: Poems from the Middle East*. New York: Aladdin Paperbacks, 2002.

————. *Habibi*. New York: Simon & Schuster, 1997.

————. *19 Varieties of Gazelle: Poems of the Middle East*. New York: Greenwillow Books, 2002.

————. *Sitti's Secrets*. Illustrated by Nancy Carpenter. New York: Simon & Schuster, 1994.

————. *The Space between Our Footsteps: Poems and Paintings from the Middle East*. New York: Simon & Schuster, 1998.

Oppenheim, Shulamith Levey. *The Hundredth Name*. Illustrated by Michael Hays. Honesdale, Pa.: Boyds Mills Press, 1995.

Rumford, James. *Traveling Man: The Journey of Ibn Battuta, 1325–1354*. Illustrated by James Rumford. Boston: Houghton Mifflin, 2001.

Shah, Idries. *The Boy without a Name*. Illustrated by Mona Caron. Cambridge, Mass.: Hoopoe Books, 2000.

Staples, Suzanne Fisher. *Haveli*. New York: Knopf, 1993.

————. *Shabanu*. New York: Knopf, 1989.

————. *Shiva's Fire*. New York: Farrar, Straus and Giroux, 2000.

Weiss-Armush, Anne Marie. *Arabian Cuisine*. Illustrated by John Berry. Beirut, Lebanon: Dar An-nafaés, 1984.

Wormser, Richard. *American Islam: Growing Up Muslim in America*. New York: Walker, 1994.

Zeman, Linda. *Sindbad*. Illustrated by Linda Zeman. New York: Tundra Books, 1999.

Native American

Begay, Shonto. *Ma'ii and Cousin Toad*. New York: Scholastic, 1992.

————. *Navajo: Visions and Voices across the Mesa*. New York: Scholastic, 1995.

Bierhorst, John, ed. *In the Trail of the Wind: American Indian Poems and Ritual Orations*. New York: Farrar, Straus and Giroux, 1971.

Brill, Marlene T. *The Trail of Tears: The Cherokee Journey*. Brookfield, Conn.: Millbrook Press, 1995.

Brown, Dee. *Bury My Heart at Wounded Knee: An Indian History of the American West*. New York: Holt Henry and Company, 1970.

————. *Wounded Knee*. (Adapted by Amy Ehrlich). New York: Random House Children's Books, 1978.

Bruchac, Joseph. *Between Earth and Sky: Legends of Native American Sacred Places*. Illustrated by Thomas Locker. New York: Harcourt Brace, 1996

————. *A Boy Called Slow*. Illustrated by Rocco Baviera. New York: Putnam, 1994.

————. *The Boy Who Lived with the Bears*. Illustrated by Mury Jacob. New York: HarperCollins, 1995.

————. *Children of the Longhouse*. New York: Dial Books for Young Readers, 1996.

————. *The Circle of Thanks: Native American Poems and Songs of Thanksgiving.* New York: Bridgewater Books, 1996.

————. *Eagle Song.* New York: Puffin, 1999.

————. *The Earth under Sky Bear's Feet.* New York: Philomel Books, 1995.

————. *The First Strawberries: A Cherokee Story.* Illustrated by Anna Voitech. New York: Puffin Books, 1993.

————. *Four Ancestors: Stories, Songs, and Poems from Native North America.* Illustrated by S. S. Burrus, Jeffrey Chapman, Duke Sine, and Mury Jacob. Mahwah, N.J.: Bridgewater Books, 1996.

————. *Fox Song.* Illustrated by Paul Morin. New York: Paper Star Books, 1993.

————. *Skeleton Man.* New York: HarperCollins, 2001.

————. *Thirteen Moons on Turtle's Back: A Native American Year of Moons.* New York: Putnam, 1997.

————. *Warriors.* Plain City, Ohio: Darby Publishing, 2003.

Bruchac, Joseph, and James Bruchac. *How Chipmunk Got His Stripes.* Illustrated by Jose Aruego, and Ariane Dewey New York: Dial Books for Young Readers, 2001.

Burks, Brian. *Runs with Horses.* New York: Harcourt Brace. 1995.

Caduto, Michael J., and Joseph Bruchac. *Keepers of Life: Discovering Plants through Native American Stories and Earth Activities for Children.* Golden, Colo.: Fulcrum Publishing, 1994.

Cohen, Caron Lee. *Mud Pony.* Illustrated by Shonto Begay. New York: Scholastic, 1988.

Cole, Judith. *The Moon, the Sun, and the Coyote.* Illustrated by Cecile Scholberle. New York: Simon & Schuster, 1991.

Creech, Sharon. *Walk Two Moons.* New York: Harper, 1994.

Cronyn, George W., ed. *American Indian Poetry.* New York: Ballantine Books, 1962.

Culleton, Beatrice. *April Raintree.* Winnipeg: Pemmican, 1984.

————. *In Search of April Raintree.* Winnipeg: Peguis, 1995.

dePaola, Tomie. *The Legend of the Bluebonnet: An Old Tale of Texas.* New York: G. P. Putnam's Sons, 1983.

Dorris, Michael. *Guests.* New York: Hyperion Books for Children, 1994.

————. *Morning Girl.* New York: Hyperion Paperbacks for Children, 1992, 1999.

————. *Sees Behind Trees.* New York: Hyperion Books for Children, 1996.

Esbensen, Barbara Juster. *The Star Maiden.* Illustrated by Helen K. Davie. Boston: Little, Brown, 1988.

Ehrlich, Amy (adapter). *Wounded Knee: An Indian History of the American West.* New York: Random House Children's Books, 1978.

Erdrich, Louise. *The Birchbark House.* New York: Hyperion Books for Children, 1999.

Freedman, Russell. *The Life and Death of Crazy Horse.* New York: Holiday House, 1996.

Garland, Sherry. *Indio.* New York: Harcourt Brace, 1995.

Goble, Paul. *Adopted by the Eagles.* New York: Aladdin Paperbacks, 1994.

————. *Buffalo Woman.* New York: Aladdin Books, 1984.

————. *The Gift of the Sacred Dog.* New York: Bradbury Press, 1985.

————. *The Great Race of the Birds and Animals.* New York: Aladdin Books, 1985.

————. *Iktomi and the Boulder.* New York: Orchard Books, 1988.

————. *Remaking the Earth: A Creation Story from the Great Plains of North America.* New York: Orchard Books, 1996.

————. *Star Boy.* New York: Aladdin Books, 1983.

Hale, Janet Campbell. *The Owl's Song.* New York: Bantam, 1991.

Haley, Gail E. *Two Bad Boys: A Very Old Cherokee Tale.* New York: Dutton Children's Books, 1996.

Hudson, Jan. *Sweetgrass.* New York: Scholastic, 1984.

Jeffers, Susan. *Brother Eagle, Sister Sky.* New York: Dial Books, 1991.

Johnston, Tony. *The Tale of Rabbit and Coyote.* Illustrated by Tomie dePaola. New York: G. P. Putnam and Sons, 1994.

King, Sandra. *Shannon: An Ojibway Dancer.* New York: Lerner, 1993.

Loat, Teri. *The Eye of the Needle.* New York: Dutton Children's Books, 1990.

Lunge-Larsen, Lise, and Margi Preus. *The Legend of the Lady Slipper: An Ojibwe Tale.* Illustrated by Andrea Arroyo. Boston: Houghton Mifflin, 1999.

Malotki, Ekkehart. *The Mouse Couple.* Illustrated by Michael Lacapa. Flagstaff, Az.: Northland Press, 1988.

Martin, Rafe. *The Boy Who Lived with the Seals.* New York: G. P. Putnam's Sons, 1993.

————. *The Rough-Face Girl.* Illustrated by David Shannon. New York: Scholastic, 1992.

McDermott, Gerald. *Arrow to the Sun: A Pueblo Indian Tale.* New York: Puffin Books, 1974.

————. *Coyote: Trickster Tale from the American Southwest.* San Diego: Harcourt Brace, 1994.

————. *Raven: Trickster Tale from the Pacific Northwest.* San Diego: Harcourt Brace, 1993.

————. *Zomo, The Rabbit: Trickster Tale from West Africa.* San Diego: Harcourt Brace, 1993.

Osofsky, Audrey. *Dreamcatcher.* Illustrated by Ed Young. New York: Orchard Books, 1992.

Oughton, Jerrie. *How the Stars Fell into the Sky.* Illustrated by Lisa Desmini. Boston: Houghton Mifflin, 1992.

Philip, Neil. *Earth Always Endures.* New York: Penguin Books USA, 1996.

Pitts, Paul. *Racing the Sun.* New York: Avon, 1988.

Power, Susan. *The Grass Dancer.* New York: Berkley Books, 1997.

Roessel, Monty. *Kinaalda: A Navajo Girl Grows Up.* Minneapolis, Minn.: Lerner, 1993.

Sanford, William R. *Chief Joseph: Nez Percé Warrior.* Berkeley Heights, N.J.: Enslow, 1994.

————. *Crazy Horse: Sioux Warrior.* Berkeley Heights, N.J.: Enslow, 1994.

————. *Osceola: Seminole Warrior.* Berkeley Heights, N.J.: Enslow, 1994.

————. *Quannah Parker: Comanche Warrior.* Berkeley Heights, N.J.: Enslow, 1994.

————. *Sitting Bull: Sioux Warrior.* Berkeley Heights, N.J.: Enslow, 1994.

San Souci, Robert. *Sootface: An Ojibwa Cinderella Story.* Illustrated by Daniel San Souci. New York: Bantam Doubleday Dell Books for Young Readers, 1994.

Slipperjack, R. *Honour the Sun.* Winnipeg: Pemmican, 1987.

Sneve, Virginia Driving Hawk. *Dancing Teepees: Poems by American Indian Youth.* New York: Holiday House, 1989.

————. *The Hopis.* New York: Holiday House, 1995.

————. *The Iroquois.* New York: Holiday House, 1993.

————. *The Navajos.* New York: Holiday House, 1993.

————. *The Nez Percé.* New York: Holiday House, 1994.

————. *The Sioux.* New York: Holiday House, 1994.

————. *The Trickster and the Troll.* Lincoln: University of Nebraska Press, 1997.

————. *The Twelve Moons.* New York: Houghton Mifflin, 1977.

Steptoe, John. *The Story of Jumping Mouse: A Native American Legend.* New York: Lothrop, Lee & Shepard Books, 1972

Sterling, Shirley. *My Name Is Seepeetza.* Vancouver: Groundwood Press, 1992.

Stevens, Janet. *Coyote Steals the Blanket: A Ute Tale.* New York: Holiday House, 1993.

Talltree, Robert. *The Legend of Spinoza: The Bear Who Speaks from the Heart.* St. Paul, Minn.: Universal Tradewinds, 1995.

Tapahonso, Luci. *Navajo ABC: A Diné Alphabet Book.* Las Vegas: Sagebrush Press, 1999.

Taylor, Harriet Peck. *Brother Wolf: A Seneca Tale.* New York: Farrar, Straus and Giroux, 1996.

Wallis, Velma. *Bird Girl.* New York: HarperCollins, 1996.

Wargin, Kathy-jo. *The Legend of Mackinac Island.* Illustrated by Gijsbert van Frankenhuyzen. Chelsea, Mich.: Sleeping Bear Press, 1999.

————. *The Legend of Sleeping Bear.* Illustrated by Gijsbert van Frankenhuyzen. Chelsea, Mich.: Sleeping Bear Press, 1998.

White Deer of Autumn. *Ceremony—In the Circle of Life.* Illustrated by Daniel San Souci. Hillsboro, Ore.: Beyond Words Publishing, 1983.

Wood, Nancy. *Hollering Sun.* New York: Simon & Schuster, 1972.

————. *Spirit Walker.* New York: Doubleday Books for Young Readers, 1993.

————. *War Cry on a Prayer Feather: Prose and Poetry of the Ute Indians.* Garden City, N.Y.: Doubleday, 1979.

Wood, Ted. *A Boy Becomes a Man at Wounded Knee.* New York: Walker, 1992.

Yolen, Jane. *Encounter.* Illustrated by David Shannon. New York: Harcourt, 1993.

Index

About the Authors

Pamela S. Gates is professor of English and currently serves as interim dean of the College of Humanities and Social Behavioral Sciences for Central Michigan University. Dr. Gates received her B.S. and M.A. from Central Michigan University, and her Ph.D. (where she specialized in literacy and learning, literature for children and young adults, language arts, and English education) in English from Michigan State University. She has taught a wide range of courses over the past nineteen years, including seminars in children's literature, fantasy literature, cultural pluralism in literature for children, and heroic traditions in literature for children and young adults. Dr. Gates has served as cochair of the Michigan Story Festival, has published more than a dozen articles and book chapters, and is coauthor of *Fantasy Literature for Children and Young Adults* (Scarecrow, 2003) and *Cultural Journeys: Multicultural Literature for Children and Young Adults* (Scarecrow, 2006).

Dianne L. Hall Mark is professor of education and dean in Spadoni College of Education for Coastal Carolina University in South Carolina. Originally from Flint, Michigan, she received undergraduate degrees from Northwood University (A.A.) and Michigan State University (B.S.) and graduate degrees from Buffalo State College (M.Ed.) and the University of Buffalo (M.S. and Ph.D.). Her research interests include urban education and parental involvement. She resides in Conway, South Carolina, with her husband, Eddie.